MW00675312

Palestinian Identities and Preferences

PALESTINIAN IDENTITIES AND PREFERENCES

Israel's and Jerusalem's Arabs

Abraham Ashkenasi

PRAEGER

New York
Westport, Connecticut
London

Library of Congress Cataloging-in-Publication Data

Ashkenasi, Abraham.
  Palestinian identities and preferences : Israel's and Jerusalem's
    Arabs / Abraham Ashkenasi
    p.   cm.
  Includes bibliographical references and index.
  ISBN 0–275–93503–5 (alk. paper)
  1. Palestinian Arabs—Israel—Ethnic identity. 2. Israel—Ethnic
relations. 3. Palestinian Arabs—Jerusalem—Ethnic identity.
4. Jerusalem—Ethnic relations. I. Title.
DS113.7.A787   1992
305.8′0095694—dc20   91–16682

British Library Cataloguing in Publication Data is available.

Copyright © 1992 by Abraham Ashkenasi

All rights reserved. No portion of this book may
be reproduced, by any process or technique, without
the express written consent of the publisher.

Library of Congress Catalog Card Number: 91–16682
ISBN: 0–275–93503–5

First published in 1992

Praeger Publishers, One Madison Avenue, New York, NY 10010
An imprint of Greenwood Publishing Group, Inc.

Printed in the United States of America

The paper used in this book complies with the
Permanent Paper Standard issued by the National
Information Standards Organization (Z39.48–1984).

10 9 8 7 6 5 4 3 2 1

CONTENTS

	Preface	vii
1.	The Structure of Ethnic Conflict	1
2.	The Political Development of Israel's Arabs until 1967	21
3.	Developments in Israel's Arab Community after 1967	33
4.	Israel's Arabs and Jerusalem's Arabs: Similarities and Differences	71
5.	Palestinian Society and Israeli Municipal Authority in Jerusalem	83
6.	Palestinian Views about Jerusalem	113
7.	Conclusion	169
	Bibliography	175
	Index	185

PREFACE

Is there a future for ethnic Arabs or the national minority, Palestinians, as an ethnic minority within the borders of the state of Israel? This book sets out to examine social fragmentation in Palestinian society and its effect on this future. Its focus is on those Palestinians who do not live under direct military occupation, but who reside within the boundaries of Israel as delineated by the state. The problem posed for these Palestinians by the integratory option and their responses form the core of our study. How the integratory option was perceived, and accepted or rejected, played a key role in the general social structuring of Palestinian society.

The choices were perceived differently by the Arabs of pre–1967 Israel, and the existence of the choices influenced their society more. Israeli-determined options were more vital there for political, social, and economic life than in Jerusalem. Nevertheless, the integratory, or cooperative, option that the Israeli government held out to the two groups was in theory quite similar. Therefore, Arabs with Israeli citizenship—those who live within the pre–1967 borders, and the tiny minority living in Jerusalem that has also chosen Israeli citizenship—had many of the same political options that the Arab citizens of Jerusalem had. They comprised a segment of Palestinian society that could—in theory at least—freely discuss its possibilities and act upon them. Theoretically, legally, nothing stopped Jerusalem's Palestinians from becoming Israeli citizens and enjoying or not enjoying the same rights of Israeli citizenship as Arabs within Israel. Nothing prevented them from joining the system and attempting to utilize it in the same fashion as Israeli Arabs, albeit with the same frustrations and limited successes.

The Jerusalem Arabs' overwhelming rejection of this option reflects the differences between them and Israeli Arabs. It was their decision, much as it was their decision not to reject the benefits of the annexation that

gave them privileges unknown by Palestinians under direct military occupation in the rest of the West Bank and in Gaza, and that set them off
again from the Palestinians in their diaspora.

Jerusalem's Palestinians have chosen to remain in the city and, with
surprisingly few exceptions since the intifada, pay their taxes, accept the
legal system, accept social security payments and national health benefits,
accept salaries paid by the Israeli government and the Jerusalem municipality, and cooperate in many informal ways with the municipality. Israeli
Arabs formally joined the system; Jerusalem's Arabs joined informally. In
both cases they succeeded in insulating themselves as ethnic Arabs against
the harshness of holding minority status in a nationalist state. Their feelings
about this state are probably no different than those of their less fortunate
compatriots in Gaza and the West Bank, to say nothing of those in the
camps in Lebanon and Jordan. Yet their actions are tempered by the
economic, social, political, and legal preferences that they enjoy within
the Israeli civic culture.

Operationally, Israeli Arabs and especially their leadership have had
very little connection with the intifada. In fact, the same can be said for
Palestinians in Jerusalem, although they are at the intifada's intellectual
center. There is a great deal of verbal support for Palestinian national
aspirations, a support far more profound in Jerusalem than among Arabs
with Israeli citizenship. The latter, or at least a significant number of them,
show more disposition to accept continued life as a minority within a Jewish
polity. Palestinians in Jerusalem show little disposition of this nature, but
they are much like many of the rejectionists among Israeli Arabs who are
not radical activists and who do not operationalize protest physically. In
other words, their protest is highly verbal, ideological, and psychological,
but not necessarily violent.

The degree to which Israel's Arabs and Palestinians in Jerusalem differ
from each other and among themselves is a central focus of examination
here. The ties of Palestinians in Jerusalem to their compatriots, especially
those in the West Bank and in Jordan, are another element of key interest.
The political, social, economic, and legal structure of Jerusalem, but especially the psychological climate there, differ from the milieu of Israeli
Arabs in ways that are starkly drawn. Basically, the fine lines of self-
identification have been blurred in Israel, while for Jerusalemites the essential psychological tie to Palestine remains unquestionable.

But what does this mean politically? How set are opinions here? How
"soft" is political support for one group or another? To what extent is
political activity a reflection of internal development and social fragmentation? And above all, do the options open by virtue of the Israeli civic
system and the obviously large Jewish demographic presence in the region
play the significant role in the political development of Jerusalemites that
they do for Israel's Arabs? To answer, our study proceeds along various

lines of comparative analysis. Developments, as we will see, can be quite asymmetrical, and therefore comparison quite complicated.

These questions are a natural outgrowth of the direction my research has taken during the past decade. I became more and more interested in the phenomenon of ethnic conflict both as a sociological problem in domestic politics and as an element of confrontation in international affairs. In 1980 I embarked upon studies of the Arab sector in Israel. I felt, as I will later elucidate, that the quiescence of the Arab sector in Israel was not in conformity to what would be expected in its situation. My investigations led to the policy paper, "The Structure of Ethnic Conflict and Palestinian Political Fragmentation," which appeared in Berlin in 1981. In the course of the 1980s, and perhaps as a result of living in Berlin, I became increasingly interested in problems of divided cities. Jerusalem offered an ideal venue for both of these interests. It also provides the researcher a political setting that can be more easily analyzed than an entire nation-state, even one as small as Israel.

Analysis of communal policies and of the administration of urban and suburban political and social structures has been the disciplinary responsibility of sociologists and urban anthropologists. Geographers as well as psychologists have also published at some length about the problems of urban society and intercommunal relationships. But analysts of international politics and international conflict have paid very little attention to the problems of cities. The difficulties of communal administration appear far removed from the causalities of international confrontation, balance of power policy, geographical strategies, and other such issues. Yet in the light of developments over the postwar period, this seemed strange to me. The problems of nationalism and ethnic conflict have impinged upon the consciousness of the international community, and it became obvious to me that without solutions to the problems of local ethnic confrontation there could be no solutions to the problems of regional and even international conflict. Although ethnic confrontation was still defined primarily in terms of large minorities within sovereign nation-states, I felt that within the urban setting many of the same theoretical and methodological analytic tools could be rigorously applied. My fascination with Jerusalem and its problems resulted in three policy studies that were published by the Leonard Davis Institute for International Relations of the Hebrew University of Jerusalem and various articles dealing with communal policy, conflict management, refugee problems, and comparisons between divided cities. This volume leans heavily on the aforementioned earlier works, but in updating the information and in modifying earlier conclusions, it can be considered to supercede all of them.

I would like to acknowledge the support I have received from various institutions and foundations. The Deutsche Forschungsgemeinschaft supported my work at the University of Haifa's Jewish-Arab Center in 1980 and 1981 and at the Hebrew University of Jerusalem in 1987, 1988, and 1989. In addition, I was supported by the Forschungsgebeitsschwerpunkt "Ethnizitat und Gesellschaft" of the Free University of Berlin, which helped to underwrite, among other things, preparation of the manuscript of this book. I also wish to thank my friends and colleagues Sammy Smooha and Majid al-Haj at Haifa for introducing me to Arab society in Israel and for assisting me in many ways in the course of the last few years. I also wish to thank the Leonard Davis Institute for its infrastructural support and its instrumental help in the research of this volume—and especially the executive head of the institute, Professor Gabriel Sheffer, for his intellectual and personal generosity, as well as administrative assistants Anna Thee, Noa Padan, and Ofra Itzhak, and the many researchers whose advice and intellectual assistance proved so helpful. I also wish to thank my assistants Akram Al-Safadi and Khalil Rinnawi for what was at times courageous assistance, and also Josef Nashef for his help in research in the East Jerusalem school system. My thanks also to Aron Sarig, until recently administrative head of the Jerusalem city government, for his advice and friendship. And last but not least, to Cheryl Beckerman for her editorial advice and persistence, and to Judie Fattal for her work on the tables.

Palestinian Identities and Preferences

1

THE STRUCTURE OF ETHNIC CONFLICT

THE CENTRAL SIGNIFICANCE OF NATIONALISM

The years since the French Revolution—what historians call the modern period—have been marked by the ascendancy of two messianic political movements that successfully competed with the established religions: socialism and nationalism.[1] Socialism is a political ideology with definable intellectual boundaries within a theoretical framework. It has developed since Saint-Simon, via Marx and Lenin, up to our own day, with a clear body of socioeconomic thought. It has come upon hard times lately, having seemingly failed to provide the social justice it proclaimed. The field has been left free, then, for other purveyors of the just and civic morality.

Unlike socialism, nationalism remains diffuse as a doctrine. Attempts at definition, both by the proponents of nationalistic ideas and by more dispassionate political scientists, have been legion. The analysis has been historically descriptive, philosophical, theoretical, psychological, structural, sociological, even quantitative. While all of these attempts have been fruitful, none have managed to pin down the phenomenon of nationalism. A chameleon-like, almost messianic movement, it has constantly changed colors over the past 150 years.

Within the developed and developing nation-states of Europe and Asia, nationalism has been the regulatory feature of nineteenth- and twentieth-century domestic systems. It functioned, as well, as a catalyst for action within these systems. The result was that more often than not, even the "socialist" nationalists would remember their nationalism while forgetting their socialism. In other words, emancipatory movements were seeking economic, political, and social redress from aristocratic oligarchy, autocratic mandarins, or "foreign" oppressors, and national "liberation" tended to take precedence over economic transformation. Although functionally the role of nationalism was to provide the integrating organizational myth for a stabilized popular consensus, and for increased domestic effi- ciency and enhanced political mobility internationally, its normative power was so great that it could be manipulated not only by leadership elites but by would-be usurpers as well. In addition, nationalism could be used to subvert more efficient functional processes in order to preserve certain socioeconomic elites, to control or to destroy modernization processes or reforming political and social groups and ideas, or both. That this is true is primarily due to one particular and major aspect of nationalism: its messianic character, its mystical quality. The fact that it appeared full- blown, as it were, on the world scene in the nineteenth century as a phil- osophical chiliastic concept does not belie the fact that it was two centuries in the making in Western Europe. It does mean, however, that the sudden breakup of earlier social forms and previously stable politics gave rise to a need for new binding myths.

Nationalism has proved to be a highly explosive as well as binding social myth. The irony of this lies in the universal asymmetry of social and political development in the world. The patterns of establishment, growth, and modification in varying times and places, and the patters of dissolution, have only been hypothesized, not proven. The patterns do not seem sym- metrical either historically, on the basis of macrosocial analysis, or even when viewed in more systematic microsocial studies of various social groups. Nor have completely accurate factor-analysis techniques been de- veloped for rigorous study—especially over significant time spans. How- ever, the resiliency of integrative myths does emerge as a central factor for these cycles. In addition, as political, social, and economic life increase in complexity, so do the thought patterns that grow out of them and serve as ideological cement. Competitive ideologies or integrative myths arise and reflect the social conflicts and power struggles both within and between political social organizations. They also reflect asymmetry of development, and this factor as well leads to volatile ideological clash.

Much of twentieth-century history has centered on this clash. With na- tionalism being the binding ideology for social control, political security, and economic growth, it was almost inevitable that dissatisfaction would be expressed in antinational or neonational terms. In many instances what has often been historically considered "working-class" dissatisfaction could well be described as "ethnic." This was certainly true of the immigrant and black workers in the United States, and true to a degree in Great Britain as well, where Celts were universally exploited. Indeed, much purely social conflict was expressed as national conflict. In recent years the concept of ethno-class has been developed to help explain this phenome- non.[2] National loyalties were often particularistic, with power and goods distribution flowing through ostensibly national but essentially "ethnic" social and political grids. These grids might be either open and assimilatory, implying a readiness to co-opt leaders and fully accept populations that accepted the national "rules of the game," or they might be "predatory" or totally closed rulership systems that permanently excluded some from full sharing of power, security, and goods.

The volatility of social conflict in national guise was enhanced by asymmetry of development. And it increased in intensity in direct relation to the social dislocation inherent in asymmetrical external and internal development. As the volatile ideology of nationalism moved eastward across Europe and into Asia, it not only lit the fires of national and social aspirations in the colonized world outside the European metropolises, but it left large ethnic or national groups—and not always minorities, at that—on the sidelines. While the English, French, or German-Hungarian Austrians might have been satisfied, the Irish, Bretons, and various Balkan Slavs certainly were not. At various points in their own social and political development and in the development of their "host" nationalities, their dissatisfaction turned to open defiance.

In some instances new nation-states arose out of the nationalist calamity of World War I. Some of these states did not outlast World War II. (But the desire for nationhood dies hard, and the death of the state and suppression of the national community does not kill the idea, as the present agitation in many former Soviet republics shows.) Some "nationalities" were only partly successful in establishing a nation-state, and national irredentism persisted and still persists. This development was not limited to Europe. The anticolonial struggles of Asia and Africa, and indeed, America, are well documented. But here too some nationalities were left behind in the rush, pell mell, to create nation-states. French Canadians, Muslim Filipinos, South Sudanese, Biafrans, Eritreans, and, it seems, countless others joined the ranks of the discontented nationalities. The "late-blooming" nationalisms and nationalities differ in some significant ways from the established nationalities and nation-states.

NATIONALITIES AND NATION-STATES

The most significant difference between late-blooming nationalities and nation-states usually lies in socioeconomic development. (In some instances size differentials, the relative lack of demographic mass, played a major role.) Most late-blooming nationalisms, which for the purposes of this study can be identified as nationalisms that had not led to nation-states by the end of World War II, were developed by a central ethnic group. In the majority of cases, the ethnic group had been left behind in the asymmetric socioeconomic development. This did not imply a lack of cultural, economic, religious, or linguistic homogeneity. Indeed, elements of such homogeneity as well as a historical sense of being one group had to be strongly felt and maintained in order for an ethnic group to articulate its sociopolitical growth and back it up with resolute action. However, nationalist agitation meant that the group had not enjoyed the same organizational growth as the "dominant" national group. It also implied exploitation. This was true not only of imperialist exploitation from without; inside the "imperialized" geographic entity, cooperative elements of society, most often reflecting a certain ethnic or socioreligious homogeneity, would help dominate and help exploit. Since such a group (Christians in Lebanon; to a degree, Zionists in Israel; and for a time, upper-class Sunni Arabs in Iraq) would develop the sinews of modern and efficient political and military life more quickly than other groups in the area, they were often able to carry their national idea forward more successfully.

This does not mean that all divisions in society had to imply a new state or a new nationalism. Even when "ethnic" in character, conflicts do not a priori lead to the building of nation-states. Fredrik Barth (1969) postulated constant division and redivision. Pierre van den Berghe (1981) stressed that physical attributes are ascribed to these divisions, as did Max Weber before him.[3] But, as Abner Cohen pointed out, the divisions can lead to the establishment of interest groups that have actually adapted to the society and are simply pressuring for benefits much as other social groups do: trade unions, women, students, pensioners. The divisions can lead as well to the formation of subcultures; people may be content to live as separate societies within the existing polity as long as nothing impinges upon the special characteristics that stem from their differences of religion or lifestyle. (Examples are widely varied: religious Jews, gypsies, homosexuals, polygamists.) (Cohen 1974). Other ethnic groups seek recognition as semi-independent entities within the polity with limited cultural autonomy for linguistic, educational, and other social characteristics, implying economic and power-sharing benefits. This symbiotic relationship between central authority and a "dissimilar" culture is the key to dynastic empires (such as the Hapsburgs and the Ottomans), and it seems to a degree to determine the success or failure of all modern multi-ethnic polities (for example, the United States, the Soviet Union, and India) as well as those in the past whose conflicts with modern nationalism are historically documented. The demand for national minority status leads at the very least to agitation for full autonomy or a geopolitical restructuring of the polity, and this can imply its demise. Nationalism is the functional ideological expression of the crossing of the line from being a domestically established society, a subculture or an interest group, to being a national minority. Although a nascent national minority can remain quiescent, with its national goals dormant, the tendency is to embrace political confrontation and conflict and achieve its ends. Success, of course, is not guaranteed a priori.

For ethnic groupings seeking to promote their nationalism, certain characteristics were commonly required. These were:

1. A clearly defined geographical area from which to operate that would develop into the nation-state.

2. Clear lines of operational legitimacy for a leadership group. In most instances various leadership groups competed with one another along distinct sociological and ideological lines. One leadership group, however, always assumed ascendancy and was able to legitimize its control over the bulk of the ethnic community concerned.

3. A keen sense of either religious, linguistic, or historical (ethno-cultural and/or economic) homogeneity and solidarity, or some combination of these, usually arising out of exploitative economic and psychologically demeaning conditions.

4. A certain demographic mass relative to other competing ethnic core groups or to the repressive agents of imperialistic national groups or nation-states.

5. A certain level of outside support. To forge a successful national movement from an internal ethnic conflict without some measure of international sponsorship appears impossible.

The nation-state always grew out of a core ethnic group in a well-defined geographical area. The development process had a valid function in the growing industrial society, where the new bourgeois class sought upward mobility and a larger geographic unit made military and economic sense. Yet the process was not as smooth as it appeared to "national" historians in the twentieth century. A continual intersocietal race was on between accommodating, integrating, or assimilating social and ethnic groups and those who rejected the emergent and dominant political structure. In the twentieth century the nation-state has lost much of its reason for existence. It does not provide much upward social mobility for the "new" classes. It is not necessarily an economically feasible unit. It no longer provides real psychological or physical security. Because of the relative weakness of the nation-state, the core groups who are left behind are able to demand their nationhood. Passive rejectionists of the past become active. The paradox is complete, because the "new" states seem less able than the old to provide the social, economic, and political elements that make nationhood more than a chiliastic illusion. Indeed, less nationalism and more social mobility in the established states is probably a more propitious solution than more and more national entities. But the nation-state remains the "emancipatory" model. The dream's disintegration allows new dreamers to implement the tired emancipatory hope of nationhood and nation-state, more often than not on the smashed yearnings of disgruntled and bitter neighbor minorities.

NATIONHOOD, NATIONALISM, AND THE NATION-STATE IN THE NEAR EAST

The nation-state fixed within its own geographical limits, with vertical mobility for those adhering to its more or less stringent codes of conduct and legal systems for those who enjoy full citizenship, is the model for the "nationless" ethnic groups or national minorities. In most instances it is a dominant national group, equipped with the paraphernalia of symbols and agencies, flags and anthems, armed forces and legends that lend it creature security, that has structured the state. This has been and is the model of success in ethnic conflict. Although much of this conflict is articulated along emancipatory, ideological, or revolutionary lines, it remains highly particularistic in its structure and goals. In the early years of the twentieth century the Balkans were considered the powder keg of the world and they reflected best the destabilizing power inherent in unfulfilled national goals and volatile ethnic aspirations. After World War II, and certainly after the establishment of the many nation-states that grew out of the imperialist experiment of the nineteenth and twentieth centuries, the focus of ethnic conflict, for a number of reasons, shifted to the Near East.

One reason for this shift was that the large number of ethnic groups in the area could function successfully side by side only under the relatively disinterested and anational Ottoman empire. While the ideas of nationalism and nation-state had penetrated the area together with the British and French incursions, especially into Algeria and Egypt, for the most part the Ottomans and the feudal social conditions of the empire did not offer encouragement, given their negative example and their repression of national goals. This changed only with the advent of the new Turkish nationalism after 1908 and especially with the growth of Kemalism in Turkey. Indeed, a strong argument could be made for the hypothesis that the influence of Middle European nationalism then became paramount in the area. Certainly, the Germans at the height of their national hybris maintained major ideological influence in Turkey, and thinking in Istanbul spread throughout intellectual circles in the empire. Zionism, too, retained many elements of German national thinking. But the Arab armies that fought with the British in World War I were still largely particularistic in aspiration and in structure and represented a preindustrial, family- and clan-oriented society. They had little contact with the burgeoning Arab nationalism among a rising intelligentsia in towns such as Algiers and especially Cairo and, later, Damascus. A nationalism like that of the present-day Palestinians did not exist at all, except perhaps in the sense that a native of the area may have considered himself or herself a South Syrian— yet it is even questionable whether Syria at that time was much more than a carryover of the geographic organization of conquerors from the Romans to the Ottomans.

The Zionist movement had begun to function in the area but it was still primarily a non–Near Eastern phenomenon. The Armenians and Assyrians were, effectively, eliminated. Only the Kurds could make themselves felt in the early twentieth century, and their bid for a nation-state was destroyed by a combination of Turkish, Iraqi Arab, and British repression. Certain ethnic groups that saw a chance of success through cooperation with the imperialist or colonial power proceeded accordingly in the period between 1920 and 1948. This contributed to a more collaborative emancipatory political organization in many ethnic groups. Consider, for example, the Iraqi Arabs, Sunni and Hashemite, who cooperated with the British against the Kurds, and the Christian Maronites who cooperated with the French against the Lebanese and Syrian Muslims. Both the British and the French in return gave a distinct advantage to these groups over others when statehood was granted, accentuating the ethnic fragmentation left by the Ottomans.

The lack of industrialization in the area and the family- and clan-oriented social structure, together with the conservatism of Islam, made it impossible for many potential national groups to organize along modern lines. Neither a working nor a middle class had developed sufficiently to be organized by others, let alone claim leadership. The heady ideas of nationalism imported from the European metropolises and Istanbul were grafted onto the particularist social structures of the past. Indeed, the modern technologies of organization, leadership, communications, indoctrination, and education were nowhere developed. This was also true of the Palestinians, and especially the Muslim community, the Kurds, and to an extent the Druze as well. The great and significant exception to this regional axiom was the case of the Zionists, but they first organized in Europe.

The strategic importance of the area, both geopolitically and economically, made it a prime venue for intervention and repression by the major powers. This further distorted a "normal" national development. It was only in the period after World War II, with the ensuing weakness of the European nation-state, that some of the late-blooming nationalisms of the Near East were able to bring about their statehood. For the Arabs, however, the advance into international recognition and national life came separately. In many instances this asymmetrical development that was characteristic among the Arabs led to a disintegration of the concept of nationalism, into various forms of particularist preference, and the organizational power of the concept was diluted. This was true although lip service was paid to the ideal of the so-called Arab nation; though ideologically appealing, it never achieved concrete geographical expression. A score of ethnically Arab states appeared, each with its own more or less highly developed nationalism and national elites. The Palestinians were left behind by this development. Likewise, the relatively rapid development of the nation-states, albeit with foreign assistance, in Iran, Iraq,

Syria, and Turkey left the Kurds behind. Some groups in the area were either too small vis-à-vis potential national enemies to firmly establish themselves (the Druze, Maronites, Greek Cypriots, and Palestinians), or too badly disorganized (the Kurds), or they were effectively eliminated (the Assyrians and Armenians). Again, probably because their movement originated outside the Near East, the Zionists were the most successful in establishing their nation-state. They established the modern organizational structures that are of key importance in successfully creating both national movements and nation-states: educated, efficient cadres, quick lines of communication, flexible policies and economically feasible goals enabling easy assimilation of potential followers, and last but certainly not least, highly motivated fighting units loyal to ideas and capable of handling new technologies (rather than individuals with particularist orientations).

THE PALESTINIAN PEOPLE: A SEARCH FOR UNREQUITED NATIONHOOD

The roughly five million Palestinians who still live in the immediate area of what was once called Palestine, or have close contacts with it, are a prime modern example of national failure. This has occurred because of internal fragmentation and the constraints imposed by external factors. Among this population, extreme asymmetrical social development is apparent. In part this is true because of the distinct differences between the different modern histories of segments of the Palestinian population, which are more or less a factor of geographic chance and of social structures prevalent in the 1930s and 1940s. At least five geographically distinct groups of Palestinians can be identified:

1. *Israeli Arabs*, or members of the Palestinian minority in the state of Israel, are those who remained behind its borders: the armistice lines of 1948, which is the so-called green line of 1967. They number 650,000 (all figures in this section are approximations).

2. *West Bank and Gaza Palestinians*, grouped together here because of their similar histories (despite differences in development), number 1,450,000. Subgroups are the dwellers of the refugee camps in the areas, who fled (or whose parents and grandparents fled) what is now Israel in 1948, and the residents of villages and towns—both those who were there before 1948 and those who have managed to leave the camps.

3. *Jerusalem's Arab Community* (150,000), the social structure of which is historically like that of the West Bank and Gaza residents, but which Israel attempts to treat politically and statistically as a part of the first group. This is yet another example of fragmentation in a list that will grow even longer before we are finished.

4. The 1,300,000 *Palestinians in Jordan* are a majority of that country's inhabitants. Yet their integration on the political level does not seem complete. Indeed, the Jordanian government has been able to co-opt elements of their fragmented society (Christians, prominent families, regional groups, and so on), and thus these Palestinians may be divided into minorities supportive of the regime (Haas 1975). Moreover, they are critical to the state: They dominate its commercial and intellectual life. But the central sinews of political control are stringently maintained by the Hashemite monarchy, and its control of various Palestinian political factions has been enormously successful. For these Palestinians, too, a distinction between those in refugee camps and out may be in order, and date of flight (1948 or 1967) is also relevant.

5. *Diaspora Palestinians* include the refugees in Lebanon, who are organized and controlled by the Palestine Liberation Organization (PLO), and those in Syria, who are closely controlled and manipulated by the Syrian government. Together, these groups number 700,000. In addition, two other groups of diaspora Palestinians have emerged. Some 900,000 live in the Middle East but not in the confrontation states. The majority of this group were in the Gulf states; their financial remittances back to the areas have been a significant factor in the local economy. Another 200,000 Palestinians live in Europe and the United States.[4]

While all of these geographical/sociopolitical categories could be broken down further, our concern in this book will be to analyze the Israeli Arab and Jerusalem groups.

No organization really maintains control over the Palestinians, who constitute one of the most fragmented political communities in the world. Dispersion, of course, has contributed to fragmentation. Central control is obviously more difficult to maintain under such conditions. The opportunity for regional and foreign intervention in policy formulation and implementation is evident everywhere. Divergent social and political development and opportunities breed distrust and operational incompatibility. Leadership groups often disagree and common policy is reduced to an ineffective and unrealistic common political denominator suitable for a political poster, not policy. The Fatah wing of the PLO in recent years has had some success in establishing tentative organization, if not ideological control, over the contentious factions, but it seems stronger outside the area of immediate concern and the border states (with the possible exception of Lebanon even after its exclusion in 1982) than within. The organizational problem of the Palestinians is further complicated by the various legal systems within which they must operate (our study involves the Israeli system, itself largely an amalgamation of other legal systems). For many

(those in Jerusalem and the West Bank), a dual monetary system based
on the Israeli shekel and the Jordanian dinar (which has given Jordan an
important conservative influence over Palestinian affairs) further compli-
cates unified policy. In addition, Israeli Arabs have had no influence on a
political center geographically removed from the immediate area. The same
can be said for Jerusalemites and, perhaps to a lesser degree, West Bank
and Gaza Palestinians as long as all continued to reside within the boundaries of historic Palestine (Sandler and Frisch 1984).

Thus, there was neither legal, political, nor economic centralization.
Under such conditions, how functional was the power of ideology as an
instrument for political organization and not simply an eschatological flight
from the former?

The passivity and fragmentation of the first group, Israel's Arab sector,
was for a long time the archetypical problem of the Palestinians in general.
These aspects of "Palestinianism" have been aggravated by the so-called
normal depredations of minority status and the long association with a
dominant, politically antagonistic but economically and (perhaps for some)
socially appealing foreign culture. But a study of Israeli and Jerusalemite
Arabs does not only reflect on the problems of the Near East and the
Palestinians generally. Certain basic questions concerning ethnic minorities
are uncovered. Like all minorities, Israeli and Jerusalemite Arabs have
problems in terms of housing, schooling, political organizations and unions,
integration, and assimilation—but they are also a national group with emotional, historical, social, and political ties (the latter limited but potentially
extensive) to a regional majority. Even if it were at peace with Israel, this
regional majority would inject a strong element of international politics
into a sociological problem. Other international actors who have shown
enormous interest in the region as yet maintain an ambivalent attitude
regarding this aspect of the problem. Israel's relations with the Palestinians
illustrate basic methodological and analytical complications in dealing with
the complex issue of domestic ethnic groups or national minorities. If a
segment of society is merely a minority, then it can be dealt with like other
segments—women, workers, students, and so forth—and the same analytical tools will be appropriate. If the problem of minority rights is really
corollary to other social problems, then they can be treated structurally
through economic, educational, and legal changes in the social, economic,
or institutional structure. Douglas Baker (1983) shows how power is manipulated through ethnic grids. Frank Parkin (1978) shows how economic
activities are manipulated. Both techniques of rulership policy are apparent
not only in Jerusalem and within Israel, but also in all Arab areas where
Palestinians live (Haidar 1988).

Unfortunately, the line between ethnic group and national minority is
blurred here. A "national" history and the history of relations, imagined
or real, with the dominant national group intrude with powerful force into

any sociological analysis. The historical setting of the conflict can be volatile and determinant. In addition, international actors and the influence of international events are far more important for this kind of analysis than for the analysis of normal social domestic conflict. Foreign powers may try but only rarely succeed in using women, students, and workers in the same successful fashion in which they are able to use national minorities to destabilize a nation-state or even tamper with a regional—or international—system.

Sociologists have not yet delivered the methodologies of comparative sociology or international sociology that are necessary for a full understanding of these problems. Although Max Weber made a powerful start at the dawn of the century, which was continued by the Chicago school in the United States into the 1930s and 1940s, and Karl Deutsch hinted strongly in this direction back in the 1950s, even the requisite codifications are lacking. The best sociologists of pluralism, minorities, and ethnic conflict (Parson, Dahl, Lijphart, Glazer, Moynihan, and Kuper, among others) have shied away from the immensely difficult problems of comparative sociology and the interplay of international politics and regional social or economic group relations with factors such as internal subjugation, integration, segregation, assimilation, and pluralism. Historians such as Hans Kohn have drawn comparisons and their work can be inspiring, but the rigor of close factor analysis is missing. The intellectual, structural weakness is immediately apparent when we consider the Israeli Arabs. Confusion and conflict arise in simple categorization: Who are these people behind the green line? Palestinians? Arabs? Israelis? Israeli Arabs? Israeli Palestinians? All of these? Categorization seems simpler in Jerusalem, but here too social division breeds identity problems and the problem of social status and future political organization remains clouded.

How did this problem come about, and are causal factors such as structure and setting in some way determinant to the evolution of further problems? Understanding structure is a function of sociological investigation. Obviously, the same broad historical antecedents—for example, a colonial history—do not produce the same political results universally, as a comparison of the United States and South Africa shows. The sociological structures of various competing groups in models of ethnic conflict are powerful determinants for the course and, indeed, outcome of these conflicts. In other words, as we have already mentioned, national minorities also have distinct social structures, with critical consequences for ethnic conflict. As society changes, the tendencies of various social groups within the "national" framework toward various courses of action (active confrontation, co-optation, integration, passivity, assimilation) also undergo change. Attitudes and actions are in flux as society is restructured. This is particularly true of societies like those of Israel's Arabs and the Arab Jerusalemites, who are fully under Israel's political and legal domination.

The Jerusalemites have other options but they nonetheless seem to reflect much that we will find among Israeli Arabs in terms of accommodation and ambivalence. In a situation of flux, who is likely to be co-opted—clan leaders? trade union executives? dependent workers? intellectuals? farmers? And who is likely to maintain a defiant national posture? Are internal developmental asymmetries causing new social fragmentations to be grafted onto old?

Sammy Smooha (1980a) confronts this problem in his search for a theoretical model for his investigation, which is by far the most thorough, of pluralism and conflict in Israeli society. He suggests three models—modernization, national assimilation, and internal colonialism—and then presents his own favored model, pluralism.

Three such theoretical perspectives attempt to cope with complex societies and their constituent status groups. One is associated with the works of Shils, Deutsch, Eisenstadt, Korhauser, Gorder, Glazer and Gans, among many others. It applies the notions of modernization, nation-building, political integration, consensual pluralism, assimilation and the like. It views change as a process of evolvement of a new social structure, in which past segmentary ties and traditions are gradually replaced by inclusive identities and institutions.

Another perspective is connected with Frank, Wallerstein, Furtado and Hechter, among others. It uses concepts of underdevelopment, dependency, internal colonialism, cultural division of labor and so on. This approach foresees growth of ethno-nationalism as a means of liberation from dependence.

In between stands the conflictual-pluralistic or neopluralistic perspective. The main contributors to this semi-deterministic, radical approach are Smith, Kuper, van den Berghe and Schermerhorn, among others. It focuses on the pluralistic-inequality structure and its repercussions for internal stability. Rather than assigning an a priori precedence to either ethnicity or class, it analyzes their interplay. It is less deterministic and more politically [rather] than economically deterministic than [is] the neo-Marxist perspective. It treats societal cohesion as more problematic than the nation-building perspective does. It traces the sources of political stability to the involuntary bulwarks of political regulation and economic dependence. (Smooha 1980a)

Smooha's approach, which he develops convincingly in *The Orientation and Politicization of the Arab Minority in Israel* (1984), is based on the writings of Esman, Francis, Macrae, and Lijphart. The major weakness in this research may be its exclusive concern with the macrosociological approach. The basic question of an antecedent typology of pluralistic ethnic conflict remains, even if one assumes that this approach is the most viable. The Middle Eastern nationalities have long historical memories. National "history" is as diffuse as nationalism and its interpretation is likely to be emotional and irrational. Structural analysis somehow neglects volatile atavisms. But the roots of ethnic conflict are inevitably historical. Causal relationships are the result of the national and international histories, often violent, of the region, and they cannot be perceived or solved through purely rational pluralistic analysis. Ethnic conflict is not only highly susceptible to international manipulation; national minorities are the creation of the historical flow of nationalisms and of international politics. Three basic typologies of ethnic conflict that evolve easily into various forms of national and international conflict are evident.

CRITERIA FOR ETHNIC CONFLICT

Identifying three broad historical patterns leading to ethnic (and/or religious) conflict in this century enables us to differentiate between various ethnic and subnational groups that are in conflict with dominant national cultures or with other ethnic cultures. We may call one category "historically ethno-regional." This type results when historical developments have served to punish one ethnic subnational group within, usually, a distinct geographical area in a nation-state dominated by another nation. This is the category of ethnic dispute that is receiving so much attention in Europe. The twin concepts of ethno-regionalism and ethnic history afford this category of dispute the possibility of a rigorous and structurally appealing, matrix-like form of analysis. Certain theories of conflict resolution, such as consociationalism (roughly defined as spoils and power sharing among ethnic elites), have been developed to deal with this category. It remains to be seen whether any ethnic group—Flemish, Breton, Scotch, Welsh, South Tyrolean, Catalan, Basque, Jura Swiss, or, in the Middle East, Southern Sudanese, Kurds, Berbers, various Lebanese and Iraqi Shiites, and perhaps Copts—can be satisfied by internal spoils dissemination. Nevertheless, ethnic regional and historical problems are probably the most open to certain territorial options of conflict resolution in addition to consociationalism: federalism, devolution, autonomy, integration, partition, and so on.

The second category is imported ethnic conflict. Such conflict may not be an exclusive feature of industrial society, but its most obvious and dramatic forms are certainly associated with societies that are technologically advanced. The highly varying need for mobile labor has typified their development. No quick or successful industrialization has taken place without bringing in large numbers of nonindigenous workers. Cheap and mobile labor has been provided by children, by women, by down-and-out farm hands. But—and this is especially true of the period after the World War II—so-called immigrant, or guest, or migrant labor seems to provide most of the needed infusions to the work force. Great Britain's utilization of such labor, first of its "cheap" Celtic periphery and then of Pakistanis and Jamaicans, has been a constant feature of its industrial development. The industrial development of the United States was certainly abetted greatly by imported labor; its ethnic immigration waves are legendary, and the current utilization of Mexicans in a period of high indigenous unemployment is much to the point. Although not generally associated with large movements of labor historically, Germany has been a particularly successful importer and assimilator of imported labor for the past 100 years.

Pure industrial or even class strife has been as often as not a reflection of ethnic differences (Birnbaum 1974). Whereas eventual assimilation was very much part of the pattern in the nineteenth century and made most conflict short-lived, other factors have altered the pattern in this century. One of the interesting features of the Israeli economy is the utilization of Arab "semi-mobile migrants." Because most of these Arabs return home to their villages every night, the basic problems of substandard housing, education, segregation, and so on have another cast in Israel. The Arab village retains much of the social problem, and this reflects a mixed or third typology that encompasses the national problem of Arab and Jew. In Jerusalem a similar pattern has developed.

It is the third category of ethnic conflict that concerns us most in this study. The broad historical framework of imperialism and colonialism lacks the analytical rigor required for any successful categorization. Concepts such as expanding, swarming, or invading nations are also unsatisfactory. The Protestant Northern Irish, Israeli Jews, Russians in the Baltic, European New Zealanders, white South Africans, Turks in Cyprus, and perhaps even Anglos in the U.S. Southwest are "transplanted" ethnic groups whose clashes with original inhabitants and others on the move into the same area lead to "transplanted ethnic conflict." In the case of Northern Ireland, Cyprus, or the Baltic, the transplantation of a population is purposive and directed from without. Sometimes populations flee and crowd the indigenous population. In some instances an ethno-regional group such as the Lebanese Christians is "restructured" internationally, so that the line between these admittedly broad categories is blurred even more. Transplanted ethnic conflict is less given to resolution than the other kinds and so it leads often, beyond protracted internal strife, to international conflict.

Despite a continuous Jewish presence throughout the centuries, the Jewish majority of Israel grafted itself onto the area. Most Palestinians either fled or were chased from their homes (it is theoretically immaterial which version is accurate). Israel as a nation was implanted by international fiat and the Jewish population's superior organization in the area. The Jews' historical claims on the area are morally interesting but do not change the model. It is definitely the most volatile model of the three. Pluralistic solutions have yet to fully succeed in Northern Ireland, Cyprus, South Africa, or even in the Baltic states or the U.S. Southwest. Indeed, Israel is the only successfully functioning implant state of its kind established in our century—but a satisfactory pluralist solution for the Arab community seems far off. Astonishingly enough, Israel's Arabs have been quiet about this. Indeed, by hard work and political cooperation they have contributed in no small measure to the success of the state of Israel. In Jerusalem similar patterns emerged, and again there is no doubt that Arab investment, labor, and economic organization have contributed much to the astonishing internal development and success of Jerusalem since 1967.

In addition to the historical typological hypotheses, I maintain that regional considerations (i.e., the venue of the problem) are critical in determining the level and course of confrontation and conflict between various ethnic groups. The Middle East has traditionally been an area of volatile and violent confrontation. It has also seen the elimination of populations, large exchanges of populations, and complete changes in population structures within various geographic areas. The patterns of ethnic conflict since the beginning of the twentieth century have been violent and confrontational. Longstanding, simmering ethnic animosities that were managed, controlled, and manipulated by the Ottomans evolved into existential struggles for statehood. The answers to the searches for identity that have marked the area and served as the justification for violence have been nationalism and the establishment of the nation-state (almost always at the expense of others). National confrontation has superseded particularist or ethnic local conflict as the dominant pattern of political strife and violence in the area. Conflict resolution, based on pluralist solutions, dissemination of political and economic spoils, and relative social and cultural tolerance (the hallmark of the multi-ethnic Ottomans), is conspicuously lacking. Instead, rule by cliques (often ethnic), clientilistic lines of control, and obedience prove resilient. National centralism has led to constant internal and international conflict, often bloody yet inconclusive. Obviously, then, the quiescence of the Arab society within the borders of Israel and indeed the relative passivity within Jerusalem as well are theoretically puzzling and demand investigation. Why was there so little internal armed resistance to Jewish domination, or so little violent conflict of any nature, in a situation and area where this could be expected to occur? Even throughout the intifada, violent confrontations by Israeli Arabs and in Jerusalem, while evident, have been marginal.[5]

WHAT DETERMINES POLITICAL ACTION?

What are the determinants of political action in a situation of ethnic confrontation? How long does one suffer what one believes to be external domination and, indeed, oppression? What does a population ask of itself individually and collectively? Let us detail the questions that are likely to shape attitudes in such a situation.

1. What, basically, do I want in life? In other words, what are my main goals and how are these goals determined? How do I define myself

and my society in terms of the expectations of my peers, my society, and myself? (This is a kind of extension to the problems of ethnic confrontation of H. Laswell's thinking.)

2. To paraphrase Fredrik Barth (1969), how do I set myself off from others, where do I draw the line between myself and others, where is my turf, and how do I define this turf? Who threatens all these aspects of my life the most? Am I interested in—as Robert Redfield, the American social anthropologist, put it in his politicized ideas on James Scott—a great or little tradition of life (Schiel 1985)? In other words, are my national goals more important to me than the particularist demands of my more immediate society? All this, of course, will determine my strategies and counterstrategies and my perception of dominance and oppression.

3. What will I risk to get what I want? Would getting part of it be enough? Am I feeling "relatively deprived," or is my relative deprivation really just the chimera of political theorists? How does my feeling of deprivation relate to my perception of power differentials (Korpi 1974)? As a corollary to these questions, is nationalism an instrument of division or of unity in the pursuit of these goals and in opposition to forces that are perceived as threatening? The diffuse and intellectually unintelligible ideological principle that is nationalism has not been as uniformly effective a tool of unity and organization in the nineteenth and twentieth centuries as national historians and political scientists would have us believe. For functional utility it has depended—as an organizational axiom of opposition or as an organizing principle of government—on certain confluences of sociological, economic, and political developments. In ethnic conflicts it does not seem that national identity alone suffices to unite or to guarantee unity.

ORGANIZATION AND DISORGANIZATION
OF NATIONAL GOALS

Successful establishment of a paramilitary organization is not necessarily synonymous with the establishment of a national movement, but such movements are very rarely successful without a viable paramilitary structure. In an earlier analysis of the paramilitary organizations of various ethnic groups in the Middle East, I showed how difficult it has been for Kurds and Palestinians to organize their paramilitary operations because of lack of cohesiveness in their societies (Ashkenasi 1986). This does not mean that the societies within their various components were not cohesive, but that a basic extended geographical unity did not exist. No sinews of

modern organizational structure united the "nationalists" in common political activity. National identification, however intense, found no trans-
lation into coordinated and "nationwide" activity. Various segments of
society all were intense in their proclamation of national goals, but particularist fragmentations remained more important than any conception of
national unity. It seems to me that this is not only still true for the Kurds,
but that it also still applies, albeit much less so, to the Palestinians—though
the point is arguable.

It appears that the Palestinians' major modern umbrella organization,
the Fatah, can only function outside the area of immediate confrontation.
It achieves open loyalty but can only integrate the various Palestinian
subunits for words and not deeds; actions are rarely within Palestine. Indeed, the PLO's international organizational success was long offset by its
dismal political and military failures in the Middle East. In fact, as S.
Sandler and Hillel Frisch demonstrate (1984), the PLO itself has seemed
to be a significant element in the lack of organizational strength of Arab
society in the territories. As we pointed out earlier, this is in part due to
its lack of immediate geographic proximity, but it is also due to the lack
of political, social, and economic infrastructure or centralized development
in Palestinian society. Many claim the PLO impedes such infrastructure or
development. Frisch (1990) has recently discussed the challenge posed by
the intifada in terms of the tension between the outside organization, which
would prefer to consolidate its control, and the leadership spearheading
the resistance within the territories.

As a corollary, the successes achieved by the Zionist forces in the battles
from 1946 to 1948 were attributable to the fact that there had been no
sizable, entrenched Jewish society in Palestine beforehand. No divisive and
traditional sociological, regional, and political restraints existed to hamper
the Jewish forces. Whatever traditional Jewish society there was in Palestine had no power to control the events of the 1930s and 1940s, so
organizing could follow the basic nationalist principle imported from Europe. There was no possibility of return to another, more comfortable or
secure position; European Jewish society had been destroyed. No social
conception or structure seriously competed with the one basic unifying
goal. The questions that were asked in the preceding section could be
answered only by founding the national Zionist-Jewish state. The trade
unions, teachers' organizations, united farm movements, and even large
elements of the organized religious community were centrally manageable
and could coordinate their actions. With Palestinian Arab society highly
fragmented, the situation was completely different for the Palestinians.
The fragmentation that worked to weaken Palestinian society in this conflict
with Zionism continued to do so in the post–World War II years, in the
post–1948 period, and indeed, to this day.

The highly localized structure of Arab society, its clan orientations, and its traditions of petit-bourgeois clientilism are still rampant within Fatah. Indeed, many of these social traditions were carried into the refugee camps themselves (Zureik 1979b). Recent research continues to verify the fissured nature of Palestinian society and politics, even when the political and ideological positions of the analysis are diametrically opposed (Baumgarten 1985, 1991; Schiller 1982). There is, in fact, no accepted structure of national Palestinian leadership within Palestine; this leads to the paradox of an ease of identification, since the national idea is designed in a most diffuse and abstract way but with a lack of organizational prowess. Everyone is a nationalist; no one has to do much to prove it. The national movement is devoid of any kind of social position; until very recently, conservative elites perforce dominated (Smith 1986a). We shall have much more to say about this later.

SELECTED SOCIAL THEORIES OF EMERGING ETHNIC CONFLICT

As societies progress, modernist theoreticians would have us believe that particularist fragmentation typically gives way to a more modern nation-state.[6] This, of course, is not necessarily the case. Such theories probably did not accurately describe even those European developments on which they were based. The more complex the society, the more complex the search for self may also become, with the process of continuing fragmentation becoming more complex as well. Out of regional, confessional, city-country, or Bedouin-farmer confrontations can come clashes of secularism and religious fundamentalism, socialism and bourgeois capitalism, clan orientation and modernism (Hudson 1981).

Tentative new research into the complicated field of ethnic urban conflict gives us some idea of the multifaceted paradigma of multi-ethnic life (Clarke 1976). The implications of spatial organization (Benvenisti 1986; Dakkak 1981; Efrat 1982; Romann 1984, 1986) are obvious in any analysis of the Middle East. Corollary demographic trends and attempts at demographic manipulation become "structural" or "situational" determinants (Clarke 1976). Their function can be to galvanize or act as controlling rods for conflict. But often socio-psychological dimensions (Barth and Noel 1972; Caplan and Caplan 1980) have an active life of their own and do not react to the logic of sociological remedies. Atavisms and pathological learning in groups and individuals result in what some call violent subcultures (Erlanger 1976; Lee 1976) and the solidification of irrational and self-delusionary belief systems, identification processes, or strategies. Spatial organization and segregation (as often as not, self-imposed and developed in response to cultural and subcultural concepts of political, social, and economic stratification) constitute but one function of belief systems that live on, self-sealed against other social or political paradigma (Clarke 1976).

Thus, "structural influences" may simply mean, on the one hand, control and co-optation and, on the other, more levels of interaction that may or may not limit the potential for violence.

Historical particularist patterns of political, economic, and especially social interchange in the Middle East, while not always leading to uncompromising polarization, have certainly been self-segregatory. They have generally manifested all of the phenomena we have discussed, and they have been especially prominent in (but not limited to) urban areas. Particularism is such a blatant Middle Eastern phenomenon that much of the theory of ethnic division can easily be applied within a given ethnic group as well. For Palestinian society this has certainly been true, and it has been complicated by asymmetrical social and economic development within the various Palestinian communities. Israeli authorities have long recognized this situation and their structural influences have successfully enhanced disunity and internal ethnic self-segregation, spatial as well as psychological.

Indeed, the diaspora of the Palestinians has also added to the complexity of their political organization and their social structures. People who grow up in refugee camps are bound to have a different psychological conception of life than those who grow up in the relative comfort of a town like Shfaram in the Galilee, or even Jenin or Nablus in the West Bank, to say nothing of the relative wealth of parts of the Ramallah community. In Jerusalem the obvious spatial and psychological boundaries between Arab and Jew are compounded by those between Jew and Jew and Arab and Arab. But the Jews have a unifying central authority, whereas Arab central authority, or authorities in Jerusalem, represent (as we shall see) only a minority of the minority in the city. Jerusalem's Arab population is also fragmented in many ways. Its ties to the rest of the Arabs in the territories are interdicted by a series of economic, social, political, and psychological paradigma. Many of these are indeed the result of structural influences. Many others, however, are imbedded in the history of the city (Romann and Weingrod 1990). In examining social fragmentation in Palestinian society, the focus herein will be on that part of the society that does not live under direct military occupation but does reside within the boundaries of the state of Israel, and on that part of the society that has an integratory option— the Jerusalemites, to whom Israel must hold out the offer of citizenship in order to claim that the city is united. Together they comprise a segment of Palestinian society that still freely discusses options and could act upon them.

NOTES

1. See my book on German and other European nationalisms, *Modern German Nationalism* (New York, 1976).

2. See, for example, Mario Barrera, *Race and Class in the Southwest: A Theory of Racial Inequality* (London, 1979), and Brigitte Mihok, *Ethnostratifikation in sozialismus, aufgezeigt an den Beispielländern Ungarn und Romänien* (Frankfurt, 1990).

3. See the posthumous edition of Weber's writings, *Wirtschaft und Gesellschaft* (Tübingen, 1972).

4. Data are from the *MERIP Middle East Report* (1987) and *Statistical Yearbook 1987* (Jerusalem, 1989); figures are increased slightly and rounded.

5. For an analysis of conflict and ethnicity, see Horowitz (1985).

6. For a thorough bibliographical analysis of much relevant theory, see the analytical papers of Donald T. Campbell and Marc Howard Ross (1989, unpublished).

2

THE POLITICAL DEVELOPMENT OF ISRAEL'S ARABS UNTIL 1967

SOCIAL STRUCTURE AND LEADERSHIP BEFORE 1948

A basic hypothesis in our consideration of fragmentation among Palestinians is that structural social cohesion of an ethnic group is the basic determining factor of its ability to organize and function under conditions of social deprivation and ethnic domination. In other words, certain basic elements are necessary for active opposition to a political, social, and economic situation that is perceived as exploitative. Dominant groups almost never evince the generosity that would be necessary to eliminate their control. International actors must have a cohesive organizational structure to work with if they are to exercise their influence in an area through an ethnic group. The transformation from ethnic group to national minority, from domestic internal conflict to international recognition, is a function of a social cohesion that, by and large, must be structured in a relatively modern fashion. As Yehoshua Porath shows (1974, 1977), during the British mandate Palestinian society proved unable to develop the modern sinews of political organization that we described in the previous chapter. In the words of I. Lustick (1980),

The struggle of Palestinian Arabs against Zionism and against the British Mandate had been dominated, since the late 1920s, by a small number of large, powerful families located in the largest cities of Palestine . . . Jerusalem, Nablus, Haifa, and Jaffa. The political strengths of the Palestinian national movement were based on the feudalistic links between these families and networks of smaller clans and extended families in villages throughout the country, as well as on the active support of a substantial urban professional and merchant class, largely Christian and nationalistic. (p. 48)

The seeds of many of the problems of the Palestinian Arabs today were planted during the mandate. "Normal" Palestinian development under the conditions of the time was, as E. Zureik stresses (1979a), hindered by the incursion of another society, more modern and more efficient, in effect freezing the existing Palestinian condition. Neither a Palestinian officer corps, a working class organized in trade unions, nor even an effective Muslim middle class developed as they presumably would have if the Jewish sector had not usurped their place. Zureik blames Zionist capitalism and British imperialism for this. But the roots of the problem can be seen in Palestinian society as well, and the efficient socialist elements of the Zionism of the period probably had far more influence on the situation than did any capitalist development. Jewish society benefitted from the creation of relatively well constructed sociopolitical entities such as trade unions, paramilitary fighting organizations, and cooperative farming units, the best of which boasted socialist theoretical underpinning and, more important, socialist cadre efficiency. In addition, a large technological gap divided the two societies, a gap that was probably wider in terms of ability to use new technologies of conflict than ability to create strategies.

Palestinian society during the mandate period retained characteristics that hindered its development and that had been tolerated or encouraged by the Ottomans because they were forms of fragmentation and ineffectual political structure that enhanced Ottoman control. Both for imperial profit and for military manpower, the Ottoman empire, which was multi-ethnic and "universalist," depended on its ability to organize various ethnic or regional, particularist "societies." It preserved tenuous regional balances in order to rule with a minimum of force or social interference, maintaining regions free of "uni-ethnic" dominance. The Levant in particular was a mosaic of communities that had never interacted politically except in the central Levant markets or else through conflict and enforced conflict resolution. This particularist model of self-segregatory social structures had to be overcome before the dream of Palestine could become more than a pious hope.

Meanwhile, much of the commerce was in the hands of one or another of the Christian sects; indeed, Christian bourgeois society dominated the commercial networks of most of the Arab cities and preempted most of the modern professions (medicine, pharmacy, law, journalism, etc.). The possible exceptions were Jerusalem and Nablus. Both were inland, but it was the family clans of these cities, especially Jerusalem, that dominated the Arab nationalist movement. Their structure was inherently conservative and their prestige and power were a function of old-fashioned infighting. The coastal cities, Haifa and Jaffa, with their young trade union movements did not play a dominant role in the Palestinian national movement. The major struggle between the Nashishibi and Husseini families was essentially a Jerusalem conflict. The Palestinian nationalist movement became inward-looking, clan-oriented, and strongly village-based. Support from the cities and urban Christians was largely verbal, while the real organizational structure was heavily Muslim and rural in character. This excluded much of Christian society from serious organizational control. Amnon Kapeliouk reports that in 1946, at the end of the mandate period, 79.8 percent of the Christians of Palestine lived in cities. Seventy percent of the Arab population, however, was living in villages of 3,000 inhabitants or less (1944 statistic). Indeed, in 1942 only 35 percent of Arab agricultural products were sold in the marketplace; this indicates that an enormous percentage of Arab society, mostly Muslim, still lived in pre-market conditions (Kapeliouk 1969). Their social loyalties reflected this situation, as Zureik points out (1979b):

Palestine's relatively small size and its homogeneous national composition did not prevent the presence of significant internal social cleavages. Regionalism, the clan system, village autarchy, not to mention the class structure, mitigated against the appearance of [loyalties that cut across clan and group]. . . . The city-country dichotomy presented a type of social differentiation which exceeded in its overall effect any other social cleavage in creating lasting social distance between the two main sectors of Palestinian society. (p. 54)

Zureik cites R. Sayigh in pointing out that the divisions persist in refugee camps in Lebanon more than three decades after the flight from Palestine:

Yet so tenacious were the perceptions of social class difference that [refugee] camp Palestinians today still use the terms *madani* [city-dweller] and *fellah* [peasant] to classify themselves and others. It is clear from the situated usage of these terms that they indicate socio-cultural differences and not simply occupational differences. (Sayigh in Zureik 1979b, p. 54)

Urban Christian society was primarily bourgeois and developed more along nuclear family lines than the *hamula* (extended family) structure of the Muslim Arab village. As we will see, it is not the fact that a Muslim is a Muslim and a Christian a Christian that necessarily keeps them apart. That certainly was the origin of the cleavage, but the resulting dissimilar social structures reinforce a longstanding regional mistrust. The events that befell the Palestinians in 1948 reflected these cleavages in Palestinian society. The extraordinary international situation that had planted a modern competitive society in their midst further exacerbated Palestinian social fragmentation. The Palestinian Muslims' indigenous, mainly reactionary leadership was more interested in its own petty feuds than in a well-organized national struggle. No impetus for change in Arab social structure to meet the Zionist challenge was possible from the leading Husseini family. Indeed, this leadership's shortsighted and selfish, dubious pro-Axis policies during World War II further fragmented and isolated the Palestinians (Gen-

Table 2–1
Arab Population by City

City	Before the war (1947)	After the war (1949)[a]
Jerusalem	75,000	3,500
Jaffa	70,000	3,600
Haifa	71,200	2,900
Lydda-Ramle	34,920	2,000
Nazareth	15,540	16,800
Acre (Akko)	15,000	3,500
Tiberias	5,310	—
Safed	9,530	—
Shfaram	4,200	4,800[b]

Source: Lustick (1980).
a The figures, especially those for Acre and Nazareth, include substantial numbers of internal refugees (on internal migration, see al-Haj 1986).
b al-Haj (1986).

Table 2–2
Arab Residents of Mixed Cities

City	1951[a]	1988
Jaffa	5,600	11,100
Haifa	7,500	20,200
Ramle	1,960	7,400
Acre (Akko)	4,220	8,500

Source: Kamon (1984); Israel Statistical Yearbook, 1989.
a includes unregistered or illegal Arab residents

sicke 1988). Much of the leadership was gone before 1946–48 and the rest fled during that period. By the end of Israel's war of independence in 1948, little was left of any kind of Palestinian leadership (except the communists) within the borders of the new state. In most instances what remained was the periphery of Arab society; completely impoverished villages such as Furadies and Jezira el-Zarka, Galilee villages such as Sakhnin without the wherewithal to flee, and the truncated Triangle towns were typical (tables 2–1 to 2–3).

Arab urban society was completely destroyed and the Arab population in what had become the state of Israel sank from some 800,000 to approximately 150,000. More important perhaps than the sudden demise of a majority population into a thoroughly marginal minority was the destruction of incipient modern structures (educational frameworks, trade unions, and the like) that had been developing in the cities. (However, it must be pointed out that the best schools in the Arab sector during the mandate

Table 2-3
Estimate of Total Palestinian Population, 1952–87

	1952 Total	%	1961 Total	%	Before June 1967 Total	%	After June 1967 Total	%	1982 Total	%	1987 Total	%
+ Historic Palestine	1,221,300	76.4	1,430,000	64.4	1,668,200	63.4	1,344,868	49.7	1,856,300	41.0	2,140,400	41.6
- Israel	179,300	11.2	242,000	10.9	318,200	12.1	325,700	12.0	550,000	12.2	645,000	12.5
- West Bank	742,000	46.4 ⎫ 65.2	814,000	36.7 ⎫ 53.5	900,000	34.2 ⎫ 51.3	664,494	24.6 ⎫ 37.7	830,000	18.3	937,400	18.2
- Gaza	300,000	18.8 ⎭	374,000	16.8 ⎭	450,000	17.1 ⎭	354,674	13.1 ⎭	476,300	10.5	558,000	10.9
+ UNRWA operational area	1,389,000	86.9	1,867,400	84.1	2,156,000	82.0	2,117,768	78.3	3,006,300	66.3	3,369,000	65.5
+ Border States	347,000	21.7	679,400	30.6	806,300	30.7	1,098,600	40.6	1,700,00	37.5	1,873,600	36.5
- Jordan	150,000	9.4	380,000	17.1	466,000	17.7	730,600	27.0	1,080,000	23.8	1,252,000	24.4
- Syria	83,000	5.2	116,400	5.2	140,300	5.4	143,000	5.3	245,000	5.4	284,000	5.5
- Lebanon	114,000	7.1	183,000	8.3	200,000	7.6	225,000	8.3	375,000	8.3	337,600	6.6
+ Other countries	31,200	1.9	110,000	5	155,500	5.9	263,162	9.7	975,000	21.5	1,125,500	21.9
- Arab world	—	—	—	—	128,000	4.9	216,162	8.0	800,000	17.6	927,000	18.0
- Non-Arab	—	—	—	—	27,500	1.0	47,000	1.7	175,000	3.9	198,000	3.9
Total	1,599,500	100	2,219,400	100	2,630,000	100	2,706,630	100	4,531,300	100.0	5,139,000	100

Source: L. Hajjar, comp., "The Palestinian Journey, 1952-1987," in *MERIP Middle East Report*, Vol. 17, No. 3, P. 10 (Washington, D.C., May-June 1987).

Table 2–4
Arab Land Possession

Name of village	Area possessed in 1947 (dunams)	Area possessed after expropriations (dunams)
Jat	12,000	9,000
Qalansawe	18,850	6,780
Jaljuliah	14,000	800
Tira	40,000	8,000
Taibeh	45,000	13,000
Ara-Arrara	26,000	7,000
Kfar Bara	4,000	2,000
Baqa al-Gharbiyah	22,000	7,000
Kfar Qassem	12,000	9,000
Umm el-Fahm	125,000	25,000
Pekein	14,000	5,500
Beir-el-Assad, Binah and Nahaf	16,000	7,000
Beit Jahn	26,500	13,000
Yirka	55,000	18,000
Sakhnin	55,000	13,000[a]
Arrabe	95,000	11,350
Deir Hanna	16,000	9,500
Majd el-Kram	20,000	7,000

Note: Compiled mostly by Lustick (1980).
a This figure is from an interview with the mayor of Sakhnin, March 1980.

period were private. Only the private Christian schools continued to operate after the establishment of the state of Israel.) Arab society in 1948, then, not only lacked any kind of real leadership—social, economic, or educational; it lacked the sinews to develop it. Even much of the old clan leadership had fled. Those of the population who remained were to see approximately 50 percent of their land disappear into the Jewish sector (Smooha 1980b). And 45,000 of these 150,000 were refugees within the state from homes that simply no longer existed after the war (UNRWA Report of the High Commissioner to the General Assembly, 1987; al-Haj 1988) (table 2–4).

Just how much of the land that was lost to the Arabs was communal or lacked verifiable ownership is a question that is hotly debated and full of rancor. Arab society perceived it as Arab land, and psychologically this hurt the most. The socioeconomic consequence was that many Arabs, probably more than half the working population, were left completely dependent upon work outside the villages and had no organizational structure beyond their own families that they could look to for economic, social, or psychological support. A strong turning inward toward village and clan was the result.

A certain exception to this rule is found in the city of Nazareth and the large town of Shfaram; still intact after the 1948 war, both places grew slightly because of an influx of refugees. Nazareth, not surprisingly, became the urban center, the intellectual heart of Arab Palestinian society in Israel (Elime 1985). Shfaram, where 55 percent of the current population of over 25,000 are either refugees or their descendants, has become a relatively successful model for social development in Arab villages. Having a much more mobile society than any other village evinces, it is mixed religiously and its citizens have wide contacts with co-religionists and Jews outside of town. (This does not indicate, however, a truly assimilatory society. There is virtually no intermarriage, even between refugee and indigenous families. And as was the case throughout Israel, the refugee community developed, socially and consequently politically, apart from the rest of the village [al-Haj 1986].) These two places were very much the exception in 1948, and even they did not offer leadership at that time to the completely fragmented Palestinian society remaining in Israel.

DEMOGRAPHY, GEOGRAPHY, AND EDUCATION

The Arab population in Israel was concentrated in three separate geographic regions. The largest was the Galilee, where about 65 percent lived. The second was the so-called Little Triangle in central Israel with approximately 25 percent of the Arab population. The remaining 10 percent were in the south. The areas developed independently, with very little interaction between them in the period between 1948 and 1967. In terms of ethnic structure the Galilee is a very mixed area, where almost all the Christian and Druze Arabs are found; for the most part, however, they live in separate villages. In 1948 Christians constituted approximately 22 percent of the Arab community, while the Druze comprised between 8 and 9 percent (18 percent in the Galilee). A separate religious group whose political affinities have been with the Israeli state since the early 1950s, the Druze are the only major group of Arabs conscripted into the armed forces, and this is by their own choice. Now constituting 17 to 18 percent of the Israeli Arab population, they maintain the highest growth rate. Their support for the Zionist state and participation in the military framework have further fragmented Arab society, for there is no doubt that the Galilee is the heartland of any developing nationalist sentiment in Israel. Those Druze who did not support Israel, and there have always been such, must be considered exceptions (Ben-Dor 1979), though at present their number may be growing. The social structure of the Druze community is similar to that of the Muslims.

About half of the Arabs in the Galilee in 1948 were Muslims. The situation that developed, as we shall see, was that Christians, whose orientation by and large was bourgeois, maintained the better educational system and were heavily concentrated in those urban areas that existed. In contrast to the Druze, their political posture was similar to that of the Muslims; however, their social structure separated them from much of the Muslim society, which was still isolated in small villages. In those Galilee villages where Christians lived in a bi-ethnic relationship with Druze, they influenced their political positions and voting patterns.

The Arab population of the second area of concentration, the Little Triangle, is completely Muslim. Having limited ties to the Galilee, it developed along different lines altogether. Moreover, Umm el-Fahm, the largest Arab town in the Triangle, was the one most truncated by the political boundaries of 1948 and by the land expropriation that occurred subsequently. Unlike the Galilee, where Nazareth reflected to a degree the mixed ethnic structure of the area and where Christian private schools could maintain a tradition of education that also affected the general standard, the Little Triangle was without an urban center to speak of.[1] Umm el-Fahm became more and more radicalized, a trend that was already evident in the 1950s, and was separated in development from the rest of the Triangle by virtue of its enormous land loss and the semi-migrant nature of much of its population. The Triangle as a whole remained an agricultural area and indeed benefitted somewhat from Israeli irrigation schemes servicing the new Jewish settlements. Although they were also meant to break up Arab concentration in the area, the result was nevertheless a substantial increase in the agricultural yield of many of the Muslim villages. Relative well-being has led to relative political moderation in the area, with the exception again of Umm el-Fahm and possibly Taibeh in the 1970s.

The third area, the south, is again ethnically and politically distinct. Most Arabs here are Bedouins, a group that has adopted a considerably more pro-Israel stance than have other Muslims. Constituting about 10 percent of Israel's Arabs, the Bedouins also suffered an enormous population loss after 1948. Of the 65,750 who roamed the Negev desert before 1948, only about 11,000 remained to become Israeli citizens. The Bedouins retained their clan structure. As Lustick points out, the Israelis

cultivated the internal fragmentation of the Bedouin and the breakup of the Tiaha confederation [to which most of the remaining Bedouins belonged]. Bedouins were required to register with the military administration according to their *tribal* affiliation (tribes being quasi-kinship groups of confederations). Bedouin tribesmen were also obliged to obtain the permission of the military Governor before crossing a boundary between one tribe and another. (1980, pp. 134–135).

This kept the Bedouins effectively separated, as was the conscious policy of the Israeli authorities throughout the country well into the 1970s. Other Bedouins who migrated north lived on the fringe of Arab society there (al-Haj 1986).

The policy, which of course applied not only to the Bedouins, maintained fragmentation of Arab society into the late 1960s through a series of regulations that encouraged an inward social orientation and restricted political, social, and economic mobility within the Arab community. The regulations of the military administration that existed until 1966 restricted mobility quite literally, requiring permits for movement between and out of areas that encompassed most Arab villages. While Israeli Arabs were allowed to work within the Jewish sector, mostly as unskilled labor, the only steady internal contact between Arabs seems to have been carried out by Christian middlemen such as doctors, pharmacists, and teachers. Although Arab society obviously changed after 1967, as we shall see, with a new generation of Arabs that was born and educated in the state of Israel, a society that was kept in place for the first 20 years has continued to maintain a conservative impetus. Fragmentation has certainly not been overcome.

Amnon Kapeliouk has documented the enormous economic head start that Arab Christians had over the Muslims and Druze in the first twenty years of the state (1968). Christians have been disproportionately represented in banking, insurance, and other commercial enterprises and also—especially—in government services (25 percent). Twelve percent of the Druze have been employed by the government, more than double the percentage of Muslims, but with this major exception, Druze and Muslim patterns are similar. Druze have made up a large part of the border police, while the Christian statistic for government services reflects a high number of teachers, but the process of co-optation is notable in both cases.

Bilingualism is the key to advancement in Israel for Arabs. Speaking Hebrew is a necessity. By the 1960s Christians had already realized this: Over half of Christian males between the ages of 15 and 44 were Hebrew speakers. The figures for Muslim males are also high but on the average are some 20 percentage points behind Christians in the same age ranges. More significant are the figures for females. By the early 1960s some 20 percent of Christian females between the ages of 15 and 44 were Hebrew speakers. The Muslim average was only 4 percent. While these figures have since changed radically, the Christian lead is apparent and significant in explaining early Christian advancement (Kapeliouk 1968).

The same phenomena hold true for educational patterns and urbanization. By the early 1960s, 74 percent of adult Christians (age 14 and up) were literate. Sixty-two percent of the Muslims were illiterate, as were half the Druze. These figures include both men and women. Christians have dominated the teaching profession. Although they represented only 20 percent of the population, they comprised 45 percent of the Arab teaching force in the early 1960s. The number of women teaching is even more significant vis-à-vis Muslims; the ratio is almost 3:1. Earlier figures would show an even greater Christian prevalence in the field as there was a large and steady increase in the numbers of Muslim teachers at the beginning of the 1960s. Christians completely dominated the teaching in the prestigious private Arab school system, while there were almost as many Jews as Muslims teaching in the Arab public system in the early 1960s. The overall ratio of Christian teachers to Muslim is 6:4.

The figures for urbanization are even more significant. Clan, or extended family (*hamula*), hierarchies have dominated the social structure of the Arab village. Few villages remained without such basic amenities as electricity into the 1980s, but in the 1960s technology was rare. With military transit laws isolating villages and hindering the development of any kind of political sophistication and social progress, the Christian of the large town was in a much better position to advance.

All of these patterns that were so clear in the pre–1967 period were further borne out by a survey by Eli Rekhess of Arab graduates of institutions of higher learning in Israel from 1966 to 1971 (1974). Forty-nine percent of these graduates were Christian, 43 percent Muslim, and 7.2 percent Druze. Proportionally the Druze and especially the Muslims are underrepresented. The regional breakdowns show similar underrepresentation of the Muslim Little Triangle, producing only 14 percent of the college graduates; fully 76 percent, whether Christian, Muslim, or Druze, were from the Galilee. The remaining 10 percent came from Jerusalem. There were no Bedouins among the college graduates.

The incorporation of Arab Jerusalem into Israel in 1967–68 affected the statistics. The Jerusalem Palestinians were counted by Israel as constituting about 15 percent of the entire Israeli Arab population. Some 85 percent of them were Muslim, but since Jerusalem had belonged to Jordan for twenty years, a completely different social structure prevailed. Indeed, Arab Jerusalem seemed everything that Arab Israel was not—more urban, highly politicized, better educated. The chances are, however, that a good portion of the 10 percent of Arab university graduates whom Rekhess found in Jerusalem came from Israel's Arab sector rather than hailing from that city or from the West Bank.[2] (They were not interviewed.) A number of Israeli Arabs have found work far from their home towns and villages in the Jerusalem municipality and as professionals in the city. This has isolated them even more since their ties to Jerusalem's Arabs are tenuous.

Statistics on the students' parents further document the patterns of advanced social and economic standing among Christians. Twenty-eight percent of the fathers of Christian university students had a high school or university education. Only 14 percent of the Muslim fathers boasted a high school education, and none of the fathers of the Druze did. Fifty-three percent of the Muslim fathers, 26 percent of the Christian fathers, and fully 75 percent of the Druze fathers were farmers. The differences in social structure between the Christian community and the Muslim and Druze communities are also reflected in the political party development in Israel during the 20 years before 1967.

POLITICAL AND SOCIAL DEVELOPMENT

Communist parties have never been particularly successful in the Arab world, nor among Muslims in general. Often, as has been the case elsewhere as well, the oppositional Communist party in the Arab world became a repository for ethnic or religious minorities, or both. Most frequently this meant urban, Christian Arabs. The Israeli Communist party is no exception. Most of the Arab political leaders who did remain in Israel after 1948 had been members of the Palestine Communist party; by and large they were Orthodox Christians. (The Greek Orthodox church claims the allegiance of about one third of the Christian community in Israel; there are five separate denominations altogether [Harari 1976, 1978b; Lustick 1980].)

The Israeli Communist party Maki, which developed into Rakah, the New Communist List, attempted to maintain a posture that would appeal to Arab ethnicity—indeed, to Arab national feeling—without disavowal of the Israeli state. It was really the only political party that developed in Israel proclaiming this stance, and certainly it was the only active one between 1948 and 1967. The Arab nationalist al-Ard (the land) movement of the late 1960s was shortlived, and although it was taken seriously enough by the authorities that some of its leadership was deported ("allowed to leave"), it was without great significance. Rakah has a veteran Jewish leadership as well as a veteran Christian leadership, and it is most probably this that discredited the party among many Arabs, at least in the period before 1968. The high proportion and activity of the Christians in the party are the phenomena of interest here, however. This development was complemented by the upward mobility of Christians, not only in the educational system, as we have seen, but in the Israeli trade union, the Histadrut.[3] Those Christians who gravitated to the Histadrut and other Israeli institutions became, if not active, at least passive supporters of the Zionist state. Their relative social and economic success proved an example to some and their children tended to follow in their footsteps. Indeed, similar patterns hold for successful Muslim and Druze families.[4]

The activity of the Christians, a minority within a minority, and their accommodation, plus that of the Bedouins and the Druze, meant that four distinct social subgroups could be identified within Arab society under Israeli control—five if those Arabs living in the mixed towns of Haifa, Lod, Ramleh, and Acre are counted separately. (Later, East Jerusalemites would comprise another group.) Regional and social differences became intertwined. Lack of contact between Muslims in the Galilee and Muslims

in the Triangle meant further breakdown of Arab unity. This fragmentation
was not lost on Israeli officials, and it was fostered in order to strengthen
Israeli control over the Arab sector, as Lustick has shown. The means
included co-opting traditional leadership for Israeli political needs (family
heads or village leaders were bought off by minor concessions and remained
quiet in the face of adverse Israeli policies) as well as recruiting working-
class Arabs for labor in Israel's economy, co-opting educated and upwardly
mobile Arabs into the Israeli structure without giving them concomitant
political say in Israeli affairs. In the latter instance, this meant that the
Histadrut, the border police, and the educational system opened their doors
a bit for Arab participation, while Jews remained dominant. Regulations
that restricted mobility so that no national political organization could
develop and a social system that effectively segregated Arab society from
the Jewish sector held back Arab social and economic development. The
phenomenon of Arab participation in—and, more important, widespread
voting for—Zionist parties without Arabs being given any influence was a
byproduct of this system.

This last aspect of control could be termed benign neglect of Arab infrastructure in Israel. However, it must be pointed out that Israel's Arabs
accepted this segregation and indeed avidly practiced a family and village
orientation. Some families gravitated to Zionist patterns, which meant
political as well as economic dependence on the state of Israel. Some sought
economic security, social mobility, or better education through Rakah.
Many Muslim day laborers continued an adherence to conservative Islam.
Some Arabs (mostly refugees) remained altogether isolated economically
and socially. But as we will see, almost all Arabs maintained social segregation along religious and geographical lines by preference.

NOTES

1. For an in-depth analysis of Nazareth, see Elime (1985).
2. There were no universities on the West Bank or in Jerusalem before 1967,
but education was universal and the school system uniform. See Mar'i (1978).
3. Kapeliouk (1969); interview with union leader Nelly Karkabi in Shfaram,
(1980).
4. Interviews and questionnaires, Shfaram, Usifiya, Taibeh, and Umm el-Fahm
(1981).

3

DEVELOPMENTS IN ISRAEL'S ARAB COMMUNITY AFTER 1967

Official contacts between Arab villages and, indeed, even ordinary contacts between residents of different villages remained low after 1967. To this day, despite the fact that contacts have grown since 1969 as the educational system has expanded, Arabs in one place may have had little contact with Arabs in a neighboring village. Furadies and Jezira el-Zarka, for example, both Muslim villages, are five kilometers from one another, but there has been almost no contact between them. Each village has strong commercial ties to different parts of the Jewish sector. High school students from Furadies are sent 35 kilometers to Ironi Aleph, a Jewish-Arab school in Haifa; Jezira el-Zarka's youth go 25 kilometers in another direction to Kfar Qara in the Triangle region.

The highest levels of intervillage contact have nonetheless been between high school and, later, university students. In particular, from answers to a 1981 questionnaire submitted to various Arab youth of high school age, in and out of high school, it was clear that contact with Arabs of other religions outside of the town was higher among students than nonstudents. (Indeed, within the religiously mixed town of Shfaram a large majority of non–high school students had no close friends from the other religious groups in town.)[1] There is no evidence that this has changed, and indeed, in such places as Nazareth or the Sakhnin-Deir Hanna-Arraba-Eilabun complex it may be exacerbated by the growth of political Islam and events in Lebanon.

Even in the Israeli cities, Arabs tend to separate themselves off and live in informal ghettos (Ben-Artzi 1980). Traditional choice and subtle and not-so-subtle pressure by the Jewish majority contribute to this situation. In the Jewish sector the mass housing that is the norm is developed by commercial concerns and thus enjoys many structural advantages. Arabs have usually built individually. With public lands withheld, the lack of room to build and enormous land costs are factors, but so is the ubiquitous Middle Eastern preference for one's own kind and the pressing financial and social need for family support in the Arab sector that persists to this day.

Another important point is that Palestinians outside Israel have made no attempt to encourage or help Israel's Arabs to reestablish the sinews of a modern society. Indeed, Israel's Arabs were mistrusted by the Arab states for cooperating with Israeli authorities (Haidar 1988). In addition, Palestinians outside Israel generally did not develop any degree of political independence from Arab states until the mid–1960s (if then). The Arab states were divided in their policy and ambivalence toward the Israeli Arab sector; thus there was no unified Arab voice to exert international pressure on Israel to strengthen this sector's economic and political position. The Israeli Arab community's flirtation with Nasserism during the 1960s did not change this basic pattern, especially since Nasserism was essentially pan-Arab and not particularly Palestine-oriented.

According to many observers the Six-Day War was the catalyst that contributed most to the changes that are transpiring in Arab society in Israel to this day. Israel's victory in that war opened the borders of the Arab world to its Arab citizens. They were able to make quick contact with their fellow Palestinians in the occupied territories and in Jerusalem. Eli Rekhess writes of

a common denominator between the different groups of Arab intellectuals in Israel in spite of their affiliation with different political currents . . . a great increase in awareness and in links with the Palestinian Arab nation. The turning point for this awareness was the war of 1967. Communication and interaction with the population of the occupied territories in the West Bank and Gaza Strip were renewed. (1976)

This contact was made all the more possible by the relaxation of military administration in 1966, which had amounted to the granting of complete civil rights to Israel's Arabs without much agitation on their part. Their loyalty to the state during the 1967 war seemed to verify the wisdom and justice of this far-reaching political step.

One essential change for Israel's Arabs after 1968, then, was their ability to contact other Palestinians outside Israel. But also and perhaps more important were social changes that were not a direct result of the 1967 war.

Increased mobility due to the rescinded restrictions allowed Arabs to move freely within Israel. Also, important demographic changes occurred in the structure of Arab society. A 100 percent increase in population meant an increase in demographic mass that brought a feeling, which was especially strong among Muslims, of belonging to a growing ethnic group. The growth of the Bedouin and Druze minorities within the Arab com-

Table 3–1
Arab Pupils in Educational Institutions

Type of institution	1948/49	1959/60	1969/70	1979/80	1988/89
Kindergartens	1,124	7,274	14,211	17,344	21,900
Primary education—total	9,991	36,903	85,449	121,985	139,220
Intermediate schools	—	—	2,457	14,803	27,230
Secondary schools	14	1,956	8,050	22,473	38,237
Post primary education—total	14	1,956	10,507	37,276	65,467
Type of post-primary education					
Secondary					
general	14	1,933	6,198	19,034	31,003
vocational	—	—	1,462	2,645	6,516
agricultural	—	23	390	794	718
Teacher training colleges	—	121	370	485	568
Other post-secondary					
institutions	—	—	—	136	68
Arab educational system—total	11,129	46,254	110,537	177,226	227,223

Note: No special Arab educational systems exist at a university level; precise statistics as to the number of Israeli
Arab students studying in Israeli universities are not available.
Source: *Israel Statistical Yearbook, 1989.*

munity also presaged political change. A large number of Arabs were
growing up in Israel who were no longer completely bound to Arab traditional society; rather, they had contact throughout their youth with a
modern, Western-oriented society. Having expectations that were different
from Arabs of a previous generation, they were soon to be the dominant
majority in their society (tables 3–1 to 3–4).

Most important was an explosion in education, as tables 3–1 through 3–
4 indicate. There has been enormous growth in the number of Arab students, particularly at the high school level. More significant perhaps is the
Arab success in matriculation examinations. Although still proportionately
considerably inferior to the level of Jewish students, the success rate has
increased dramatically (fully 1000 percent in the first decade after 1967 and
progressively since). A continued proportional advantage is enjoyed by
Christians and males in high school education. The highest proportional
increase, however, was made by Muslim high schoolers, and a trend toward
more Muslims in universities has continued (Institute for Israeli Arabs
Studies 1992).

There was an enormous increase in teaching hours in the Arab school
system in the 1970s and the number of teachers within the Arab sector
after 1969 increased almost threefold. This is an increase of 2.5 percent in
Arab teachers in the Arab sector as compared to approximately about 1.5

Table 3–2
Pupils Aged 6-17, by Sex and Religion (Rates per 1,000)

	Religion			Girls	Boys	Overall
	Druze and other non-Jews	Christians	Muslims			
			Aged 6-13			
1969/70	882	973	846	806	932	871
1976/77	942	978	915	896	952	925
1984/85	978	984	938	935	960	947
1987/88	979	986	944	938	963	951
			Aged 14-17			
1969/70	209	550	234	200	380	294
1976/77	324	(703)	415	365	526	449
1984/85	620	807	590	581	656	621
1987/88	620	819	596	586	661	624

Source: Harari 1976, 1978b; *Israel Statistical Yearbook, 1989*, p. 613.

Table 3–3
Matriculation by Sex and Religion, 1986-87

	Examined	Passed
Muslims	3,451	1,442 (41.8%)
Christians	582	360 (61.9%)
Druze	822	446 (54.3%)
Boys	2,595	1,219 (47.0%)
Girls	2,289	1,043 (45.6%)
Total	5,174	2,351 (45.4%)

Source: Israel Statistical Yearbook, 1989, p. 626.

percent in the Jewish sector. In addition, there was an enormous increase in the number of high schools in the Arab sector, from 1 in 1948 to 90 in 1979 (Harari 1978b). There has been a stagnation since. As important has been the influx of trained individuals into Arab society. Sami Mar'i (1978) claimed that it was the Arab worker going from his village into the modern Jewish sector every day and returning that brought ideas of educational tolerance and utility into the Arab village, allowing and indeed helping to galvanize the explosion in education. The eight-year compulsory education law of the early stages of the Israeli state applied to all citizens and it likely contributed to early Arab educational development.

Table 3–4
Graduates of Matriculation Examinations[a] (Cumulative Numbers)

	Arab education	Hebrew education	Total
1948/49	—	802	802
1956/57	77	2,904	2,981
1960/61	94	3,464	3,558
1969/70	212	10,831	11,043
1971/72	486	11,469	11,955
1974/75	780	12,030	12,810
1976/77	1,080	12,050	13,130
1979/80	1,300	12,700	14,000
1983/84	2,200	18,300	20,500
1986/87	2,351[b]	—	—

a Excluding technical trend graduates (2,000-3,000 in 1976-1977).
b 23,000 matriculations in the Arab sector can be assumed in the past decade (1980-1990), as opposed to some 5,000 for the entire period between 1950 and 1980.

Table 3–5
Employment Patterns among Israeli Arabs by Religion

	Muslim	Christian	Druze	Total
ALL EMPLOYEES	103,710	29,400	11,190	144,505
Agricultural	6,140	600	440	7,180
Industrial	18,835	5,695	2,660	27,220
Electrical	630	180	50	860
Construction	20,225	3,475	1,630	25,335
Commerce	10,535	3,105	560	14,245
Transport	6,005	1,395	750	8,160
Financing	2,270	1,495	335	4,115
Public services	17,330	7,755	2,645	27,790
Personal services	5,215	2,440	275	7,933

But the principle of benign neglect for the Arab area held sway and efforts to enforce compliance with the law were lacking. The subsequent increase in compulsory education to 10 years probably had less to do with concern for Arab education than Israel's need for skilled Arab workers, who make up 42 percent of the Arab working population (table 3–5). This, plus Arab recognition of the material and social benefit of education, caused the boom. Here again we are probably witnessing the influence of Christian society.

Computer analysis utilizing Smooha's raw data (1976) indicates levels of economic well-being among the three religious communities—Druze, Muslim, and Christian.[2] The relevant findings follow.

As expected, Christians showed a much higher incidence of education and a significantly higher level of economic achievement. Obviously the two go together and obviously the significance of this has not been lost within the Arab sector. Only 6.1 percent of Muslims have completed post-primary education. They comprise 56.2 percent of the groups of Arabs having such an education and 4.4 percent of the total number of respondents. The raw percentage for Christians in higher educational brackets in 1976 was consistently higher than their percentage (18.2) of the total: 38.6, 23.6, and 37.8 in the three highest groups complete, respectively, post-primary, incomplete higher, and complete higher education. Although the Druze do slightly better than the Muslims, it is significant that the bulk of this education is still primary or incomplete post-primary (8–10 years). The trends here have not changed appreciably in recent years, but as the Christian sector with its lower birth rate and higher levels of emigration has diminished, the raw numbers of Muslims have grown.

The computer breakdown for economic success is based on six categories of material indicators (table 3–6). Again we have three rows and rounded numbers. Again we find the Christian raw percentage in the last three categories (possession of telephones, automobiles, and televisions) higher than their total. Christians possess more material goods than do Muslims or Druze. In this category the difference between Druze and Muslim is more significant. The Druze, although only slightly more educated, is significantly better off than the Muslim. The Christian Arab not only far outstrips them both but indeed may well at this point have outstripped the North African Jew. My own interviews in the Arab sector between 1979 and 1981 convinced me that economic achievement is the strongest motivating factor in the community. John Hofman's more rigorous analysis seems to bear this out (1977). And education was seen as the key to economic advancement.

This also holds true for the education of women, which has increased enormously within Israeli Arab society, especially within the Muslim and Druze communities. A typical interview answer was "If my girl is going to have to work anyway, she might as well go to school and make more money when she is through." The example of female schoolteachers, mostly Christians, in the late 1960s and early 1970s made a deep impression. Sami Mar'i stresses this as an important element in convincing Muslim families to send their daughters as well as their sons to school. It is fair to say that the increase in education generally, the increase in education of women, and women's consequent integration into the employed sector of society (with the biculturalism and bilingualism inherent in these developments; Hebrew is almost as important as Arabic in the Arab high school curricula) mark the great exception to the principle of segmentation and

Table 3–6
Economic-Material Well-Being

Count, Row % Column %, total %	Druze	Muslim	Christian	Row total
	7	73	1	81
	8.3	90.2	1.6	11.7
	10.3	14.5	1.0	
	1.0	10.5	0.2	
	11	92	8	111
Housing density	10.2	82.6	7.1	16.1
	17.5	18.4	6.3	
	1.7	13.3	1.1	
	14	88	19	121
Separate bedrooms	11.5	72.9	15.6	17.4
	21.3	17.5	15.0	
	2.0	12.7	2.7	
	14	130	26	170
Hot water	7.9	76.6	15.5	24.5
	20.7	25.9	21.0	
	1.9	18.8	3.8	
	11	77	33	121
Telephone	9.0	63.7	27.3	17.5
	16.7	15.4	26.4	
	1.6	11.2	4.8	
	6	4	12	22
Private car	8.8	54.1	37.0	10.1
	9.4	7.5	20.6	
	0.9	5.4	3.7	
	3	4	12	19
Television	14.4	19.8	65.8	2.7
	4.1	0.7	9.7	
	0.4	0.5	1.8	
Column	66	468	111	642
total	9.4	72.5	18.1	100

self-segregation encountered in the 1960s. This exception is what is causing a dramatic change in the structure of Arab society.

A change in political activity is another result of education. Political activity can also be associated with the increasing numbers of academicians within the Arab sector. In 1973–74 there were still only about 1,000 Arabs studying in Israel at all universities combined. The figure now probably exceeds 4,000, including graduate students not formally enrolled. The Arab Student Council at the Hebrew University of Jerusalem estimated that during the 1989–90 academic year there were 1,200 Arab students at the university's two campuses in the city, and an additional 450 at Tel Aviv University, 200 at the nearby Bar-Ilan University, 700 at the University of Haifa, 300 at the Haifa Technion, and 500 at the Ben-Gurion University of the Negev in Beersheva, with another 1,000 pursuing studies in education, nursing, and similar areas at various colleges.[3] (The figure for Bar-Ilan University may be growing and the Tel Aviv figure declining as conservative Muslim parents choose to send their children to a conservative religious university, albeit Jewish.)

The student body at the University of Haifa is almost 15 percent Arab. This reflects the concentration of Arabs in the northern areas of the country and their more advanced social structure there, plus Haifa's long tradition of relative tolerance and biculturalism. The 300 Arabs studying at Haifa's Technion have close contacts with the University of Haifa Arab student body. There are no figures available for the religious breakdown at the University of Haifa and other universities. A ratio of 50:40:10 of Christians, Muslims, and Druze seemed a reasonable conjecture in 1980. The percentage of Christians fell during the 1980s and Muslim students are probably the majority now. During the late 1960s and early 1970s the Hebrew University of Jerusalem was the center of Arab student activity. By the 1980s Haifa had surpassed Jerusalem in this regard, and it is interesting to note that the Haifa student body probably more accurately reflects the politics of the Arab sector. The bulk of the Haifa Arab students return to their villages every evening. The 1,200-odd Jerusalem Arab student body stays on campus or elsewhere away from home in Jerusalem. They do not have much contact with East Jerusalemites or other Palestinians and their participation in the intifada has been virtually nil, with the possible exception of some members of Sons of the Village and a growing body of Islamic-oriented students. The political implications of this will concern us later.

Approximately 700 Arab students are studying outside Israel. The number has remained unchanged over the past decade. Approximately 250 have studied each year in Eastern Europe, their educational fees being covered by the Communist party. This situation changed in 1989–90 as part of the upheaval in that area, and as these students have generally been recruited through Rakah, the Israeli Communist party, a major change may be in process. We will discuss this later on. Those who study in the United States, Canada, and Western Europe must finance their own studies or seek aid on the same footing as other foreign students. Close to 80 percent return to Israel to find work after graduation, while 10 percent stay abroad. The remaining 10 percent who do not graduate are split between returnees and expatriates.

There are no accurate figures for this, but verbal information given to me indicates that especially in certain subjects such as medicine, the numbers of foreign students are out of all proportion to the size of the Arab community. From Kfar Qara 25 students were studying medicine in 1980, 22 of them outside the country, and 150 students from Shfaram were studying medicine outside. Some 30 or 40 students from Sakhnin have been sent to universities outside the country every year. There are approximately 40 premedical students from Baqa al-Gharbiya, most of them studying abroad.

What political significance should be attached to the phenomena of these students who are studying outside Israel is unclear. For Christians, the pattern has been that many students simply do not return. (The fact that educated Christians leave the country reflects a development that is observable in the Jewish sector as well). The Christian population in Israel has declined from 22 percent of the Arab population in 1948 to approximately half that at the present time. This is partly due to a birthrate, more or less equivalent to that in the Jewish sector, of approximately 25:1000— again an indication of "modernization." The birthrate for Druze and Muslims is almost twice this, but it is also declining. It is the Arab young men and, in increasing numbers, women who are studying in Israel's universities who will have a profound effect upon the Arab sector. Unlike their Jewish colleagues, the Arab students are highly politicized. They do not accurately reflect the political divisions within the society; like most students they are generally more radical than the society from which they have come. But their radicalism is for the most part well within the bounds of legality.

The majority of Arab students have generally supported the Israeli Communist party, Rakah, or the Front as it is often called now. At Haifa, where the Arab student body is most representative, Rakah has won most of the elections since 1980. The main opponent to Rakah on campus is the Progressive National Student Movement (PNSM) affiliated with the Sons of the Village (or Sons of the Homeland). The Sons are a rejectionist, loosely organized political grouping with an ideological affinity for the Palestine Liberation Organization, especially its more radical or rejectionist elements, which the progressive student movement reflects. It has rejected the state of Israel entirely. Rakah, as we shall see, is much more cautious. It is a non-Zionist political party that nonetheless accepts the existence of the state of Israel and is committed to work within it through legal means for basic changes that are not always clearly delineated.

We will deal more fully with political articulation later. It is important to realize, however, that within the burgeoning educational structure of the Galilee an acceptance of the state of Israel still seems to be central to students' politics, if not their psyches. It is significant that the Sons of the Village–oriented student groups have been consistently successful only at the Hebrew University of Jerusalem. They defeated Rakah there in 1990, and the intifada period in general has seen a growth in their strength, but only at the university level.

In addition to the problems within Israel, the Hebrew University reflects the political currents of East Jerusalem and the West Bank. Jerusalem continues to function, if not as it did in the 1930s, nonetheless as a marketplace of Palestinian ideas and a significant coordination point for Palestinian organization. But East Jerusalem's influence on Israel's Arabs is marginal at best. The social and political ambivalence of their situation is brought home to Israeli Arab students there daily. It is not only that their relationships to indigenous Jerusalem Palestinians are limited by many of the social considerations and restraints that fragment Arab society generally. The political situation in Jerusalem implies inordinate pressure. The city's more "nationally" oriented political life presupposes a level of Palestinian activism that is perceived as impracticable by the Israeli Arab students. Yet returning to their own towns or villages may not be easy, as was made clear from interviews in 1980. Students from the Hebrew University who had lived in East Jerusalem seemed politically isolated in the moderate town of Baqa al-Gharbiya. This situation has not changed significantly; the reason, however, may be more social than political.

In general, there has been an increase in radicalism in terms of rejection of the political status quo, but moderate legal protest continues to be the dominant mode of dissent within the Arab student community. Investigations at the University of Haifa showed the most radical students to be freshmen, and the most radical members of the Arab community at large were those in the last years of high school. This radicalism declined as the student's university career progressed, and it decreased yet further when the student left the university to actively partake in the life of the outside Jewish and Arab sector (Smooha 1984). Interviews in Jerusalem in 1990 showed no change in this trend. The weakness of the Sons of the Village in Arab society may confirm this.

Investigations within the Arab community in the 1970s showed a large but slowly and steadily decreasing inclination (especially on the part of young Arabs) for contacts with Jews (see Hofman, various works). This trend reflected rejection of certain aspects of the Israeli political, social, and economic structure. My investigations in 1981 revealed that some 55 percent of the Arab students in the 11th and 12th grades in Shfaram were anxious to have contacts with Jews (and there was very little difference— about 10 percent—between Muslim, Christian, and Druze students in this respect). This figure sank to almost zero, however, when the Jews were posited as having Zionist affiliations. Indeed, even in the Druze village of Usifiya, where almost 100 percent of high school students evinced a desire for contact with Israeli Jews, only two of twenty respondents were unequivocally willing to have social contacts with Zionist Jews (nine of the Druze were ambivalent in this respect, or almost 50 percent). In Shfaram 14 of 51 high school respondents indicated that they would perhaps or sometimes be willing to get to know Zionist Jews. Here again the percentage was much higher among the Druze than among the Christians or

Table 3–7
Willingness for Interethnic Contact

	Arab Public	Establishment-Affiliated Arab Leadership	Rakah-Affiliated Arab Leadership	Rejectionist Arab Leadership
Willingness to have Jews as friends	69.4	100.0	100.0	83.9
Willingness to live in a mixed neighborhood	47.4	52.0	53.1	64.5

Source: Smooha, 1989.

Muslims, but there were no unqualified positive responses. It is somewhat surprising that a similar investigation at municipal youth clubs in Shfaram among young people who left school before the 11th and 12th grades revealed a more positive attitude toward Jews in both areas of the questionnaire. This was especially true for the youth club of mixed Druze and Muslim membership. (The other youth club, about a kilometer away, was Muslim and Christian). Adult attitudes, which were explored by Smooha (1989), show leaders as the most willing to mix with Jews (table 3–7).

My field research revealed direct correlations between positive responses to such questions as "Would you like to have more contact with Jewish Israelis?" and "Are your parents in some way directly employed by Israeli organizations?" and "Do you feel that there is a future for you in the state of Israel?" In addition, responses to the question "Do you notice a significant difference in attitude between the generations?" showed that for the most part (although there is a great deal of ambivalence about other matters), Arab high school students do not perceive a generational gap in attitudes within their own religious groups. These results were much more pronounced in the Triangle—and indeed generally among Muslims, regarding their perceptions of themselves and perceptions of them by non-Muslims—than among Christians and Druze. This indicates a special Muslim sense of solidarity, which in all venues has been germinating for 40 years and now seems ready for articulation. The same can be said of the Bedouins as well. But respondents from all groups saw themselves as being less split by generation than Arab society in bigger towns or in Israeli cities.

These results tie in well with Smooha's research.[4] Family contacts with the Jewish sector and economic success therein go hand in hand with optimism and national moderation (Smooha 1980). But a sense of historical grievance is handed down from parents to children as well. This factor further solidifies regional and communal political fragmentation.

As we mentioned previously, questionnaire returns reflect the high level of religious segregation that is still evident in Arab society at large. Random interviews with university students in Tel Aviv and Jerusalem in 1990 have reconfirmed this phenomenon. The results in the most "radical" of the Triangle towns, Umm el-Fahm, and the much more "moderate" or accommodating Taibeh, were remarkably similar. Approximately 40 percent of the respondents, all Muslim, desired contacts with Jews, about 20 percent were ambivalent, and 40 percent were negative. The ambivalence in these towns is much greater than in Shfaram or Usifiya. Only one respondent in Umm el-Fahm and two in Taibeh wanted more contact with Jewish Israelis who had Zionist proclivities. But the level of negative ambivalence was much higher in Taibeh (11 out of 42) than in Umm el-Fahm (4 out of 58). Of course, "Zionism" is a most unpopular and loaded term. (Additional contacts with Taibeh residents throughout the 1980s would cause us to modify our assessment.) Politically, Taibeh has differed markedly from Umm el-Fahm. It is economically much better off and its politics have remained moderate in the face of the intifada and the rise of Islamic politicization. Nevertheless, Taibeh witnessed violent pro-Palestinian demonstrations on Land Day in 1990, the anniversary of the day in 1976 when six Israeli Arabs were killed protesting land confiscations in the first Israel-wide Arab political demonstrations. Whether or not the demonstrators in 1990 were indigenous is a question hotly debated in Taibeh.

Higher levels of desire have been established in Arab society for contacts with Jews than in Jewish society for contacts with Arabs (see Hofman, various works). There is no doubt that whatever the wishes of the Jewish and Arab communities, more and more contact is going to develop between the Jews and Arabs in Israel, primarily as a result of the explosion in education that has taken place in the last 20 years. Previously, contact was between employer and employee; there were the unfortunate interactions characteristic of a guest worker being inducted into industrial society. Social contacts and friendships, while clearly evident, have not replaced the basic boss-and-worker or official-and-supplicant patterns of the past. Yet broad contact is taking place on a level of social and intellectual equality. Two critical social elements are (1) the increased knowledge of Hebrew that the Arab community has gained and (2) the political and social savvy of university campuses. Previously, "integration" occurred exclusively between 8:00 a.m. and 4:00 p.m. Both groups then returned to their own sectors. Arabs retreated far into their own psychologically secure but segmented and particularist societies and regions.

While this scenario still prevails, three social factors mitigate for further contact and increased integration. One is the sheer weight of demography (tables 3–8, 3–9). Arab society is simply growing too fast to be contained in its villages much longer. Statistics from my earlier research showed not only a natural growth rate that is twice as great as among Jews and a 500 percent increase in Arab society since 1948; they also pinpointed the rising

Muslim demographic predominance among Israel's Arabs. Muslims have been, and by and large still are, village dwellers. As the villages become too small to hold them, they are being forced into a more cosmopolitan setting. The fact that new needs in education, housing, and other infra-structural areas were not really addressed in the 1980s is a major cause of friction in Israel and may be more important in the long run for Arab-Jewish relations than the intifada.

A second social factor is the aforementioned educational explosion, which I believe is the critical social variable. Third, Arab membership in the Israeli trade union movement, the Histadrut, has kept pace with the educational explosion both in raw numbers and in terms of quality of employment. The unionization of Arab society is remarkable; 209,417 Arabs hold membership in 130 centers—well over half the adult popula-tion.[5] This creates a significant amount of interaction with Jews. Crucial union concerns such as strike votes and strike effectiveness sometimes hinge on the Arab workers, and they have proved very loyal to their union leadership.

The basic changes that have occurred since 1968, then, are (1) the in-crease in internal mobility and international contact in Israel's Arab com-munity and (2) the increase in this community's demographic strength and socioeconomic, educational, and bicultural functioning. However, these changes were superimposed on the still fragmented communities. Religious differences still had an impact, especially given that the educational system, even at the high school level, has failed to integrate students psychologically and equalize social structures through equal opportunity. The familiar clan structure (*hamula*) is still significant within the Muslim and Druze com-munities, especially at the village level. The smaller the village, the more important these factors remain. The intifada to the east has not changed either social structures or attitudes. Nor, as we shall see, has it changed political practice significantly.

REGIONAL PATTERNS REVISITED

There remain significant regional differences between various elements of the Arab community in Israel. The south with its tribal-oriented Bedouin population is the most moderate area. Changes here have been slow indeed, but municipal election results in Rahat demonstrate that political resent-ment is growing. Since 1967 the mixed cities (not including Jerusalem), with about 10 percent of the Israeli Arab population, have emerged as a distinct geographical grouping with its own specific problems. In general (excluding Acre) a moderate attitude prevails, although here the traditional conservative Arab social structure has been broken. Particularist communal ties of family and religion nonetheless seem paramount. Changes in social

Table 3-8
Natural Growth by Religion

	Year	Live births	Per thousand	Deaths	Per thousand	Natural growth	Per thousand	Infant mortality	Per thousand
Muslims	1960	8.130	55.2	1.098	7.5	7.032	47.7	404	49.7
	(1970)	(13.123)	—	(1.386)	—	(11.727)	—	(509)	—
	1970	16.130	50.2	2.094	6.5	14.036	43.7	685	42.5
	1978	19.378	42.6	2.136	4.7	17.242	37.9	557	28.7
	1988	22.188	35.5	2.190	3.5	19.998	32.0	371	17.0
Christians	1960	1.752	35.8	352	7.2	1.400	28.6	77	43.9
	1970	1.989	26.7	520	7.0	1.469	19.7	67	33.7
	(1970)	1.754	—	368	—	1.386	—	48	—
	1978	2.007	23.7	507	6.0	1.500	17.7	35	17.4
	1988	2.298	22.1	570	5.4	1.728	16.7	24	10.5
Druze and other non-Jews[a]	1960	1.139	50.0	199	8.7	940	41.3	43	42.1
	1970	1.515	43.0	195	5.5	1.320	37.5	53	35.0
	1978	1.930	41.6	251	5.4	1.679	36.2	47	24.4
	1988	2.348	30.5	238	3.1	2.110	27.4	44	18.7

Note: Figures as of 1970 include East Jerusalem. Figures in parentheses are without.
a "other non-Jews" serve to lower the figures for Druze Israelis by a few percentage points.

Table 3–9
The Proportion of Non-Jews in the Population under Israeli Control and the Proportion of Non-Jews with Israeli Citizenship, by Age

Age (apparent)	Within the entire population	Within the population of citizens
0 - 4	50.8	24.0
0 - 14	48.2	24.0
0 - 19	47.3	23.7
0 - 24	46.9	23.6
0 - 34	44.5	22.1
0 - 44	41.7	20.6
0 - 54	40.5	19.9
0 - 64	39.4	19.0
Total	37.6	17.9

Source: The Central Bureau of Statistics, 1988, p. 48, p. 706, in: Landau, 1989.

structure are inexorable, however, and are grafting new pressures on this traditionally divided society.

The Galilee, the Triangle, and the South are still not integrated into one political community, for there is not yet a national political party to do this. A coordinating organization such as the Democratic Front for Equality (Hadash) could not function without Rakah, which is in essence its sponsor, and has consistently failed as a true integratory agent. Bodies that are developing, such as the Committee for Defense of Arab Lands, the Committee of Heads of Arab Local Councils, and the Arab student councils (the National Committee of Secondary School Students and the National Committee of Arab Students), all of which were tied in some way to Rakah in the early 1980s, have failed to unify Israeli Arab society, much as Rakah has failed as a political party in articulating the goals of the entire minority community. New groups with new ideas have since emerged, such as the Progressive List for Peace, the Arab Democratic party (headed by former Labour party Knesset member Abdul Wahab Darawshe), and the Islamic movement, which evolved out of the Muslim Brotherhood.

The differences within the regions are reflected in divergent political patterns. There is no doubt that the Triangle remains more moderate politically, more conservative socially, and more ready to accept the status quo than large sections of the Galilee. Of the 18 heads of local councils in Arab villages associated with the Rakah-sponsored and dominated Front in the early 1980s (there are now only 13), only one was from the Triangle, from the town of Umm el-Fahm where Rakah was defeated in 1989. On the other hand, it is in the Triangle that the Islamic political movement has fully blossomed. It is for the present moment "moderate," oriented toward social equity and communal development, and it advocates the classical Muslim Brotherhood strategy of evolutionary religious and political change (Rekhess 1990). But Islamic politics can turn quickly volatile, and Muslims in general are the most likely ethnic group to reject the state and Israel.

Election returns in the Triangle over the past 10 years, for Knesset elections and especially for the municipal councils, reveal (with the exception of Umm el-Fahm) that despite heavy Rakah gains throughout the Arab community (because of numbers of voters, if not percentages), there are stronger ties to the previous government parties (those that formed the Labour Alignment) than exist in the Galilee (Harari 1978a, 1978b). This pattern persisted in 1988, with the Islamic movement not yet campaigning. In municipal elections in 1989 the Islamic movement took the mayoralty (elected directly in Israel) in Umm el-Fahm, Kfar Qassem, Jaljulya, and Kfar Bara, all in the Triangle, and in Rahat, a major Bedouin town in the Negev.

Size of community was until recently the determinant factor in predicting election returns (table 3–10). The smaller the place, the more moderate or conservative it was. This apparently played an even greater role in the past. The fact that the Triangle is exclusively Muslim is also significant. The recent successes of the Islamic movement may call such determinants into question. One can apparently be socially radical in Umm el-Fahm (25,000 inhabitants) or conservative in Kfar Bara (3,000 inhabitants) or Kfar Qassem (10,000 inhabitants) and still support candidates with an Islamic orientation. We will have more to say about this development later. Awni Habash illustrated the conservative workings of Triangle politics and social structure in his dissertation comparing Taibeh and the village of Kfar Qara (1973). Both places have developed further since then. Taibeh, now a city of over 25,000, evinces today deep social cleavage and a high rate of criminal activity, whereas in the smaller Kfar Qara traditional structures are still dominant.

Family social structure and position, if not *hamula* politics, still heavily influence the attitudes and political behavior of Israel's Arabs. *Hamula* solidarity, on which many lists are based, is especially strong in local elections; national elections may be a private or factional matter, leading to apparently paradoxical voting behavior in many cases (Ginat 1990). Majid al-Haj, a sociologist at the University of Haifa, has claimed that family politics dominate the inner Arab social and political decision-making process and that not even the intifada has changed such patterns. He says that although the effect of the intifada was to sharpen the contrast between finely balanced nationalistic and civilian components and it had an important impact on election propaganda in the Arab sector, ultimately "the change wasn't radical enough to influence voting patterns and political behaviour."[6]

Table 3–10
The Vote in Arab Settlements by Type
(Percentages)

	1981 Urban	1981 Rural	1981 Bedouin	1984 Urban	1984 Rural	1984 Bedouin	1988 Urban	1988 Rural	1988 Bedouin
Arab & Mixed Lists									
Hadash (DFPE)	45.5	27.8	5.0	40.0	23.6	4.8	36.7	17.3	4.3
PLP	—	—	—	20.4	15.2	11.7	15.9	6.1	1.1
ADP									
	—	—	—	—	—	—	9.8	9.1	41.7
Center & Left									
Labour	21.9	30.6	51.0	18.0	28.2	50.7	15.7	23.6	18.6
Mapam	—	—	—	—	—	—	2.9	9.0	5.2
Citizens' Rights	0.2	0.9	0.6	0.6	1.6	0.9	4.0	7.5	2.3
Shinui	4.8	5.1	0.9	5.5	5.1	0.5	2.7	3.5	0.4
Yahad	—	—	—	5.0	7.5	10.8	—	—	—
Religious Parties									
Mafdal	2.9	6.3	2.3	3.6	5.8	5.6	2.8	5.6	1.3
Tami	0.3	0.5	0.7	1.5	2.5	1.5	—	—	—
Shas	—	—	—	0.0	0.1	0.6	0.4	0.9	0.3
Agudath Israel	0.1	0.1	0.3	0.1	0.1	0.2	0.1	0.1	0.8
Degel haTorah	—	—	—	—	—	—	0.2	0.1	0.6
Morasha/Poalei Agudath Israel	0.1	0.1	0.3	0.1	0.0	0.4	—	—	—
Right									
Likud	4.7	9.8	10.0	3.4	7.2	6.7	5.8	11.5	12.8
Tehiya	0.2	0.2	0.2	0.1	0.5	0.4	0.1	0.1	0.4
Tzomet	—	—	—	—	—	—	0.1	0.2	0.4
Moledet	—	—	—	—	—	—	0.1	0.5	0.3
Kach	0.0	0.2	0.6	0.1	0.1	0.3	—	—	—
Other Lists	19.3	18.6	28.1	1.6	2.5	4.9	2.7	4.9	9.5
Total	100	100	100	100	100	100	100	100	100

Source: The Central Bureau of Statistics and others, 1986, p. 36; 1988, p. 108-109, in: Landau, 1989.

SOCIAL AND IDEOLOGICAL FRAGMENTATION

A fourth area of division has reemerged in Arab society in Israel that will undoubtedly both rival and complement the divisions of family, religion, and region in the future. Issue-oriented sociopolitical cleavages are causing serious rifts in Arab society. Conflicting conceptions of identity, economic status, and social structure have certainly grown in the past decade. Even 10 years ago internal divisions in a town like Umm el-Fahm meant that meetings were held behind bolted iron doors and political clubhouses were burnt down; political physical violence and an atmosphere of mutual distrust were endemic. A few kilometers down the road in Arara-

Ara, the Muslim conservative character was—and is—still relatively intact. The differences between the two places are those of inner city and suburbia. But the conflicts of Umm el-Fahm, based on social and economic deprivation, are spreading to other areas. The south and the urban centers appear likely targets. In the Triangle the pattern of conservative economic and political accommodation versus activism is becoming ever more apparent, and in the Galilee expressions of separatism by "have-nots" are considered by some to be a distinct possibility (Rekhess 1990).

No doubt there is intertwining of issues, geography, and religion. But the social structures of the past are giving way and their insulatory power is fraying. Smooha's extensive macrosociological research long ago pinpointed deep-seated political and social divisions within Arab society.

Compared to 46 percent of Arabs defining themselves as Palestinians, there are 54 percent who defined themselves as Israeli Arabs. As against 42 percent desiring Palestinian-national education, 58 percent desired education based upon the love of Israel as a homeland shared by both peoples or another similar goal. The internal split is particularly striking between the 50 percent denying or having reservations about Israel's right to exist and the 50 percent who recognized this right without reservations. The same 50–50 division occurs between those dissatisfied and satisfied with Israeli citizenship. (Smooha 1980b)

More recent polling than Smooha's bears out much of the ambiguity in national identification for Israeli Arabs. In 1989 71 percent said they would not be interested in living in a Palestinian state, should one be established. Seventy-five percent would remain in Israel if given the possibility of living anywhere else (as would 80 percent of Jews). Eighty-three percent believed or strongly believed in the possibility of peaceful coexistence between Jews and Arabs within Israel's green line, while 53 percent believed that it will *not* work beyond the green line. The Israeli Arabs here make an interesting distinction between themselves and their neighbors in Jenin, Nablus, Gaza, or elsewhere in the territories. Yet 45 percent felt "not at home" in Israel and 69 percent felt that they were discriminated against often or very often.[7]

The basic question of identity causes great problems. I used Smooha's raw data for a 1981 computer breakdown by religion (Druze, Muslim, Christian) on Palestinian identity among Israeli Arabs (table 3–11). If we take the two most nationalistic categories, Palestinian Arab and Palestinian, we find enormous Muslim response (84.9 and 80.7 percent). Whereas over 70 percent of the Druze referred to themselves as Israeli or Israeli Arab, 40 percent of the Muslims called themselves Palestinian Arabs or Palestinians. Notice the Christian ambivalence here. Fifty percent of the Christians referred to themselves as Israeli Arabs or simply Arabs, and only 26 percent identified with non-Israeli Palestinians.

The Druze maintained strong identification with Israel; they do so to

Table 3–11
Self-Identity among Israel's Arabs

Count Row pct. Col pct. Total pct.		Druze	Muslim	Christian	Row total
	1. Israeli	12 47.6 18.7 1.7	8 31.3 1.6 1.1	6 21.1 4.1 0.8	26 3.6
Non- Pales- tinian Israeli	2. Israeli Arabs	35 12.9 52.9 4.9	199 73.1 38.2 27.6	38 14.0 28.7 5.3	272 37.8
	3. Arab	14 16.2 21.6 2.0	45 51.2 8.7 6.3	29 32.6 21.6 4.0	88 12.3
	4. Israeli Palestinian	2 1.8 2.5 0.2	64 70.7 12.3 8.9	25 27.5 18.7 3.5	91 12.6
Pales- tinian	5. Palestinian Arab	1 0.5 1.4 0.1	167 84.9 32.0 23.1	29 14.7 21.6 4.0	197 27.3
	6. Palestinian	2 4.1 2.9 0.3	38 80.7 7.3 5.2	7 15.2 5.3 1.0	47 6.5
	Column total	66 9.2	521 72.3	134 18.5	723 100

this day. Christians have shown a more hesitant attitude (despite their verbal nationalism) toward Palestinian nationality and political divorce from Israel than have Muslims (Hofman's data analysis also supports this development). Christian students in Shfaram were generally but not significantly more open-minded toward the Jewish sector than the Muslims there. But all high schoolers in Shfaram were considerably more open to contacts with the Jewish sector than 12th graders in Taibeh or Umm el-Fahm; this may reflect the considerably better economic situation of the Galilee town, as well as its relative cosmopolitanism. Both social phenomena have in the past been associated with Christian Arabs. Indeed, as we have seen, Christians have been opinion leaders and conduits for the transfer of culture on all sides of the political and social spectrum. This has resulted in more political sophistication in the Galilee and an acceptance of bourgeois-oriented Christian lifestyles in many mixed villages.

What we have here is probably bourgeois nationalism that stops short at great material sacrifice. Responses to my questionnaire indicated that Arabs with contacts or good jobs in the Jewish sector tended to be the most optimistic. It seems safe to say that socioeconomic and political position rather than region or religion may become more important in determining Arab action, even within religiously oriented movements. What is developing in a significant segment of the Arab sector is a materially and family-oriented society that may be verbally "radical" or "moderate" but socially conservative and politically hesitant. For the time being, however, this development is not ameliorating Arab political fragmentation in Israel. Indeed, it may be exacerbating it, especially if the opportunities for economic advancement fail to keep pace with the growth of the population, in particular among high school and college graduates and in the Muslim sector.

ACCOMMODATORS, FENCE SITTERS, REJECTIONISTS

Sammy Smooha's sociopolitical typology of Israel's Arabs (1980b, 1989) not only appears accurate, it is an excellent analytical tool (tables 3–12, 3–13). In 1980 he divided Arab society into three groups: accommodators, fence sitters (fairly and strongly reserved), and rejectionists or dissidents. These groups represented about 20, 60, and 20 percent of the population, respectively. The middle 60 percent, which has since grown to 80 percent, he now categorizes as two groups, reservationists and oppositionists. Their positions are the most fluid or opportunistic or both, and they seem most susceptible to either integrationist Israeli or nationalist Palestinian blandishments. Smooha has employed a lengthy series of issues, including acceptance of the state of Israel, equality between Arabs and Jews, Palestinian identity, repatriation, independent Palestinian statehood, and land expropriation, in his categorization of Israeli Arabs. Communal and religious differences still pertain as well, despite the other variables.

Updated figures show a continuation of previous trends.[8] Druze by and large support the state. Over half of the Christians are on the positive side, by a ratio of about 5:4, and there is a 2:1 relationship between accommodator and rejectionist. The Bedouin figures are less "moderate" than the Christian but are still well within an accommodationist-reservationist majority. The Muslims make up the bulk of the oppositionists and rejectionists. There is a 3:1 relation of Muslims who reject rather than accommodate, although here too the overwhelming percentage are fence sitters, with a slight preponderance of oppositionists. This is interesting, for in the

Table 3–12
Selected Indicators of Radicalization versus Politicization

Arab Radicalization Perspective	Arab Politicization Perspective
1. Rejection of Israel's right to exist	Acceptance of Israel's right to exist
2. Desire to restrict contacts to Arabs, or to operate only in independent, national Arab organizations	Willingness to have unrestricted contacts with Jews or to integrate into Jewish or mixed organizations (short of assimilation)
3. Support for all means of struggle, including illegal and violent means, if necessary	Support for democratic, parliamentary or extra-parliamentary, but legal means of struggle only
4. The struggle for civil equality is considered as part of the struggle for national liberation	The struggle for civil equality is considered as a struggle for equal rights and opportunities between Arabs and Jews
5. Israeli Arabs have a right to self-determination; their fate and future are tied to the Palestinian people; and their status as a minority in Israel is rejected	Israeli Arabs do not have a right to self-determination; their fate and future are tied to Israel; and their status as a minority in Israel is accepted
6. Rejection of the territorial integrity of Israel in its pre-1967 borders, including the separation of the Galilee and Triangle from Israel	Acceptance of the territorial integrity of Israel in its pre-1967 borders, including the retention of the Galilee and Triangle as parts of Israel
7. Support for a non-Israeli Palestinian identity for Israeli Arabs	Support for an Israeli Palestinian identity for Israeli Arabs
8. Repudiation of the existence of a Jewish nation in Israel	Recognition of the existence of a Jewish nation in Israel
9. Support for a secular-democratic or a Palestinian state in all of Mandatory Palestine in place of Israel	Support for a Palestinian state in the West Bank and Gaza Strip alongside Israel
10. Support for the Rejection Front	Support for the PLO mainstream
11. The PLO is the sole, representative body of all Palestinians, including Israeli Arabs	The PLO is the sole, representative body of the Palestinian people, excluding Israeli Arabs

Source: Smooha, 1989.

continuing polarization among young Arabs (ages 18–25) we find that there is less weight in the middle and the numbers on both extremes are greater; the relationship between the middle and the extremes is 7:2, as opposed to 8:2 for all age groups combined. The continuing moderate trends in the smaller villages (under 5,000 inhabitants) are revealing as well as the defiant larger villages. The relatively more moderate results in larger communities certainly reflect the inclusion of the mixed cities in the poll. Notice that although level of education is the least critical variable here, those whose education terminated in high school are the most opposed, while those

Table 3–13
Arab Orientation Types by Social Background

	Accomodationists	Reservationists	Oppositionists	Rejectionists
Total	11.3	38.9	39.8	8.9
Age				
18-25	32.8	32.9	43.6	50.0
26-35	19.3	27.5	23.1	18.6
36-45	24.4	19.1	18.4	13.4
48-55	13.4	10.9	9.6	10.3
56+	10.1	9.7	7.2	7.2
Education				
0-8 years	61.7	60.9	52.0	56.9
9-12	25.8	30.0	35.5	35.3
13+	12.5	9.1	12.5	7.8
Size of community				
15,000 or more	15.0	26.0	33.3	24.8
10,000-14,999	1.7	6.8	13.5	23.8
5,000-9,999	38.3	26.9	26.1	25.7
Under 5,000	45.0	40.3	27.0	25.8
Community				
Druze	42.5	10.4	3.3	1.0
Bedouin	14.1	17.5	10.2	11.5
Christian	12.5	13.6	15.9	5.7
Non-Bedouin Muslim	30.8	58.5	70.5	81.9

Source: Smooha (1985 data).
Note: "Total" figures refer to percentages of the Arab community. Figures that follow are raw percentages of these figures. (For example, of the 11.3 percent of the Israeli Arab population that accomodates, 10.1 percent are aged 56 or over.) The raw percentages can be factored by the total to obtain an accurate picture of relationships within and between groups in the categories of age, education, community and size of community. (Thus, approximately 14 percent of the 56+ age group are accomodators, versus some three percent of those aged 18-25.)

with the most education are the most accommodating. Smooha's most "dissident" Arab theoretically would be a Muslim high school–age youth from a large village or town who is less educated (under eight years of schooling). Yet we know that most Muslims live in smaller communities, and most high school–age youth are high school students and by definition have more than eight years of schooling. The intertwining of variables is obvious in a society that is becoming more and more differentiated.

Smooha's older data (1976) indicated a high level of verbal conflict readiness among Israeli Arabs. A direct correlation was found between those who felt "land-damaged" (63 percent) and confrontation readiness. Those with the closest contacts in the Israeli political and social structure (in my research, Druze and those directly employed by Israeli agencies) are the most accommodating. My own observations confirm all elements of Smooha's far more extensive polling. For example, the importance of the land question cannot be overemphasized. Visits to Umm el-Fahm and interviews

with the Sons of the Village and Alignment-oriented (Labour party) school
teachers showed a city with an enormous radical potential back in 1980. I
speculated then, however, that the dominant force was the Muslim Brotherhood (about which I will have more to say later). This conjecture was
dramatically borne out in the municipal elections of 1989. There is no
doubt that the loss of the land started Umm el-Fahm along the road to
radicalism and its present self-isolation.

Sakhnin, in the Galilee, is another story. It was a relatively moderate
town until the Land Day disturbances of 1976, when three residents of the
village were among those killed by the Israeli security forces. The town is
in a hollow surrounded by hills with towers that kept squatters off the hills
that are considered government land by the state and village land—parts
of Sakhnin, Arraba, and Deir Hanna—by local Arabs. According to former
Sakhnin mayor Jamal Tarabaya, a member of the Democratic Front, about
40,000 *dunams* were confiscated from the town. The Israeli government
maintained that this land, known as al-Mal, was ownerless and was being
reserved for development, though whether development was actually en-
visaged is a question. No matter what the rights and wrongs of the issue,
the Arab community is growing fast, here and elsewhere, pressing against
the boundaries of villages whose lines were drawn in 1948. Although
Sakhnin, Arraba, and Deir Hanna appear as tiny specks on maps of Israel
(if they appear at all), they are growing together and becoming a large
urban conglomerate of more than 50,000 people. The villages used to share
(significantly enough) a high school, as well as lovely mountain views and
not much else. (There are now high schools in both Sakhnin and Arraba,
while students from Deir Hanna attend the one in the nearby Christian
village of Eilabun.) The "prosperity" of the area is a tenuous product of
an external economy. Expansion is blocked and no funds for investment
and internal development seem available. A simple stroll around village
outskirts a few years after the explosive Land Day events could leave no
doubt that it was the land issue that radicalized Sakhnin. (In recent years
some of this area was returned under conditions that remain unclear; the
villagers are at least able to work the land.) Yet overall, the politics of the
town, with its Rakah mayor, are still relatively moderate today. Located
in the Galilee and having a still strongly materialist orientation and successful educational programs, Sakhnin is not nearly as internally fragmented and socially isolated as Umm el-Fahm; and the pressure of the
expanding population still does not compare to the crowding experienced
by that town or Nazareth. Socioeconomic concerns of Arabs within Israel
may have more to do with self-identification than with the intifada.

Nearby Eilabun also shows the significant fragmentation and strong political articulation in the area. A prosperous, "modern," largely Christian
village, it is politically dominated by two major Christian families (Sruhr
and Zureik). In the last municipal elections the Sruhr family supported the

Table 3–14
The Vote in Arab Localities, 1955-88

Election year	Rakah/ Hadash (DFPE)	Israel Communist party	PLP	ADP Darawshe	minority lists	Labour & affiliates[a]	Other lists	Total	Valid votes[b]
1955	—	15.6	—	—	57.9	20.7	5.8	100.0	69
1959	—	11.3	—	—	58.6	19.9	10.2	100.0	72
1961	—	22.5	—	—	45.5	24.9	7.1	100.0	77
1965**	23.5	0.6	—	—	42.9	21.6	11.4	100.0	88
1969**	29.4	0.7	—	—	40.6	13.3	16.0	100.0	102
1973**	36.9	—	—	—	36.0	10.0	17.1	100.0	115
1977**	50.7	—	—	—	21.5	8.7	19.1	100.0	129
1981	37.9	—	—	—	13.4	26.2	22.5	100.0	143
1984	33.0	—	18.3	—	—	23.0	25.7	100.0	177
1988**	33.0	—	14.1	11.2	—	20.4	21.3	100.0	218

Source: The Central Bureau of Statistics and others 1974-1986, The Central Bureau of Statistics, 1988.
[a] Between 1955 and 1959 this column included Mapai, Mapam and Achdut haAvodah (Labour); in 1959, the Labour Alignment, Mapam and Rafi; between 1961 and 1988, Labour and Mapam (in 1988 Labour won 16.7% and Mapam 3.7% of the votes in Arab localities).
[b] In thousands.
** Candidates (not including mixed cities).

Front (Rakah), while the other family supported the largely Muslim, pro-Palestinian nationalist Progressive List for Peace (PLP). Like many others, the village has a marginal but growing community of sedentary Bedouins. Most of the men serve in the Israeli police force or the army. This did not stop this group, however, from supporting the PLP in order to better their own social and economic position in the village. (In other words, the price was right.) The residents of Eilabun by and large maintain an "accomodating" profile that is not reflected in their voting patterns.

The town of Maghar, down the road with 20,000 inhabitants, is completely different socially from Eilabun or Sakhnin–Arraba–Deir Hanna. The town has a large Druze population, as well as Christians and Muslims. The latter complain of being pushed around by the Druze, who have weapons because they serve in the Israeli forces. Be that as it may, the mixed town was less than a model of harmony in the fall of 1990.

POLITICAL ARTICULATION

The political articulation of Arab positions within Israel has reflected the fragmented, inward orientation of the Arab sector (tables 3–14, 3–15). For much of the state's existence, certainly until 1969 and probably through 1973, the Arab community by and large has supported Israeli government parties (generally Labour) or associated minority (traditional religious or family) lists. National, local, and trade union elections all demonstrated

Table 3–15
Results of Elections to the 11th and 12th Knessets within the Arab Population in Israel

	Qualified voters	Valid votes	Rakah/ Hadash	PLP	ADP	Labour	Yahad	Likud	Shinui	Citizen's Rights	Mapam	Mafdal	Others
11th Knesset (23.7.84)	276,973	199,968	63,818	35,214	—	51,546	11,006	9,720	8,802	1,942	—	7,723	9,119
% of total	100.00	72.0	32.0	17.6	—	26.0	6.0	5.0	4.4	1.0	—	4.0	4.0
12th Knesset (1.11.88)	326,242	241,601	81,714	32,879	26,385	41,636	—	15,981	5,959	10,785	9,001	6,951	10,311
% of total	100.00	74.0	34.0	14.0	11.0	17.0	—	7.0	2.0	4.0	4.0	3.0	4.0

Source: Landau, 1989.

this phenomenon. The entire political construction was watched over and
manipulated by so-called "Arabists" located mostly in the Ministry of the
Interior, as Lustick, Smooha, and Ben-Dor have all described. The Israeli
government, its civil servants, and the Labour Alignment—and they were
to all intents and purposes one unit, politically and organizationally, until
1976—structured this political edifice with the diverse building blocks of
Arab society.

As we have seen, the edifice is showing cracks, but changes, which reflect
transformations in Arab society, are only beginning to take place. Political
articulation has long been primarily manifested within the boundaries delineated by the Israeli government and within political parties that do not
really challenge the political structure in Israel. I include Rakah in this
group.

Since Rakah, a non-Zionist party, is politically isolated in Israel, a vote
for it has been a vehicle for low-risk protest. Rakah's opposition has been
mostly verbal and strictly within the law. Rakah is, in short, a bourgeois
nationalist party masquerading under a communist label. Although its old-
line leadership, almost exclusively Jewish and Christian, was made up of
dedicated Moscow-true communists (which is indeed one reason that it has
been challenged by younger party members), much of its membership
(Christian, by and large) is nationalist and opportunist; its supporters are
protesting a series of national indignities and seem completely uninterested
in communism. A high proportion of these voters are well-educated and
middle class Israeli Arabs who are, if not Christians, either Muslims and
Druze who have benefitted from new social, economic, and political values
transferred to their society through the Christian Arabs. These values are
middle class and materially oriented. They include nationalist identification
processes but are not "socialist" or collectivist. Just the opposite is true.
The susceptibility to material co-optation is manifest. A percentage of
working-class Arabs (often Muslims) and residents of small villages have
retained their loyalty to Labour, though these may be moving to the Islamic
movement. But Rakah, even in its organization of nationalist or disenchanted Arab sentiment, has remained a factor for order and status quo
in Israel. Moreover, its rejection into the 1980s of the PLO as a voice for
Israel's Arabs and its support in this position by the Soviet Union have
probably had as much effect as any factor in recent years in preventing
rejectionist Arab sentiment from gaining a firm foothold in Israel. It does
now firmly support the PLO as the representative of the Palestinian people
beyond the green line. As in the past, its policy has mirrored that of the
Soviet Union, another factor in its current crisis. Rakah's organization
stands against any brand of adventurism. It is a dominating force, or tries
to be, in various "national committees."

Rakah's influence was on the increase until the mid–1980s. By 1984 it
received 33 percent of the Arab vote in national elections.[9] Its policies

until the intifada suited the new majority in Arab society in Israel: intellectual, verbal, middle class, materially oriented Arab nationalism (not necessarily Palestinian) with a very low risk level. Rakah's own retreat from further land demonstrations after the violence of Land Day in 1976 is symptomatic. Its support for one-time traditionalists in municipality bargaining, which has not changed, underlines this element of accommodation in its current ethos. At present, social changes in Arab society are taking their toll. While Rakah maintained its prominence in 1988, keeping four of six mandates in the Arab sector in national elections, its percentage of the Arab vote declined. Younger, less ideologically oriented Arabs are forcing out old-timers such as Tewfik Toubi, who left the Knesset in 1990, and Meir Vilner, a Jew. A new party newspaper has appeared in opposition to *al-Ittihad*, the party mouthpiece. The events in Eastern Europe may have signalled the demise of the party, and there is talk of an Arab Christian Democratic party. As the last decade of the century begins, Rakah's domination of Arab politics in Israel is ending.

Three new political parties appeared in the Arab sector in the 1980s. All seem to have been founded as much in opposition to Rakah as in opposition to established Jewish Zionist parties. The first was the Progressive List for Peace (PLP), founded to prepare for the 1984 Knesset race—successfully, for two candidates were elected. The party was and is distinctly Western and anticommunist in attitude, as well as non-Zionist. It places much emphasis on the Palestinianism of Israel's Arabs, but it mirrors Rakah's "two states for two peoples" platform. Its intellectual and middle class orientation has kept it from achieving a mass base, but according to Rekhess (1990) it has "fostered ties with the Fatah mainstream." Given the social structure of its leadership, established Muslims and members of the middle class, this seems logical. Its ineffectiveness at translating its verbiage into action (a problem that Rakah has as well) led to its decline in 1988 to only one seat, held by leader Muhammad Miari, and its influence in municipal elections has been negligible.

In 1988 Abdul Wahab Darawshe founded his Arab Democratic party. A Knesset member who calls himself "Palestinian by nationality and an Israeli by citizenship," he left the Labour party over Labour party Defense Minister Rabin's hard line policies in suppressing the intifada. His party is supported by middle class Muslims and *hamulas* who were associated with him while he was with Labour. He believes (and he, essentially, is the party at this stage) that at present Arabs should be represented by Arabs. (Rakah has Jewish parliamentary deputies, as did the PLP until 1988.) Darawshe's party is socially conservative and still close to Labour, but it advocates Palestinian rights to self-determination and a separate state. He was elected to the Knesset early in 1988 but the party's performance in municipal elections was disappointing.

A third Arab political movement, operating in Israel since the 1970s but originally outside the pale of Israeli Arab politics, was the Muslim Brotherhood, which evolved into the Islamic political movement in Israel. The Muslim Brothers, connected through common religious training of leadership to similar movements in Egypt, the West Bank, Gaza, and Jerusalem, reject the state of Israel and call for an Islamic state. It is unclear what the boundaries of this state would be. The Muslim Brothers were strong in the Triangle in general and in Umm el-Fahm specifically and, according to my observation, they controlled the streets there by the early 1980s. They once set fire to a communist club building there; they are antisecularist, anti-Zionist, and socially conservative. They had ties, apparently, to the underworld in Taibeh. In the early 1980s weapons caches belonging to the Gaza branch of the Brotherhood were uncovered in the Triangle. Indeed, their activities in the Triangle area may have been coordinated from the West Bank town of Jenin. They were strongly represented at the Palestinian nationalist Bir Zeit University on the West Bank: They claimed almost 50 percent of the representation to the student union until the spring of 1980, when their numbers fell to about 30 percent in a swing to secular nationalism (see chapter 4). This is especially significant because Bir Zeit is a university with a large Christian student body and backing. They dominated the student body in Gaza and at Al-Najah University in Nablus, thus mirroring their strength in Egyptian undergraduate circles. They operated only when they felt strong, organizing regionally, town by town. They seem to have pressured school teachers for more "Islam-oriented" education, especially in the Triangle, but their activities were not limited to that region. They established themselves, perhaps as the dominant force, in the mosques of the mixed towns of Shfaram and Acre. They were well financed and their appearance in Israel coincided with an enormous upsurge in their activities in Gaza and, to a lesser degree, the West Bank. Their appeal to the Muslim community—especially the unskilled workers, dislocated farmers, and the traditionalists, antifeminists, and those left behind by the educational boom—must be significant. Their political activities were spontaneous, and their recruitment and organization took place under religious auspices and control. It is hard to assess the future level of their political influence in Israel, but their influence in the Muslim community has grown and they certainly represent a potentially highly divisive force in Arab society (Druze, Christians, and Rakah are for them outside the pale).

The consolidation of the Islamic movement as a national political force, led by Sheikh Abdallah Darwish of Kfar Kana, was crowned with success in the municipal elections of 1989. It has yet to campaign in national elections. Whatever its connections to the intifadist Hamas (see chapter 5) on the West Bank, the Islamic Jihad in Gaza, or the Muslim Brotherhood in Jordan,[10] it has maintained a moderate, completely within-the-law profile in Israel since its official entry into the political arena. Indeed, the exigencies of moving into this wider arena, which Sheikh Darwish seems to understand well, perforce have a moderating effect. As of 1990 it was attempting to form an all-Arab list in opposition to Rakah, but including "secular" political groups such as Darawshe's Arab Democratic party and the PLP. It is aiming for a potential six seats or more in the Knesset, with intentions of becoming a force in national Israeli politics. It remains to be seen whether the various positions in Israeli Arab Muslim society alone can be brought under one political umbrella.

Among the primary losers to the fundamentalists have been the Sons of the Village. Operating since the early 1970s, they too have never campaigned nationally. The Sons and the Progressive National Student Movement are loosely organized rejectionist movements, popular especially with college and older high school students. Both groups support the PLO as the representative for all Palestinians and essentially call into question the existence of Israel as a Jewish state. PLO acceptance of the state has caused a dilemma for them. Both groups are actively anti-Rakah ("the handmaiden of Arab Reaction") according to M. Kewan, one of the Sons' most prominent elder spokesmen in the early 1980s. Neither group, however, has any plans for unilateral action.

Still young (they seem never to age, as older members move on and out), relatively disorganized, and under constant government surveillance, the Sons of the Village managed some success in municipal elections (they boycott the Knesset elections) and more at universities. But like many similar popular youth groups, the Sons and their allies are prone to infighting (they now have three factions with fluid organizational lines and ideologies), penetration by informers, and tactical error. Moreover, the revolutionary romance of the 1970s has withered in the face of the "put up or shut up" demands of the intifada. The Sons adhere to a typical antibourgeois, anticolonialist, and anti-Moscow Third World ideology. In the early 1980s they seemed more in conflict with Rakah, which was determined to destroy them (by their own account, given behind bolted iron doors in Umm el-Fahm in January 1980 and April 1980), than with Israeli authorities.

Rakah has long been feeling the "national" pressure generated by the Sons of the Village and by others in the Arab sector, perhaps even more acutely since the ascendance of the Islamic movement. The so-called national meeting in summer of 1980 in Shfaram, at which Rakah strengthened its support for the PLO as the representative of the Palestinian people outside Israel and moved closer to a rejectionist posture (albeit without doing anything differently), was an attempt to regain support among nationalist Arabs who were "strongly reserved" about the Israeli state. The open and formal meeting of Rakah Knesset members with Yassir Arafat in fall 1989 was another step in this direction. Hostile tongues claim that such moves are nothing but an attempt by Rakah to hold on to flagging support. But as longtime communist and Knesset deputy Tewfik Toubi put it, "[Taking in] radicals [means the] risk of bringing in the authorities." Indeed, the Sons of the Village were content to chip away at Rakah's position without organizing in a similar fashion. They could not really organize and maintain their opposition to the Israeli state and their seeming support for the more radical elements, such as Habash, in the PLO without immediately running afoul of the Israeli authorities. The result of an Israeli crackdown could be arrest, perhaps even exile. The lessons of the militant nationalist Al-Ard movement of the late 1950s, which was suppressed by the authorities, are still clear, so although the nationalist Sons may be conspiratorial, for the time being they too are "legal." In short, the Sons were for a time a more significant national danger for Rakah than they were for Israel. Their ingenuous Arab-Palestinian nationalism (their positions are relatively unclear) and the fresh-faced idealism of their members made them a distinct threat to Rakah's youth movements. Indeed, they were the first Israeli Arab group of any kind that adopted the ideologies of the so-called Third World and are embedded in that intellectual and political tradition. Their ally group (both may be one loose structure) at the university level, the Progressive National Student Movement, has controlled the unofficial Arab student council at the various universities at various times, but their strength has traditionally been in Jerusalem. (In 1989 their lists prevailed at the Hebrew University of Jerusalem and Beersheva's Ben-Gurion University of the Negev, while Rakah's Democratic Front for Peace and Equality carried Tel Aviv, Haifa, and the Technion.)[11] Somehow, the Sons always remained Sons. The group never grew up and its activism remained generational. As Arabs left the university they left the Sons and its policies. The intifada could have been expected to strengthen the movement, but it has not appreciably done so. The tradition remains of success on campus and failure on the streets of the towns. Running in the 1989 municipal elections in 11 localities as the Patriotic/ National Action Front, the Sons did quite poorly, taking only seven of a total of 125 seats altogether (5.6 percent). Their performances in the major towns of Nazareth and Umm el-Fahm were dismal failures (Paz 1990).

VOTING TRENDS

Smooha's early 20:60:20 breakdown of accommodationists, fence sitters, and dissidents has corresponded to political events on the national level; I have a feeling that it may be more representative than the new 10:40:40:10 breakdown (into accommodationists, reservationists, oppositionists, and rejectionists). Rakah's support, which increased significantly until the 1980s, incorporated much of the 60 percent group. The accommodators are probably still voting for extra- or ex-government–affiliated parties and groups. The 10 percent of the vote received by the left-wing Citizens'

Rights, Mapam, and Shinui parties in 1988, together with 17 percent for Labour, add up to almost two-thirds of the Arab vote for dovish Jewish Zionist parties. The Israeli right—Likud, Liberals, and the far right—have never had much contact with the Arab sector and have not really organized well there (though they may receive some marginal support among, particularly, Bedouins and Druze). This is not completely true of Mafdal, the National Religious party, which has been somewhat successful and whose religious orthodoxy, social conservatism, and, especially, open coffers have proved alluring to some Arab villages. The combined share of the Arab vote won by Mafdal and other right-wing parties in 1988 was 10 percent, leaving half of the vote to the three Arab parties—a jump of 10 percent over the previous election to the Knesset.

While Rakah also may have once attracted a minority of Smooha's 20 percent rejectionists, they were generally likely to be those who boycott the vote (or have been too young to do so, for as we mentioned earlier, the most "radical" Israeli Arabs are found in the 11th and 12th grades). Those of voting age who do not boycott may have other options in the future, such as the Islamic movement.

The picture in Histadrut elections is at variance with national voting patterns in the Arab sector. Election returns confirm a demonstrable trend. In an area of immediate economic and personal concern, Arab voters tend to vote for Labour. The returns in the Muslim Triangle and among the Druze show this particularly clearly. If Umm el-Fahm is removed from the Triangle returns and likewise Abu Snan and Maghar (Mazaar), whose Druze communities are more open to mainstream political development (both Galilee villages are exceptional, with approximately 55 percent Druze and 45 percent Christian inhabitants), the figures show an even more impressive accommodating trend benefitting Labour. The same has been true for all the Knesset elections in the Druze sector. It should also be noted that most of the Bedouin community is still aligned with Labour (although current government land policies in the south, economic difficulties, the intifada, and growth of the Islamic movement are cutting into Labour strength and changing political thinking) (Ben-David 1989). A picture of significant local Labour strength in the municipalities and villages emerges, in part because of Labour's relatively successful recruitment, or co-optation, in the 1960s. In the case of the left-wing Mapam (United Worker's party), this process took place in the 1950s. There are hundreds of Arab appointed and paid officials of the Histadrut, mostly in the villages. Thousands of Arabs teach in the school system and numerous Druze, as well as a significant number of Bedouins and Christians, are members of the border police and the regular army.[12] Indeed, many of the mayors in the Rakah-backed Democratic Front for Peace and Equality of the 1980s started their careers in association with Labour and are now more assertive in their views—but not necessarily more daring in their actions. The im-

Table 3–16
Nazareth Electoral Results, 1989

Nazareth Histadrut Council		Nazareth Municipal	
Mixed list (family oriented)	8	DFPE (Rakah)	10
Islamic movement	6	Islamic movement	6
Labour	5	Progressive List for Peace	2
Mapam	1	National Religious Party: Fahed	
Achvah (Christian party)	1	Mazawi's *hamula* (local)	1

portance of "national" elections here is also open to question, and patterns are changing. Unfortunately, there are no new statistical materials to update the detailed work of the late Yechiel Harari, but scattered data are available. A combined Arab list for the Histadrut was able to muster only 4.17 percent of the total vote. In the parliamentary elections of 1988 the Arab lists took some 60 percent of the Arab vote. The percentage in the Histadrut would be about half of this.

Municipal elections have seen a definite weakening of the Labour-oriented parties. This confirms the trend observed in the 1970s. Indeed, the Committee of Heads of Arab Local Councils, founded in 1974, may have become more of a spokesperson for Israeli Arab society than the Arab Knesset members. Its militancy has grown with the increase in non-Zionist party mayors. It has organized general strikes of the Arab sector, the first major one having been on June 24, 1987 (Rekhess 1990), and generally operates in a pragmatic fashion within the boundaries of Israeli law. Here the fragmentation has played a key role in Arab politics. The *hamula* conflicts of the past are still in evidence, but nationwide preferences are becoming more important and the successes of the Islamic movement in 1989 may lead to more unity or to bitter internal confrontation.[13]

The election returns of the Histadrut and municipal elections in the major Arab city of Nazareth cast some light on these developments (table 3–16). Recall that Nazareth is the intellectual and political Arab center of the Galilee, the most populous Arab region in Israel, and it is the heart of Rakah territory and of Israeli Arab ethnic aspirations. The population by now is divided equally between Christians and Muslims. The Islamic movement in its first real campaign in a traditionally Christian town shows a clear breakthrough in the Galilee and its most urban center. The traditional Zionist left shows residual strength in Histadrut but not municipal elections. Here, too, if the PLP and the Islamic movement joined together for local or national elections, we would see the Christian-Rakah bastion of Israeli Arab politics under siege. There is no doubt that Christians are ill at ease at the prospect.

In Kfar Kana, another town in the Galilee, although the mayor was elected on a Rakah-PLP joint list, the vote for councilors favored the Islamic movement. (The results were as follows: Islamic movement, 4; Hadash (the Front), 2; a *hamula* list, 1; and Sons of the Village, 2.)[14] Only a tenuous coalition kept the Islamic movement out of power.

Municipal elections indicated strong pockets of support for the Islamic movement in the Triangle, and apparently many of Darawshe's Knesset voters in the Negev turned out for them in municipal elections as well (Paz 1990). The movement appears to be somewhat more radical in the Galilee than in the Triangle. This was apparent at Land Day demonstrations in Deir Hanna in 1989. Youth appeared with the green flags of Islam, thereby alienating the rest. Their radicalism in this corner of the lower Galilee is probably tempered by their rumored ties to certain financial institutes in the area.[15]

The Islamic movement's concern for principles of social betterment and development within a conservative moral framework and its modest and dignified political profile played especially well in the four Triangle locales of Umm el-Fahm, Kfar Qassem, Jaljulya, and Kfar Bara, all of which are particularly close to the territories. Ties to Hamas are not now as politically evident as when the movement was still the Muslim Brotherhood, but the fact that all Islamic religious leaders of the region attend the same seminaries creates a high potential for cooperation and coordination. At the Hebrew University of Jerusalem the growing number of Islamic movement supporters are the students with the most contact with Palestinian society, through joint prayer and religious meetings. Yet Palestinian activism and possible interaction with Hamas were not important in the movement's election campaign. The Sons and the Progressive List for Peace, who stressed Palestinianism, did poorly; the latter won only one village chairmanship, in Arraba (Ginat 1990). The Islamic movement has a broad platform for religious social justice, which is part of the Muslim Brotherhood's approach of "eternal cultural struggle" to political conflict (Paz 1990).[16] It is interesting to note that Sheikh Raid Mahajinah, leader of the most successful branch of the movement in Umm el-Fahm, is part of a large *hamula* noted for its connection to and support of Labour.[17]

SOCIAL LABELS AND POLITICAL ACTIVITY

Where do such trends leave Smooha's rejectionist percentage, or even the more reserved of the fence sitters, the Israeli Arabs with high Palestinian identification and ideals? It has left them outside the pale of Israeli politics and ripe for new movements, such as the Sons of the Village and the Progressive National Student Movement. Now the fundamentalist Islamic movement seems to be more to the taste of many of these people.

When looking at the fundamentalists, we run squarely into the weakness of a macrosociological analysis, even such a thorough and extremely perceptive one as Smooha's. A religious movement like the Brotherhood recruits from all segments of Muslim society. In terms of the typology, it would seem that voters for Darawshe and the Zionist parties tend to be accommodators, many Rakah backers are reservationists, PLP backers are oppositionists, and Sons of the Village are rejectionists. But everything depends on the power on the ground. The key question is: What is the Islamic movement?

An accommodator can continue to remain politically moderate or conservative, enjoying the psychological balsam of religious fundamentalism. (This seems to hold true in Israeli Jewish society as well.) Religious renaissance, with its strongly irrational overtones and atavistic impulses, is a powerful political variable throughout the Islamic world, and not only there. In all analyses, Muslims evince a higher level of dissidence, rejectionism, and even self-segregation than other elements of Israeli Arab society. But the difference between a nonsectarian, well-educated Son of the Village and an activist Brother is ideologically and psychologically enormous. Rejection of Israel, the "Zionist entity masquerading as a state," has been their only common ground. The Brotherhood's demand for an Islamic Palestine ran counter to all pluralistic (albeit primarily Western) modern and emancipatory social prognostication and analysis. Thus, the influence of militant and ascetic Islam on large segments of Arab society in general and Palestinians in particular (not only in Israel and, indeed, probably much less there than on the West Bank or Gaza) was underestimated. Their ability to temper their own inclinations, to concentrate on social or moral and not political problems, and to unify disparate groups in a political movement is still open to question. But the first steps have been provocatively successful.

It is significant that Israeli authorities may have underestimated them. Religious activities were encouraged in the Arab sector, and the Brothers enjoyed a great deal of freedom in Israel and in the occupied territories as well. The authorities are now confronted with an unpleasant new political variable partly of their own making. Their reaction has been as ambivalent as the policies of the movement.

THE FUTURE OF ARAB SOCIETY IN ISRAEL: FRAGMENTATION, INNER CONFLICT, AND EXTERNAL PRESSURES

Arab society in Israel today, we have seen, evinces old and new elements of fragmentation. The regional, familiar, and religious differences of the past, and the resulting social differences, retain an atavistic hold on significant portions of Arab society. Indeed, correlative differences of social structure have developed that may prove just as fragmenting. The village Muslim may continue to fly in the face of modernization through Islamic politics, as may the Bedouin. In addition, basic political and social conflicts similar to those encountered in all pluralist societies,—but complicated by the extreme form of the "national" question inherent in Israel's historical and geographical setting—are developing quickly. New internal conflict is being grafted on the old, and there is no doubt that Israel's Arabs internally face a more overtly conflict-ridden future. There is also no doubt that all elements of Arab society will demand political, social, and economic equality within Israel. The new generation will set limits to the self- and Israeli-encouraged segregations, self-abnegation, and isolations of the past. Although its potential for divisiveness is great, the Islamic movement may play a role as the unifying political element that has eluded the majority of Israeli Arabs.

The basic dividing lines between groups will be erected at the risk threshold of national demands. But autonomy schemes that hint at irredentism will definitely meet determined and widespread Israeli Jewish opposition. This has been a deterrent for all Arab political groups in Israel. Just how much material advantage will Israeli Arabs be willing to sacrifice for Palestinian national goals? Not much, if the past be an indicator of the future. But how much do past indicators mean in the light of social transformation? Much will depend on developments outside the Arab sector. The new social groups within Arab society will undoubtedly seek political partners to reform this current untenable situation. Current Israeli governmental impasses do not seem likely to offer much in the way of increased political influence and material well-being within Israel. Nationalist-clerical coalitions offer little hope for more than the status quo or suppression. Theorists of "total Zionism"—further Jewish expansion within and beyond Israel—such as Yisrael Koenig, Uriel Lynn, and Ariel Sharon, would not seem to offer a moderate Israeli Arab much hope. The Labour party has within it, especially in the trade union movement, elements that could ally with Mapam and the intellectual left within Jewish society to offer Arab moderates as much participation in the political, social, and economic life of Israel as they desire. Specific issues such as investment in the villages, cultural autonomy, political equality, and land usage—in other words, socioeconomic problems—are all negotiable. Will the Islamic movement accept that and become a reliable partner for the Israeli left? Perhaps stranger things have happened in the Middle East, but only perhaps. No significant party in Israel is willing to change the Jewish character of the state. Just as Iraqis do not seem willing to change the Sunni Arab character of Iraq, or Egyptians the Islamic character of Egypt, nationally oriented Jews (precisely those who live in Israel) will not wish to alter the Jewish national character of Israel. It is immaterial here that no one can define that character.

As we said earlier, nationalism is diffuse in nature and none the less powerful for that as a mover of minds. The basic price for Israeli Arabs of state-institutional cooperation is, as it always has been, total acceptance of the current structure. This is not a palatable choice for a majority of Israel's Arabs, but realistically it is the only choice that will allow socio-logical cures to be applied to the growing structural problems of Arab society and that will blunt Jewish chauvinism, which is especially strong among "Oriental" Jews, as well as segments of the Orthodox community. So far Israel's Arabs have had no real international support except for the former Soviet Union's questionable and now useless embrace of Rakah. The applied pressures not only of Israel's governmental institutions but also of its Jewish citizenry on Israel's Arabs create a constantly nagging national tension that is on the one hand socioeconomic in origin but on the other a constant historical reminder of national Arab losses and hu-miliation. The ballast of history, imagined and real, is an external pressure that may warp any social structure and destroy any attempt at a pluralistic solution. The weight of nationalism whips the scales more and more out of the balanced arc of judicious, equitable, and acceptable social accom-modation. This is especially true if international actors weight the balance even more.

NOTES

1. In Usifiya, a predominantly Druze village, none of the Christians (5 of 28 respondents) had close Moslem friends and all had more contact with Jews than Moslems outside of town; 17 out of 23 Druze had more contact with Jews than Moslems, and 15 out of the 23 had more contact with Jews than with Christians. In Triangle towns such as Taibeh and Umm el-Fahm, over 50 percent of high school students had no non-Moslem friends. (In Taibeh, of 42 respondents, only 9 had a non-Moslem friend.) The same held true for contact outside the village. Fifty percent of the students in Umm el-Fahm and 75 percent in Taibeh had more contact with Jews than with non-Moslem Arabs outside their village.

2. Smooha (1989) draws on this data, but he has not broken it down by religion.

3. No precise statistics are available from the universities.

4. See Smooha's chapter on ethnocentrism (1984).

5. *Al-Histadrut: Kel'a Hasina min Ajil al-'Omal* (The Histadrut: A fortress for the worker, who must protect it) (Tel Aviv, August 1989), in Arabic.

6. See al-Haj (1989), in Hebrew. The six-paper collection is discussed in Marda Dunsky's article, "Analyzing the Israeli Arab Vote," *Jerusalem Post,* November 15, 1989.

7. The corresponding figures for Jews follow: 53 percent believe that peaceful coexistence is possible within Israel and 69 percent believe that it is not possible in the territories; 11 percent feel "not at home" in Israel. The findings are from the 255th edition of the Continuing Survey of the Israel Institute of Applied Social Research. The subjects were a representative sample of 1,194 Jews and 247 Arabs, age 20 and over, from 80 cities, towns, and villages within the green line, polled in June 1989. This was reported by researchers Elihu Katz, Majid al-Haj, and Hanna Levinsohn in "Jews Think Israeli Arabs Would Leave to Live in a Palestinian

State—But Arabs Want to Stay Here," *Jerusalem Post*, September 1, 1989, and in Hebrew, *Yedioth Achronoth*, August 25, 1989.

8. 1989 figures, from Smooha, *Arabs and Jews in Israel*, vol. 2, *Change and Continuity in Mutual Intolerance* (Boulder, 1991). In Professor Smooha's words, the differences between the religious communities, age groups, and other categories on political orientations have not really changed since the 1980 survey (personal communication, April 27, 1990).

9. See R. Cohen, "Processes of Political Organization and Voting Patterns of Israeli Arabs," (M.A. thesis, Tel Aviv University, 1985). The Progressive List for Peace received 18 percent of the Arab vote in 1984; Labour, 23 percent; Likud, 5 percent; Mafdal, 4 percent; and independent left-leaning Zionist groups such as Mapam, the Citizen's Rights party, and Shinui, 17 percent.

10. Cf. Rekhess (1990) and Ziyad Abu Amr, *The Islamic Movement on the West Bank and in the Gaza Strip* (Acre, Israel, 1989), in Arabic (discussed by Michal Sela in "The Islamic Factor," *Jerusalem Post*, October 25, 1989).

11. Bar-Ilan University has no political parties.

12. See Ben-Dor (1979) for a discussion of co-optation among the Druze.

13. See Sela, "The Islamic Factor," *Jerusalem Post*, October 25, 1989, and Sela, "The Potential of a United Arab Electorate," *Jerusalem Post*, March 23, 1990.

14. Figures were compiled by Khalil Rinnawi, 1990.

15. Paz (1990, p. 21, n. 15) cites editions of the Arabic press, namely, *al-Ittihad*, *al-Watan*, and *as-Sinara*, in the first week of April describing the events of Land Day in Deir Hanna. The information on Sakhnin is taken from interviews in Maghar in 1990.

16. See also Rekhess (1990).

17. Paz claims that the policies of the Islamic movement are akin to the admonitions of Hasan al-Bana, an Egyptian Muslim leader of the 1930s.

4

ISRAEL'S ARABS AND
JERUSALEM'S ARABS:
SIMILARITIES AND DIFFERENCES

During the post–1967 period, characterized by continuing fragmentation of Arab society and the Palestinian national movement in Israel, skillful Israeli manipulation of this endemic feature of Palestinian life could be observed in Jerusalem and in the West Bank as well (Benvenisti 1979, 1983, 1985, 1986, 1989). Teddy Kollek may not be the new Haroun 'al-Rashid, but it is obvious that he adheres to the Ottoman principle of keeping the wolves satisfied and the sheep happy. Whether one considers this policy to be managed coercion (as Lustick would) or a mask to hide domination (as Benvenisti would), a certain amount of autonomy, socio-economic self-indulgence, and indeed "progress" is granted to Arab society. This is what allows it to operate within its own communal structures along levels that it can choose for itself. This is true of any and all elements of Arab society as long as the Palestinian national question does not lead to direct confrontation.

Arabs have been permitted quite fiery rhetoric; this was tolerated as long as nothing was really concretized. The organization of the national question was also long successfully interdicted by the Israeli authorities. I have shown at some length in the previous chapters how these policies have succeeded on the electoral and communal level in Israel itself. Smooha's recent work (1985, 1989), like al-Haj and Yaniv's previous research (1983), strengthens again the thesis that Arab political protest finds its outlet within political parties sanctioned in Israel (Israelization). While one could expect dissimilar developments in Jerusalem, where the sinews of urbanity and social cohesion were not dismembered (unlike what happened in the territory of Israel after 1948), many of the same processes are evident, albeit in distinctly different form and intensity.

HISTORICAL DISTINCTIONS

Jerusalem is clearly different in many ways from any of the Israeli Arab towns or villages. The annexation of the city by Israel immediately after the 1967 war did nothing to change this fact. The most basic difference is historical. As we have seen, Arabs in Israel never had—and lack to this day—a real urban center, with an intellectual life to filter and disseminate ideas and to unify and organize the intelligentsia of a nation. The society has no cultural core. The effects of its geographical dispersal are reflected in its fragmented social and cultural life. There is no amalgam or really active intellectual focal point; this is the function of an urban center.

Jerusalem serves this role for Palestinians on the West Bank. Although Jerusalem suffered intellectually and economically at the hands of the Jordanians in the 1948–67 period, and its population decreased during these years, there is no comparison to the social, intellectual, economic and political deprivation that Israel's Arabs underwent. There was no truncation of the Arab body politic. Family structures, the city's intelligentsia, and its connections to the Arab world remained intact. The ties to the Hashemite monarchy in Jordan retain an almost institutional character to this very day, King Hussein's declaration of July 1988 notwithstanding. Commercial activity became more and more centered in the hands of the conservative families. Many of them, especially those from Hebron, further consolidated financial and social positions first established in the 1940s.

After occupation, the Israelis made as few changes as possible that would alter the basic makeup of the society. The social infrastructure of the leading families was left intact; indeed, the Israelis encouraged these petty oligarchies to act as a kind of surrogate administration, very much along the lines of an indirect British colonial rule.

The Jerusalem city administration further encouraged these developments and also sought to develop its own independent Arab leadership for cooptation within Palestinian society in Jerusalem. In this it has been far less successful than the Israeli government had been in dealing with Israeli Arabs. It could never really command a significant level of strength among Palestinian leadership families in Jerusalem. The relationship was one of cautious bargaining and tentative one-time deals. Those who were co-opted, as we have seen, were really on the fringe of a still intact urban society within Israel. On the other hand, fringe members of a fringe Israeli Arab society after 1948 were able to establish themselves as at least the economic and intellectual equals of many of the Israeli Arab families whose professions and economic positions allowed them to remain outside the direct embrace of Israeli administration. This economic—if not social—equality was maintained.

Jerusalem's urbanity, its intellectual and economic independence, and its traditions have shielded its Palestinians against Israeli penetration and have allowed the city to maintain itself as a hub of Palestinian political activity. Yet the political benefits of this development in Jerusalem have not been as profound as might be imagined. Although Jerusalem's Palestinians did not suffer the same intellectual debilitation as Arabs in Israel, they were not able to organize political life on the West Bank, nor does it seem that they attempted to do so. And they represent no factor whatsoever in Gaza.

Activity was limited to publications and to economic development. The limits to joint developments between Jerusalem and the West Bank and Gaza were delineated by the Israeli government. A step too far, a step outside of the structure of Israeli civic permissiveness, meant entering the foreboding realm of direct military control. Because established Palestinian leadership in Jerusalem shied away from much direct operational involvement, especially after the intifada began, its influence on events became marginal. Neither the population of Jerusalem nor its oligarchical leaders spearhead the intifada. They are followers. Certainly, there is more direct involvement than among Israel's Arabs, but the urban intellectual center of Palestinian affairs has in a sense been truncated in its operational effectiveness.

Although there is universal popular rejection of continued life in a Jewish polity, there is at the same time a keen awareness among Jerusalem's Arab elite and large segments of its population of the need for some form of future cooperation. Perhaps they correspond to Smooha's Israeli Arabs who accommodate and to another large percentage of rejectionists (half of Israel's Arabs) who continue to sit on the fence. This is, of course, a reflection of intellectual ambivalence and a certain absence of viable alternatives, which is especially obvious in an urban society (Ashkenasi 1988). Geographically and economically, Jerusalem's Palestinians are tied to a national web not of their making. Urbanity and communal particularism, ironically, work here to both heighten and diminish the differences between Palestinians in Jerusalem and Israel's Arabs, and indeed between the former and other Palestinians, at least in terms of radical rejectionism and operational activism.

JERUSALEM—A GROWING ISLAMIC POPULATION

A second major difference between Arab Jerusalem and Israel's Arabs, one that may be gaining in significance, is in the religious sector. Although Jerusalem has a small and active Christian minority, it does not mirror the strength of the Christian minority in Arab Israel (which, however, is also waning). Arab East Jerusalem has become by and large a Muslim city. The size of its Christian community has been declining both relatively and absolutely (Tsimhoni 1983). In addition, the Christians are divided into many different denominations. The structure of administration in the post–

1967 period, when the Israelis cut Bethlehem and Ramallah off from any
administrative political entity associated with Jerusalem, strengthened the
Muslim character of the city. It also weakened the economic structure by
dismembering the Christian community. It became most difficult for Bethlehem and Ramallah Christians to invest in Jerusalem or maintain their
economic standing in the territories, and this reflected on their ability to
support the community in Jerusalem.

Moreover, the steady influx of new residents from the Hebron area and
their economic advancement have increased Islamic concentration and
strength in the Arab section of the city. Indeed, economic expansion has
both caused an increase in conservative family control in the entire area
from Hebron to Ramallah and strengthened traditional family-oriented law
within the Palestinian society. This development further highlights certain
fragmentary tendencies in the structure of the community and increases
social conservatism (see Zilberman 1988, 1990). The influence of the more
fundamental and traditional Hebronite Islam is starting to affect East Jerusalem's previously relatively tolerant and moderate religious character.

While the basic element of Arab religious and regional fragmentation
in Israel is missing, people nonetheless are keenly aware of the differences
between "Hebronite" and "Jerusalemite," especially in the family oligarchies that dominate Arab life. These oligarchical families, through control
of the chamber of commerce and to a degree the Supreme Muslim council
(both institutions were closely tied to Jordan, and they still are, albeit not
as directly), are able to maintain social and commercial control of Arab
East Jerusalem. The underdeveloped economic and banking structure of
East Jerusalem and the West Bank (Harris 1986, K. Rouhana 1985) abets
this control. The result is social and political conservatism and tradi-
tionalism.

I myself noted the strength of political Islam in Israel as early as a decade
ago (Ashkenasi 1981). It was informal in nature, at the time taking no
direct political form. Political parties were not organized and most Arab
intellectuals—many of them, of course, Christians—arrogantly rejected
Islam as a political factor of any significance. Much the same attitude was
prevalent in Jerusalem shortly before and during the early stages of the
intifada. Arab Jerusalem itself was considered, and indeed was, a secular
entity. The society was less susceptible to Islamic political blandishments
than was the West Bank and, certainly, Gaza. Responses to recent questionnaires, however, show the strong and growing support for an Islamic
polity in Jerusalem.[1] This does not mean that all the supporters are potentially radical or fundamentalists. Further analysis of the responses demonstrated that approximately half of them, or about 20 percent of all
Jerusalem Muslims in the sample, do tend to be politically and socially
intolerant. This would mean that within Israel and in Jerusalem alike,
political Islam is an ascendant force.

Political Islam is also, obviously, a divisive force within Palestinian society, and at its core it rejects any Israeli polity. Its future in Jerusalem is probably not propitious but its chances in outlying villages of the West Bank, refugee camps, and especially Gaza are very good indeed. It tends to be strong outside the established families, among working-class Muslims, and among the young. It has the same diffuse appeal to the underprivileged, the lower middle class (those who think of themselves as middle class and are in economic terms still underprivileged), as other simplistic, socially populist, radical political movements. This makes it, both in Israel and within Jerusalem, a factor of inestimable danger for Palestinian political aspirations. As a political alternative to Palestinian nationalism it is unpalatable to many members of society who would normally be able to lead a national movement, particularly Christians and college graduates. There is a relatively high level of socialist and reformist political preference among unemployed college graduates in Jerusalem. These tendencies conform to those held by the Sons of the Village in Israel. But these groups have little in common with either the Islamic movement in Israel or the Hamas Islamic political organization in the West Bank and Gaza. On the other hand, on Israeli university campuses and in village councils Islamic groups have been courting the Sons of the Village and are seeking a national consensus. By and large, however, Islamic activism is a sociopolitical development that may frighten many potential activists away from anti-Israeli policies.

This tendency is already obvious among many Christian groups, despite tax strikes and similar measures of resistance that are in one sense admissions of being operationally ineffectual. Indeed, in Jerusalem proper there has not yet been any action comparable to political activity in either Beit Sahur, which has refused as a community to pay taxes, or the more volatile Beit Jalla. Both are lovely Christian villages just outside Jerusalem and both are politically active, but their protest remains particularist; it is not part of a comprehensive Palestinian strategy.

Both Jerusalemites and Arabs in Israel continue to support the intifada verbally, and in the case of Jerusalem's families, financially as well. Although Muslim oligarchic families may support Hamas financially, they remain politically cautious; more often their financial support is directed to the conservative Fatah wing of the PLO.

EDUCATIONAL DIFFERENCES

Jerusalem's Palestinians by and large are unicultural, and the educational structure of the community has remained, linguistically, purely Arabic and essentially under Arab control.[2] Israel's Arabs know Hebrew and the Israeli *bagrut* (matriculation) tests have become the key to entrance to Israel's universities. Through the education of their elites in Israeli universities, these Arabs become more susceptible to ideas in Israeli society. Social, if not political, ideas are prevalent. This does not mean that these Arabs have become Zionist Israelis or that they accept the Israeli polity. It means, however, that they understand the system and how to live within it, and that they are more adaptable to it than are their compatriots in Jerusalem.

Municipal authority in Jerusalem has not intervened significantly in the structure of Arab education. Early attempts to do so were thwarted by Arab parents withdrawing their children from the schools, and private schools especially have continued to maintain their basic curricula intact. Jerusalem's schools continue to adhere to the Jordanian curriculum, and English is the most common second language. The Israelization process that concerns pluralistic thinkers such as Smooha and Al-Haj and that is so apparent in the educational explosion for Arabs in Israel was not functionalized in Jerusalem.

Furthermore, since the intifada began, schools in Jerusalem have been subject to the humiliating unpleasantness of occupation, and students are changing their attitudes. A significant proportion of the young have been jailed at one time or another. Relations with Jews are less acceptable in Palestinian Jerusalem than among Israeli Arabs. High school students in particular seem ethnically polarized.

A whole series of intellectual contacts are maintained and a whole series of social and economic relationships influence the lives of Israeli Arab students in high school and university. The geographical spread of the university system in Israel and the lack of a central Arab university there further support this tendency. Although Jerusalem is clearly the intellectual center of Palestinian society, it has no Arab university. The universities in the areas, Bir Zeit and Bethlehem, are small and their influence within Jerusalem, although important for some, does not dominate. The essentially conservative Arab political, social, and educational superstructure has managed to keep itself more or less immune to political and social radicalism from below.

Palestinian Arab universities on the West Bank take Arab students from Jerusalem, so that Arab (indeed, Palestinian) university training was and is available to an Arab elite in the city. However, the university system (a function and result of Israeli occupation, as there were no universities before 1967) has created an Arab academic proletariat, often unemployed, a growing articulate, divisive social group. The younger, university-educated Palestinians in Jerusalem have a great deal of difficulty finding suitable employment. They have gravitated to the councils of the intifada, but since they are not, politically or socially, directly involved in the economic, legal, and political superstructure of the city (either in the established oligarchical families or in Islamic Hamas), their overall influence in the city remains limited. It is more limited than in a town such as Nablus, which is probably the real capital of the intifada and the next largest Palestinian urban center after the Jerusalem area. Nevertheless, there is no doubt that the autonomous Arab educational system in Jerusalem is a major factor separating its Palestinians from Arab Israelis, to say nothing of Jews. In attitude, in political proclivities, and in the search for future alternatives, this may cause a heightened activism in Jerusalem in the near future.

THE REFUGEE FACTOR

The boundaries of municipal Jerusalem encompass one refugee camp, Shuafat, and some of the school buildings of Kalandia, as well as international facilities including the United Nations headquarters, UN schools, and central religious institutions. This sets the city off from Arab society in Israel. It has been this way since at least the early 1950s, when all registered refugees behind the green line were taken off the UNRWA (United Nations Relief and Works Agency) rolls and were more or less integrated into Israel's Arab society. West Bank camp dwellers pour into Jerusalem every day seeking jobs and services. (Camp dwellers also work in Israel itself, but rarely in areas inhabited or frequented by local Arabs as well.) The refugee factor has made Jerusalem's Arabs highly aware of their common relations with the West Bank.

The camps themselves have always been centers for Palestinian nationalism and for radical politics (Ashkenasi, "The International," 1990). Although Israel can and does exert pressure on UNRWA, the schools maintain a Palestinian national profile. Radicalization is evident everywhere that people are crowded without much hope, and the Middle East is one such area. There also seem to be significant psychological differences between camp dwellers and other Palestinian Arabs, especially those who live in Israel (Nashef 1984, 1991). (Balata camp near Nablus was a center for, and perfect example of, volatile Palestinian nationalism and Israeli repression even before the intifada.)[3]

Today many camps seem more like urban slum areas than like traditional refugee camps. The development of Jerusalem's refugee community nonetheless demonstrates the difference between Jerusalem and the West Bank and Gaza. Shuafat refugee camp became an urban slum with a high percentage of working-class Palestinians; a segregated camp life sustained by the UN ceased to exist. All data seem to indicate that it resembles a slum area such as Silwan in a whole series of sociological paradigma (income, housing, education levels, mobility, and so forth).[4] The fact that Israeli social services such as trade union membership, social security, and health insurance were available to Shuafat made it easier for its residents to integrate into Jerusalem's economic structure, which in essence meant the dissolution of many of UNRWA's services. A camp thus no longer existed within Jerusalem's boundaries. The UNRWA schools, however, continued to function alongside private and municipal schools, so that a third distinctive element of Jerusalem's Palestinian educational system was maintained. And many of UNRWA's operations in the West Bank were organized out of the administration building of the Sheikh Jarrah area of Jerusalem.

It is not easy to assess the influence of this on Palestinian Arabs in Jerusalem. Palestinians in international employ, including UNRWA workers, differed significantly from others in a series of questionnaire responses. Generally, however, one can say that Jerusalem's development has further separated its Palestinians from those in the West Bank, but also from Arabs in Israel. With Shuafat having been urbanized, there are no longer any real refugee camps per se in Jerusalem. Yet numerous international organizations drawing their raison d'être from the internationalization of the Palestinian refugee problem and of the Palestinian problem in general exist within the city. Awareness of the refugee problem is the rule. Because the camps are not far away, their misery cannot be overlooked or repressed.

OUTSIDE CONTACTS

A fifth major difference between Jerusalem and Arab Israel, no longer as significant but certainly historically important, is that Jerusalem's Arab community has been able to maintain informational contacts with the Arab world. West Bank and Jerusalem Arabs were not snubbed by either the diaspora Palestinian organizations or other Arab states as their Israeli counterparts were. Arab television and radio were easily heard. Jerusalem's communication system is penetrated by the Arab world and an array of "national" newspapers are published in East Jerusalem—indeed, there are so many that they themselves may be an element of fragmentation within the Arab society. Again, as with the universities, the newspapers are a function of Israeli control but also of Jerusalem's special status. They are, as the universities are, focal points of intellectual and cultural expression not only for Jerusalem. Their connection to Palestinian nationalism, even to various segments of the PLO, seems relatively clear. But their ability to publish depends on their geographical location in Jerusalem, for they are ostensibly illegal on the West Bank and in Gaza. Because the universities are outside Jerusalem, they have been subject to more stringent military occupation law.[5]

DEMOGRAPHIC MASS

A sixth difference is demographic. Within the boundaries of Jerusalem, as drawn by the Israeli government after 1967, we find a population that is a little more than 70 percent Jewish and a little less than 30 percent Arab. The proportion of Arabs to Jews within greater Jerusalem is

almost twice that within the green line. The 1983 census lists 306,312
Jews, 108,531 Muslims, and 13,730 Christians in Jerusalem. The figures
for 1986 were 336,000 Jews, 118,500 Muslims, and 14,300 Christians;
71.6 percent Jews and 28.4 percent non-Jews. For Israel the 1984 census
including Jerusalem reported 82.6 percent Jews and 17.3 percent Arabs.
Since 1967 there has been a 90 percent increase in the number of Arabs
and a 75 percent increase in the number of Jews in Jerusalem (*Jerusalem
Statistical Yearbook 1986*).

Perhaps a more important factor than numbers is that different segments
of Jerusalem's Arab population had the possibility of easy contact with
one another. Geographic and political barriers are in essence minimal. The
fact that contact is still not developed is the function of a social structure
that is in many ways similar to that of Israel's Arabs. Self-segregative, low-
mobility, and fragmented social profiles are typical of Palestinian society
everywhere. Nevertheless, Jerusalem is the center of intellectual activity,
publishing, theater (what little there is), and popular legal activity for
Palestinians in the territories—or at least for all Palestinians in the areas
from Hebron to Nablus. Furthermore, if we disregard the socially artificial
boundaries that were drawn in 1967 (although they have come to have
political, social, and psychological significance), the numbers change radically. With the inclusion of all areas of the metropolitan district of Jerusalem, the towns of Ramallah, Bethlehem, al-Azariya, (Bethany), and
others, the population percentages balance off at roughly 50–50. Also,
some 130,000–150,000 Jews live in areas that were not part of Jewish
Jerusalem before 1967. This residency in a rather concentrated geographical area will weigh heavily in any solution in the future. The Jews in
Jerusalem are very much in evidence. Arab and Jewish boroughs are in-
frastructurally and geographically intertwined. This fact of life further sep-
arates Jerusalem's society from that of the West Bank and from Arabs in
Israel.

Numbers and self-perception of demographic mass are critical for determining action. Self-perception of available alternatives plays a basic role
in the acceptance or nonacceptance of possible options. There is a more
distinct awareness in East Jerusalem's society than among Israel's Arabs
of belonging to a large Arab community to the north, south, and east. The
intifada obviously intrudes more on the lives of Jerusalem's Palestinians
than on the lives of those in Israel. Palestinians in Jerusalem are aware
that they are (1) a minority within the city in the absence of the West
Bank, yet (2) a potential majority or at least an equal demographic factor
in the metropolitan area that includes West Bank areas. This is an important
psychological consideration that affects their strategy of confrontation with
Jewish society. As we have seen, the more contact one has with Jewish
society, the more likely one is to accept the need for continued contacts

in any kind of future political solution. This pragmatic or cognitive option is embraced despite a subjective or ideological anti-Israel inclination that does not vary from that of the rest of the society.

Arab demographic patterns in Jerusalem are again at strong variance with those of Israel's Arabs and those of the West Bank, to say nothing of Gaza (figure 4–1). Although it is growing, Jerusalem's Arab population is not growing as fast as its Jewish counterpart. Jewish immigration will probably swell the numbers of Jews in new housing outside the pre–1967 boundaries of Jerusalem. Arab immigration to Palestine and legal migration to Jerusalem remain interdicted. The character of demographic development is probably the most critical factor in any future choice of options by Jerusalem's Palestinians. It has also definitely mitigated against a high activist profile during the intifada.

For Israel's Arabs this consideration is even more critical. They are, or at least they consider themselves, a minority island within a Jewish sea. Where this holds less true—in the Triangle and especially in places that are really border towns, such as Umm el-Fahm on the Israeli side of the green line—it may be necessary to temper this analysis. On the other hand, developments in these areas seem to favor the growth of Muslim fundamentalism.

FRUSTRATION AND NATIONAL CONFLICT

The aforementioned differences between the Israeli and Jerusalem Arab communities do not belie the fact that both groups are able to exercise options. Religion seems to be the most volatile and divisive variable. Religion in itself offers a way of sidestepping the pressures of Palestinian nationalism and embracing a more universalist but still distinctively Arab political position. Nonviolent Islamic political activity transcends the narrowness of the Palestinian national revolution and also keeps adherents relatively safe from the political pressures and retaliations of the state and the surrounding Jewish community. Of course, no one can be sure that politicized Islam in Israel will remain nonviolent, or that in Jerusalem it will not become a more potent and divisive factor. In both Israeli Arab society and among Jerusalem's Arab community, frustration and social malaise grow as we enter the 1990s. Hope for an Israeli government attuned to Arab/Palestinian needs and susceptibilities has diminished. The young are restless; they seem willing to embrace more volatile solutions and give way to heady emotionalism (as the reaction to Saddam Hussein's invasion of Kuwait in the summer of 1990 indicated). Established Arab political leadership in both venues seems unable to organize effectively. The social structures that we will analyze more fully later in this book have been shaken, but they are still the only structures. Mistrust between the two communities is widespread. The path may be set for some new activist

Figure 4–1
Arab Demographic Concentrations in Israel, Jerusalem, and the West Bank

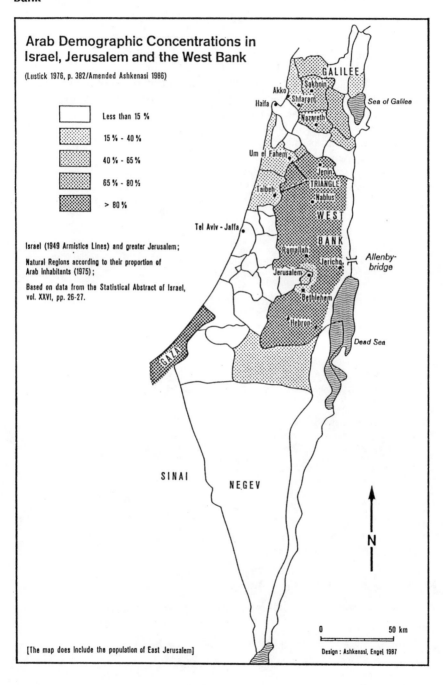

Arab Demographic Concentrations in
Israel, Jerusalem and the West Bank

(Lustick 1976, p. 382/Amended Ashkenasi 1986)

Less than 15 %

15 % - 40 %

40 % - 65 %

65 % - 80 %

> 80 %

Israel (1949 Armistice Lines) and greater Jerusalem;

Natural Regions according to their proportion of
Arab inhabitants (1975);

Based on data from the Statistical Abstract of Israel,
vol. XXVI, pp. 26-27.

GALILEE

Akko
Haifa
Shfaram
Sakhnin
Nazareth
Sea of Galilee

Um el Fahem

Jenin
TRIANGLE
Taibeh
Nablus

Tel Aviv - Jaffa

WEST
BANK

Ramallah
Jericho
Allenby-
bridge
Jerusalem

Bethlehem

Hebron
Dead Sea

GAZA

SINAI

NEGEV

N

0   50 km

[The map does include the population of East Jerusalem]

Design : Ashkenasi, Engel 1987

unifier—messianically Islamic or national or both—but for the present, the divisions still outweigh the differences and the rhetoric of unity.

NOTES

1. See chapter 6, where the study is discussed in detail.
2. A. Hareven, interview, February 1986.
3. Balata Refugee Camp Report 1986, private papers of Feisal Husseini. Information on Balata was presented by Husseini at a press conference at the National Palace hotel in East Jerusalem in the winter of 1986.
4. Ashkenasi, Jerusalem Data Project (1987).
5. For an analysis of the influence and positions of the newspapers, see Eli Rekhess, "Partisan Press," *Jerusalem Post*, April 22, 1987. Jordan is belatedly trying to recoup ground in the publications battle with the introduction of *al-Nahar* in 1986; cf. as well Shinar (1987). Obviously, this development was not a "conscious" element of Israeli policy.

5

PALESTINIAN SOCIETY AND ISRAELI MUNICIPAL AUTHORITY IN JERUSALEM

CONTROLLING EAST JERUSALEM

The task of controlling and dominating Arab society in Jerusalem after 1967 was more difficult than the task of co-opting large portions of Arab society and coercing the rest in Israel. Nevertheless, the Israeli municipal authority in Jerusalem has generally been successful in maintaining smooth control of the Arab community in the city, and the city has been a borderline model of communal development, always teetering on the brink of volatility, especially since the intifada, but always drawing back to guarded coexistence. Acts of intra-ethnic violence in Jerusalem (by Arabs and Jews) have almost invariably been perpetrated by those from outside the city or from its marginal groups. Indeed, elements of the Jewish community in Jerusalem, such as some anti-Zionist ultra-Orthodox groups, have been politically far more volatile in their opposition to the secular municipal authority than are the Arabs, and less likely either to perform municipal duties such as paying taxes or to obey the law.[1]

Since 1979 there has been an overall jump in crime in Jerusalem; there were 19,766 recorded offenses in 1984, still quite low by most standards. In 1979, 457 cases were brought against adults and there were 384 convictions. Of these offenders 99 were non-Jews (almost exclusively Arabs). The figures for 1983 were 2,472 charges, 557 against non-Jews; this represents a drop in the percentage of Arab or non-Jewish cases in relation to population. The conviction totals were 1,648 Jews and 498 non-Jews. It is significant that the conviction rate is similar in both ethnic groups. The statistics tell the same story for recidivists. Some 36.7 percent of the non-Jewish population and 40.3 percent of the Jewish criminals repeat their crimes. Juvenile delinquency figures for 1979 were 460 Jews and 207 non-Jews; for 1984, 441 and 168, respectively (*Jerusalem Statistical Year-*

book 1984). The number of security case convictions in Jerusalem municipal courts is also minimal; there were 13 against Jews, 39 against non-Jews in 1983. (These are exclusively adult charges and convictions; juveniles are not charged in open court in Israel for security offenses—a major difference from the West Bank, where they can be prosecuted.) In 1986 there were 2,210 charges brought against adults, with 2,036 convictions; 634 of those charged were non-Jews. Of those convicted, 1,453 were Jews and 583 were non-Jews. Recidivists accounted for 28.2 percent of the non-Jewish and 43 percent of the Jewish population. In 1987 there were 23,582 recorded offenses, more than a 20 percent increase over 1984, but the population, particularly the young adult population, grew as well.

Nonetheless, the crime and violence situation is not rosy. The number of security cases has been rising in Jerusalem; these often find their way to central Israeli jurisdiction in the town of Lod. The so-called security briefs reflect, conservatively, a 1 to 10 ratio to the Arab population of the West Bank, who are tried directly by military courts.[2] Jerusalem's Arabs enjoy Israel's civil legal system and apparently appreciate it. The occupied territories are under an ambitious, arbitrary, and often provocative military system and the Arab population responds accordingly. Prominent defense attorney Lea Tsemel, like others in the legal profession, points to the significant legal benefits of living with a Jerusalem identity card as one reason for Arab quiescence in the city. Since the intifada the level of incidents has jumped in Jerusalem, but to what degree this has occurred is not clear. Reports vary according to reporting officers and soldiers. The number of reported "incidents" on the West Bank for 1988 was 17,111; for Jerusalem, 2,957. Thus, the intensity would seem to be about the same. However, Jerusalem's incidents are much less serious. The throwing of a stone there would be reported, while it might well be ignored on the West Bank. In addition, a majority of "activists" in Jerusalem seem to come from the West Bank, from towns such as Ram, al-Azariya, or Abu Dis on the border. An examination of administrative arrests clarifies the picture a bit. From 1987 to 1989 there were 18 administrative arrests in Jerusalem and thousands on the West Bank (Shalev 1990, pp. 94, 95, 226). In 1988 there were 2,780 security arrests in Jerusalem but only 1,568 files and only 663 court cases.[3] Clearly there is an intifada in Jerusalem and clearly it lacks the intensity of that in the occupied territories. The violence tends to be concentrated on certain days, for example, in 1988 after the killing of Abu Jihad or in December 1989 after the closure of schools and institutions in East Jerusalem (Zilberman 1990).

Several complicated reasons, which are related to the questions we asked in the previous chapter, account for this phenomenon. The Jerusalem municipal authority, headed by Teddy Kollek, has always tried to maintain a low profile in dealing with the Arab community in Jerusalem (Kraemer

1980, Romann 1984). The mosaic of ethnic life is buttressed by this admin-istration. In this they were aided, consciously or not, by Jordanian social and financial policy in the city. Major organizations that are supposedly Jordanian-influenced, such as the Waqf[4] and the chamber of commerce, are conservative in nature and dispense considerable funds to conserva-tively oriented clients. In other words, a composite of political communities and political-social groups is not only tolerated in Jerusalem but is en-couraged in the Arab and the Jewish community alike. This leads to highly fragmented social groupings within the city, and the mosaic of Arab life may be a corollary to the regionalism of Arab life in Israel. The Arab community in Jerusalem is also socially heterogeneous. Many villages have been incorporated into the municipal structure of Jerusalem. Village areas such as Issawiya, A-Tur, Sur Bahir, Silwan, and Beit Safafa are very dif-ferent from middle class areas such as Sheikh Jarrah, and they again are different from new Arab quarters such as Beit Hanina with its recent influx of Israeli Arabs. Indeed, sociological data for 1983 showed that some differences between Beit Hanina and Silwan or Shuafat, especially in terms of income and mobility, may be greater than between Beit Hanina Arabs and Jews generally (Ashkenasi, Jerusalem Data Project, 1987).

The data for 1983 show that 42.4 percent of the Jewish population of Jerusalem earns in the lower 50 percent bracket, from 14,198 Israeli shekel to 29,450 Israeli shekel. (The shekel was replaced by the new shekel in 1986.) The raw figures mean very little because of the fluctuations in Israeli currency; what is important here is the comparison between Jewish and Arab society in Jerusalem. Fully 79.5 percent of Arab society earned under the Jerusalem mean. It is interesting to note that in comparing the third quarter of income—that is, the 25 percent of the population that earns from the upper 50 to 75 percent of income—Jews and Arabs come closest to parity: 27.3 percent of the Jewish population and 16 percent of the Arab population. The divide grows significantly again in the upper 25 percent grouping, with fully 30.3 percent of the Jewish population and only 4.4 percent of the Arab population in the upper 25 percent income bracket.

Given that these figures are for family income, earned by the head of a household, the income spread becomes even greater. Interestingly enough, if we break these figures down even further we notice that with increased education the differences in the upper income percentage, at least in the upper 50 to 75 percent, tend to decrease sharply. In fact, they reverse in the group with 16 years of education. What is significant here, however, is the large proportion of Arabs relative to Jews who still remain in the lower percentiles of earning capability even with significant levels of ed-ucation. Consider, for example, the high school graduates (13–15 years), over 65 percent of whom earn in the lower half of the income scale. Over 50 percent of the Arab population with university degrees earns under the average for the population in Jerusalem as a whole. These figures again exclude a rather significant percentage of Arab unemployed college graduates (the figure is estimated at something like 12,000 for the West Bank and Jerusalem together), and they exclude significant differences that become obvious when one analyzes individual income rather than income by household. Here, Arab income in terms of Jerusalem as a whole moves significantly toward the lower 50 percent; indeed, into the lowest quarter, where fully 47.7 percent of Arabs are found. (This figure is, by the way, a good 10 percent less in gross income per month than family income.)

Among the third quarter, that is, those who earn an average of 50 percent to 75 percent of income, significant movement—3.4 percent—appears. The numbers for Jewish citizens of Jerusalem remain fairly constant here. But as the educational level rises this difference becomes less significant. One of the reasons for this may be that educated Arab women in civil service positions (such as teachers) earn as much as educated Arab men, and this tends to help the better educated in the Arab community (provided, of course, that they have or are willing to accept these positions). These figures tend to take on added significance if one divides them in terms of age. Without wishing to appear elitist, it can be maintained that influence in society is probably greater for people with a high school education and above. This is especially true of Arab society, where an increasingly large percentage of the population is being educated (Mar'i 1978; Safadi 1987; Shinar 1987). In terms of individual income, 18.8 percent of the Jews and 14.3 percent of the Jewish population from the ages of 15 to 24 with 11 to 12 years of schooling are in the upper two quarters, respectively. The figures for the Arab population are 5.1 percent and 0 percent. For 13 to 15 years of school, the figures for the Jewish population are 16.9 and 3.4 percent, respectively, and for the Arab population 1.6 percent and 3.1 percent, respectively. For those with university degrees, figures for the Jews are 15.5 percent and 5.0 percent; for the Arabs, 10.0 percent and 0 percent. These figures are certainly open to question because in some cases they are based on answers by five or six members of the population in the upper brackets. However, in the lower brackets we have rather large numbers of responses in most instances. Therefore, by means of negative elimination we can also show that the young Arabs in Jerusalem were mired before the intifada in an economically hopeless situation, one that implied familial dependency, emigration, and/or deprivation. The situation has since deteriorated.

The figures for the population from the ages of 25 to 44 tell a different story. Here, the group with 11 to 12 years of education among the Jews are 36.7 percent and 25.5 percent in the respective upper income quarters. The Arab figures are 20 percent and 5.2 percent. For those with 13 to 15 years of education, the figures are 35.2 percent and 31.5 percent among the Jews, among the Arabs 22.3 percent and 10.9 percent, and in the post-baccalaureate grouping (16 years plus), 30.1 percent and 40.2 percent among the Jews, 30.9 percent and 21.3 percent among the Arabs. There is still a large percentage of "post-'67" highly educated Arabs making less than the average income in Jerusalem, but among the most highly educated Arabs more than 50 percent earn more than the average income. This means that one could speak of the development of a small, educated, perhaps new Arab bourgeoisie in Jerusalem before the intifada.

Responses by people over 45 indicate that the statistical trend evidenced from the age group of 24 to 45 continues. Among those Arabs with more than 16 years of education and over 45 years of age, 35.3 percent are in the highest quarter and 41.2 percent are in the second highest quarter. In other words, 76.5 percent of Arab society with post-college schooling over the age of 45 are in the upper half of income earning in Jerusalem. Because these figures are based on only 26 responses they are not conclusive.[5] At the same time, however, they do verify what we have determined impressionistically about the state of affairs in Jerusalem and about Arab society generally. Sociological class differences have developed and these depended to a large degree on education, an overt acceptance of the economic and sociological status quo, and repressed national chagrin.

The data on income by religion did not give a good enough statistical basis to explain differences between Christians and Muslims. This was because of the rather low number of Christian respondents and the inability to ascertain how much institutional assistance Christians receive in Jerusalem. Many assume that this institutional assistance is significant and, at least in the short run and in pecuniary terms, more important than what the Waqf can or will do for individual Muslims.[6] By all indications, Christians as a group are economically better off.

It is also interesting to compare Jewish and Arab society with regard to means of employment, a problem that Romann and Weingrod have considered in depth (Romann 1984, Romann and Weingrod 1990). There are, of course, obvious differences in occupational status, but in terms of percentage of salaried or self-employed members of the work force, the statistical differences are hardly significant (table 5–1). However, 25.3 percent of Arab society is employed in the public sector as compared to 44.6 percent of Jewish society. What this figure indicates is that the salaried Arab's position is less secure in a large percentage of employment situations, especially since the intifada with its repeated strikes and pervasive economic restrictions. In addition, although a small number of Arabs have prestigious jobs in city administration and in the school and hospital systems, almost no Arabs are in middle management and highly technical positions (Romann and Weingrod 1990)

So far we have been dealing with income differences between Jews and Arabs. The problem of two societies within one city is apparent. What lurks under the surface are the differences within Arab society. To investigate this statistically, I broke down Arab society into various living quar-

Table 5–1
1983 Employment Figures (Percentages)

	Arab	Jew
OCCUPATIONAL GROUP		
Academic scientists	4.9	13.9
Free professions	12.1	19.3
Managers	0.9	6.6
Clerks	8.4	23.6
Sales	11.2	7.4
Service	17.8	12.2
Agricultural workers	1.7	0.5
Industry, skilled (production)	18.5	6.7
Industry, skilled (service and building)	16.3	8.5
Industry (other)	8.2	1.3
STATUS AT WORK		
Salaried	87.2	89.4
Self-employed	12.8	10.6
PUBLIC SECTOR		
Other	74.7	55.4
Public	25.3[a]	44.6
PLACE OF EMPLOYMENT		
East Jerusalem	58.8	10.2[b]
West Jerusalem	29.0	82.7
Outside Jerusalem	12.2	7.2

a A word of caution here: public sector also means nationally employed Jerusalemites (police, university, etc.) and, in the Arab employment sector, "private" public service (Waqf, charities, etc.).
b The 10.2% of the Jewish working population employed in East or Arab Jerusalem is found almost entirely in the public sector (hospitals, courts, police, etc.).

ters: the Muslim quarter in the old city of Jerusalem, the new and expanding suburb of Beit Hanina, the interesting village of Beit Safafa with its high percentage of Israeli Arabs, the refugee camp of Shuafat, and the depressed village quarter of Silwan. The breakdown here by occupation (table 5–2) is almost as revealing as the breakdown for Jews and Arabs.

Compare Beit Hanina's job statistics—8.8 percent in academic scientific occupations, for example, and 14.3 percent in the independent professions—to those of Shuafat. Notice the high percentage of industrial workers in Shuafat, especially in comparison to Beit Hanina. However, although Beit Hanina has the highest percentage of Arabs in the public sector, 25.4

Table 5–2
1983 Residential Figures (Percentages)

Subquarter of residence:	Muslim Quarter	Beit Hanina	Beit Safafa	Shuafat	Silwan
OCCUPATION					
Academic scientists	3.0	8.8	1.5	1.2	0.7
Independent professions	8.8	14.3	8.9	6.2	6.5
Managers	0.2	1.4	0	0	0
Clerks	7.8	11.4	6.1	5.6	6.5
Sales	12.5	19.5	2.8	9.3	10.5
Service	18.7	10.2	18.8	20.4	30.7
Agricultural workers	1.9	0.7	5.1	1.9	1.3
Industry, skilled (production)	22.9	15.2	19.6	25.9	19.0
Industry, skilled (service and building)	18.5	11.9	20.9	19.8	15.7
Industry (other)	5.8	6.6	16.3	9.9	9.2
WORK STATUS					
Salaried	88.6	83.5	95.4	84.6	84.9
Self-employed	11.4	16.5	4.6	15.4	15.1
MUNICIPAL EMPLOYEES					
Other	78.1	74.6	79.2	77.8	76.4
Public sector	21.9	25.4	20.8	22.2	23.6
PLACE OF EMPLOYMENT					
East Jerusalem	62.6	75.0	43.8	57.4	48.3
West Jerusalem	29.0	19.6	28.2	31.3	35.1
Outside Jerusalem	8.3	5.3	28.0	11.5	16.6

percent, the difference between it and the other quarters (or boroughs) is minimal. In all quarters, over 20 percent of the population works in the public sector. At what occupational level do we find these workers? It seems fair to assume that the Beit Hanina community has higher-level jobs within the Jerusalem municipality.

Within the quarters there is a definite difference in mean income. The mean income in Beit Hanina is significantly higher than that of the rest (table 5–3). It is interesting in this regard to look at the mean income of all of Jerusalem, including Jews and Arabs: in 1983, it was 20,521 shekel. Compare this with the 17,123 mean in Beit Hanina. In other words, Beit Hanina is an Arab borough whose mean income is close to that of the

Table 5–3
Income: Analysis of Variance, 1983

Value label	Income in shekels	Mean	Standard deviation	Respondents
Muslim Quarter	5,383,993.0000	12,758.2773	8,334.4463	422
Beit Hanina	8,167,888.0000	17,123.4549	20,743.2550	477
Beit Safafa	4,419,122.0000	14,347.7987	7,556.6714	208
Shuafat	1,422,145.0000	12,155.0855	5,172.4809	117
Silwan	1,293,653.0000	11,978.2685	7,624.7363	108
Total	20,686,801.0000	14,446.0901	13,654.6591	1,432

mean income for all Jerusalem including Jews. Beit Safafa, while not doing as well, still manages to place in the third lowest quarter for the whole city. It is noteworthy that there are rather large variances in income in Beit Hanina, some of the most striking being very high levels of income for Christians from the ages of 24 to 45 and with higher education. But again, these figures are based on rather limited samples. Indeed, the mean income for heads of households does not change the overall picture significantly. In fact, it reaffirms it.

Spatial segregation is as important a differential as income level in an analysis of sociological paradigma. The map in figure 5–1 indicates the level of segregation between Jews and Arabs within Jerusalem. The ethnic areas are distinct and compact, but Arab and Jewish quarters crisscross. (In fact, in the Old City one can walk on the roofs of part of the Arab town to get from one Jewish area to another.) There is no neat physical division between an Arab and a Jewish town. Borders are sometimes no more than a few meters, a road, a little park, a playground, an official building (Romann 1984, Romann and Weingrod 1990). The psychological lines between areas, as Romann has pointed out, are more important than the physical ones.

Within the Arab community there is a distinct tendency toward spatial immobility. If we compare Jewish and Arab society in Jerusalem (table 5–4), it is easy to see that Jewish society is far more mobile. Some 85 percent of Arab society remained rooted in the same place from 1978 to 1983; this was true of only 63 percent of the Jews. Of the Jewish community, 19.5 percent has moved within the city boundaries, whereas only 6.9 percent of Arab society moved from one quarter to another in Jerusalem; as many Arabs have moved into certain areas of Jerusalem from places completely outside the city (probably rejoining family members within Jerusalem or moving in from Israel proper, since it is very difficult for an Arab who was not registered in the city in 1967 to return to Jerusalem). Among the Jewish

Figure 5–1
Jerusalem: Quarters, Subquarters, and Statistical Areas, 1983

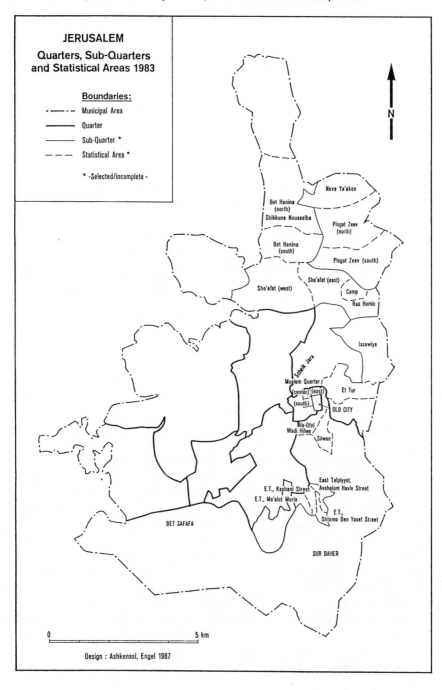

Table 5–4
Mobility, between 1978 and 1983

Count Row pct. Column pct. Place of residence	Arab	Jew	Row total
Unchanged	55,620	118,190	173,810
	32.0	68.0	68.0
	85.9	63.1	
Same statistical area	700	4,070	4,770
	14.7	85.3	1.9
	1.1	2.2	
Other Jerusalem	4,450	36,485	40,935
statistical area	14.7	85.3	1.9
	6.9	19.5	
Unknown	65	300	365
statistical area	17.8	82.2	0.1
	0.1	0.2	
Other locality	320	14,080	14,400
	2.2	97.8	5.7
	0.5	7.5	
Abroad	1,995	11,945	13,940
	14.3	85.7	5.5
	3.1	6.4	
Unknown	1,610	2,340	3,950
locality	40.8	59.2	1.6
	2.5	1.2	
Column	64,760	187,410	252,170
total	25.7	74.3	100

community, there is more movement within the city than there are other Jews coming in from either abroad or other localities in Israel. (One cannot posit from this that Jewish society is completely integrated and that there are no fissures within Jewish Israel. There are quarters in Jewish Jerusalem that are not only sociologically completely distinct but also cordially detest one another.) A large percentage of Jewish society, however, is mobile within the city. And although this causes much social friction, it leads to mutual problem solving as well. This is not true of the Arab community.

Again, an analysis of mobility within the boroughs is significant (table 5–5). Almost all the quarters evince a tight spatial segregatory pattern except Beit Hanina. Fully 13.3 percent of the population there was living in some other part of Jerusalem before moving to Beit Hanina. Compare this with Beit Safafa (1.9 percent) or Silwan (3.6 percent). A figure of 6.6 percent in the Muslim quarter indicates, interestingly enough, that there

Table 5–5
Mobility by Neighborhood, 1978–83

Count Row pct. Column pct. Tot pct.	Muslim Quarter	Beit Hanina	Beit Safafa	Shuafat	Silwan	Row Total
Unchanged	2,482	2,553	2,244	835	821	8,935
	27.8	28.6	25.1	9.3	9.2	87.7
	89.0	78.1	95.1	92.5	94.5	
	24.4	25.1	22.0	8.2	8.1	
Same statistical	38	50	7	2	6	103
area	36.9	48.5	6.8	1.9	5.8	1.0
	1.4	1.5	.3	.2	.7	
	.4	.5	.1	.0	.1	
Other Jerusalem	183	435	44	38	31	731
statistical area	25.0	59.5	6.0	5.2	4.2	7.2
	6.6	13.3	1.9	4.2	3.6	
	1.8	4.3	.4	.4	.3	
Unknown	8	4	3	0	1	16
statistical area	50.0	25.0	18.8	0	6.3	.2
	.3	.1	.1	0	.1	
	.1	.0	.0	0	.0	
Other locality	5	18	11	0	0	34
	14.7	52.9	32.4	0	0	.3
	.2	.6	.5	0	0	
	.0	.2	.1	0	0	
Abroad	36	126	18	7	7	194
	18.6	64.9	9.3	3.6	3.6	1.9
	1.3	3.9	.8	.8	.8	
	.4	1.2	.2	.1	.1	
Unknown locality	37	81	33	21	3	175
	21.1	16.3	18.9	12.0	1.7	1.7
	1.3	2.5	1.4	2.3	.3	
	.4	.8	.3	.2	.0	
Column	2,789	3,267	2,360	903	869	10,188
Total	27.4	32.1	23.2	8.9	8.5	100

are many returnees to the Old City. This trend is probably increasing as the quarter is renovated and property increases in value. However, it is less an indicator of mobility within the quarter than a sign that people are returning to where they once lived. These statistics do not indicate that Arab quarters are closed communities. They simply suggest that new families rarely move into the village-type Arab community, and certainly not into the refugee camp unless they are forced to. This mobility is a function, to a degree, of income, opportunity, and new housing, all of which are available to an extent in Beit Hanina.

It is hard to say what social or political ramifications ensue from this kind of pattern, but in table 5–2 we can see that by and large the population of Beit Hanina is least dependent on occupation in West Jerusalem. Fully 35 percent of the population of Silwan work in West Jerusalem and another 16.6 percent work outside Jerusalem, probably in Israel as guest workers of one kind or another. It is not surprising to see a high percentage of Beit Safafans working in Israel, since many have Israeli citizenship. (They constitute the only significant number of Arabs in Jerusalem within the villages with Israeli citizenship, for the dividing line between Israel and Jordanian-claimed territory from 1948 to 1967 ran through the village.) What this does mean, however, is that large percentages of some of the Arab quarter residents work within the Jewish community and live entirely within their own neighborhoods. It is questionable, then, what kind of ties they can develop that are integratory for the whole Arab community. On the other hand, the Beit Hanina Arabs, the best educated and the best off financially and therefore the most mobile, are generally those who differ most from the rest and have less structural integrity and less unity as a quarter.

These figures alone would mean little if they were not abetted by a distinct policy of quarterization by the Jerusalem municipality. This is done through the utilization of traditional political leadership, especially within the villages, and through the establishment of neighborhood councils in some of the other quarters. Neighborhood councils also typify a growing number of Jewish neighborhoods. Although often enough both systems—traditional leadership and councils—function parallel to one another, they are to a degree competitive and represent another element of political fragmentation.

NEIGHBORHOOD COUNCILS AND BOROUGH ADMINISTRATION (MUKHTARS AND MINHALOT)

The self-administration of much of Arab Jerusalem, especially the semirural areas, was carried out via individuals known as mukhtars. Their largely autonomist social and cultural "turf," as well as their informal relationship with and influence upon the municipal authority of Jerusalem, is certainly a throwback to Ottoman administration. There are some 56

mukhtars; the number varies. The mukhtars who function in the West
Bank and Jerusalem were and may still be informally sanctioned by the
Jordanian government, which has empowered them with various forms of
civil and economic authority. Not all mukhtars deal with the Jerusalem
administration. Nevertheless, the edge is taken off the potential conflict
inherent in the ethnic structure of Jerusalem by the support of borough-
oriented self-administration. Representation of interests is held at the lowest possible level. The municipality's policies and activities are disseminated
throughout the city by means of the mukhtar system to other contact
persons, and political intensity as such is lowered. The early concentration
on political conflicts within the neighborhoods and quarters makes an early
identification of problems possible, and local political planning and ac-
knowledgement of local wishes make the administration of the city easier.
By activating a mosaic of communal political structures and by establishing
firm social and administrative institutions or informal hierarchies, the municipality creates a series of active addresses to which not only the municipal
organizations but also the Arab community can turn. Traditional patron-
client relationships, and even modern middle class interest groups, become
manageable. The lines for disseminating goods and services become political but predictable; reciprocities that can be both political and ethnic
are open and flexible. Informal structures—the mukhtar system is the most
obvious example—can also be used to limit political conflict resulting from
extra-municipal political confrontation.

It should be noted, however, that the role of the mukhtar has declined
in importance as new social groups (unionized workers, religious organizations, university graduates) proliferate. The system of minhalot (singular,
minhelet) is a system of neighborhood councils that at their inception in
1980 were financed equally by the Jewish Joint Distribution Committee
and the municipality of Jerusalem. This system had already functioned in
Israel in purely Jewish communities, most of which were Oriental and were
being encouraged to develop communal democratic systems. In Jerusalem,
some Jewish quarters were brought into this system and it was possible to
initiate the system in one Arab quarter of Jerusalem, A-Tur. Also, in 1984
a neighborhood council was established in a section of Beit Hanina, in the
so-called Nusseibeh quarter, inhabited in part by Israeli Arabs but mainly
by Arabs from East Jerusalem. (Many residents of this portion of Beit
Hanina are Arab employees of the municipality—teachers, nurses, and the
like.) The budgetary structure of the neighborhood councils at their inception and their organizational form were quite similar, with minimal
financial support and one and a half or two civil servants' positions for
utilization in social affairs in the neighborhood councils. The councils reported back to a directorate that was not part of the municipality of Jerusalem. Since that time, however, the success of the minhalot has resulted
in the planning of new Arab minhalot, beginning in Beit Safafa. A by-

product of the intifada has been the shelving of plans for minhalot in Silwan and Sur Bahir. Beit Hanina's minhelet is limping along. As in Beit Safafa, it is Israeli Arabs who are major participants. The Jewish minhelet of East Talpiot, an area of new housing in what was once no-man's land and Jordanian-controlled farmland, had begun to represent Arabs as well—through the mukhtars of neighboring Arab villages such as Sur Bahir and Jabal Mukaber, which were incorporated into Jerusalem's boundaries. The overwhelming majority of these mukhtars were previously unwilling to deal with the municipality of Jerusalem and are still reluctant to do so, all the more since the intifada.[7]

The municipality, however, has taken direct control of coordinating the operations of minhalot, granting them budgetary and communal autonomy while so far avoiding concurrent political development. Within the Arab community of Jerusalem the minhalot operate with a mixture of, on the one hand, Israeli Arabs and, on the other, Arabs who identify fully as Palestinians in the modern suburb of Beit Hanina and in the intact village of A-Tur. The latter minhelet is interesting because it includes the representatives of the old Jordanian village council and, indeed, was budgeted not only by the municipality of Jerusalem and the Joint Distribution Committee but directly by the Kingdom of Jordan through the old village council. Its Israeli Arab secretary insists that it still is. This neighborhood council is a mixed structure; municipally appointed civil servants, most from East Jerusalem but in some cases Arabs from Israel as well, coordinate social, cultural, educational, and other communal services initiated by the Arab community through old Jordanian notables (some of whom were or are mukhtars) and newly co-opted, well-educated younger professionals. In addition, the minhelet in exclusively Jewish East Talpiot maintains political contacts with mukhtars of the southern villages. Villagers are increasingly using the social and health facilities of East Talpiot. In 1986 the structure of the minhelet system changed, as successful minhalot were given a degree of financial independence. They could write their own budgets and could also attempt to raise money independent of the city administration. A-Tur, as well as the Jewish minhalot of Gilo and East Talpiot, are now so privileged. This amounts to communal autonomy.[8]

Minhalot have continued to function throughout the intifada. The municipal neighborhood councils also seem to offer a mutually beneficial structure for Israel, for the municipal administration of Jerusalem and, to a limited degree, for Jordan. Both Jerusalem's administration and the Hashemite kingdom were interested in the co-optation of a new category of communal personalities (teachers, new professionals, social workers, etc.) into the local decision-making process. The viability and eventual political development of the councils were an important aspect of the so-called borough program advanced at one time by Mayor Kollek and others. The mosaic structure of the city would seem to be a self-segregatory neighborhood council scheme that allows a great deal of autonomist local life but leaves the predominantly Jewish city government in control of the overall, citywide aspects of life. Indeed, the national question would play a very minor role in this kind of structure, as long as Arab society in Jerusalem ignores the electoral process in Jerusalem for pressing ethnic demands. (While a minority of Jerusalem Arabs vote in municipal elections—the trend was ever more in each election, reaching 18 percent before the intifada when the trend reversed sharply—others scorn participation as a recognition of the occupier.)

VOTING PATTERNS AND OTHER POLITICAL INDICATORS

Any analysis of Israeli Arab returns in national elections indicates the differences between Arab communal voting practices and policies and overall ballot comportment (al-Haj and Yaniv 1983). Arabs in Jerusalem are not, by and large, Israeli citizens (they can opt for Israeli passports if they wish, but the overwhelming majority maintain Jordanian passports). But they can nevertheless vote in municipal elections in Jerusalem. Almost all Arab adults living in Jerusalem are eligible voters. Yet no Arab political party has developed in Jerusalem; no political party represents Palestinian nationalism. Political favors and political clientilism are maintained through the system of local neighborhood or quarter leadership or through the various family organizations. Significantly enough, however, in 1985 almost 18 percent of Jerusalem's eligible Arab voters voted for Teddy Kollek's One Jerusalem list (this represents about 10,000 of the 66,000 eligible Arab voters and more than 95 percent of all Arabs voting). Kollek received 64 percent of the overall vote in Jerusalem, 79,515 of a total of 134,778 voters and 124,540 valid votes. (Apparently some 10,000 votes were invalid.) Only 48.5 percent of all Jerusalem's registered voters, Arabs and Jews, cast ballots. Over 80 percent of all eligible Arab voters boycotted the election. Most of Kollek's Arab support came from the village areas, as does a large portion of Arab support for Israeli Zionist political parties in Israel.

Interestingly enough, no real correlation can be made between voting patterns and participation in neighborhood councils. The villages whose voters supported Kollek's One Jerusalem list were Beit Safafa (about 40 percent), Sur Bahir (25 percent to 30 percent), and Issawiya (30 percent), whereas A-Tur (under 20 percent) and especially Beit Hanina (5 percent to 15 percent, depending on polling areas) remained under the Jerusalem Arab average voting participation. Communal cooperation may reveal nothing about national identification processes, and voting patterns may be suspect as an indicator of national goals in ethnically divided cities. (In winter 1988 A-Tur proved, after the refugee camp, to be the most violence-prone Arab borough, and both Issawiya and Sur Bahir were troubled. Beit

Hanina and Beit Safafa remained calm.) Nevertheless, the city administration keeps precise figures by polling area (about 800 voters per area),
and there may be good reasons for these voting patterns.

Part of Beit Safafa was in Israel before 1967; more than half of the Arab
population there holds Israeli passports. Although Israeli Arabs, as we
have seen, may also identify with Palestinian nationalism, they are not
averse to bettering their communal situation through utilization of the
Israeli political system or cooperating with those who identify with it. In
Sur Bahir, Mayor Kollek (but especially an ad hoc committee of villagers
and residents of the nearby Jewish neighborhoods of Talpiot, East Talpiot,
and Arnona) supported the community against the Israel National Land
Authority. For the time being, although precious agricultural land has been
expropriated for public development (roads, etc.), Sur Bahir has use of
the land. (Cynics have claimed that Sur Bahir's Jewish neighbors prefer
adjacent, handsomely tilled Palestinian fields and olive and almond trees
over smelly Zionist bulldozers and traffic.) Ironically, part of East Talpiot
is built on land acquired in earlier expropriations from Sur Bahir, as well
as nearby Jabal Mukaber. As for Issawiya, its returns may reflect a very
high rate of employment in West Jerusalem, especially at adjacent Ha-
dassah hospital and the Hebrew University. The negative voting pattern
in A-Tur seems in part to have been a function of its residents' and especially its elite families' orientation toward Jordan. This orientation seems
to be eroding; the village now evinces a high nationalist Palestinian profile
(see chapter 6). Beit Hanina's upwardly mobile Arab society seems to
evince a stronger intellectual attachment to Palestinianism. They reject
formal contacts with Israel and the Jerusalem municipality, but they are
interested in schools, playgrounds, health and child centers, and the other
local communal services that upwardly mobile people everywhere desire.
Thus, they are willing to participate to a degree in a communal decision-
making process but refuse to commit themselves psychologically by voting.

Again, this is an impressionistic analysis. The level of attachment to
Palestinian nationalism, the depth of the national identification process
within Arab society in Jerusalem, and the level of risk that is accepted for
participation in Palestinian political organization and activity will be analyzed statistically later. The participation or lack of it in the Israeli election
process, albeit municipal elections, seems to be an indication of the overt
and verbal attachment to Palestinianism and the rejection of the political
structure of Jerusalem; a rejection that is widespread in Arab society, other
forms of communal participation notwithstanding. Of course, it has been
by and large a passive form of protest.

In the 1989 elections a record low of fewer than 3,000 Arabs voted,
mostly for Kollek's list, but some apparently for the conciliatory and dovish
Zionist combined list of the Citizens Rights and Peace party and the Shinui
("Change") party. They defied the threats of intifada activists to do so. A

large percentage seem to have been Israeli Arabs from Beit Safafa; concrete figures are still missing. The One Jerusalem list lost seats, in part due to the decline in Arab voter participation. In the weeks preceding the elections, intensive efforts to win the Palestinian vote were made by both One Jerusalem and the dovish list. The attempts by these groups to move most Jerusalem polling places to the west side to reduce Arab fears of reprisals were vociferously opposed by right-wing and religious factions who claimed this was tantamount to redividing the city.

Nevertheless, it is obvious that in Arab society a clear political distinction is still made between Kollek's low-profile, city manager's conception of the city of Jerusalem and the more nationalist-centralist policies of the right-wing Likud. This is in part because of the generally conservative social structure of Arab Jerusalem and the corollary social and economic power of the major families and clans, whether they be old-Jerusalem (Nusseibehs, Dajanis) or more recently arrived Hebronites (Barakats, Nasser al-Dins, and others). This power is heightened by the lack of Arab banking and central financing facilities in Jerusalem or elsewhere in the West Bank or even in Israel (Harris 1986). There seems to be no interest in these circles in a centralized Palestinian political organization that might curtail the major Jerusalem oligarchies. But even mainline Fatah people in Jerusalem such as Ibrahim Kara'een, editor-in-chief of *al-Awda*, evinced definite preference for the Kollek administration.[9] In 1985 *al-Awda* urged those Arabs in East Jerusalem who felt that they had to vote to support the One Jerusalem list. Of course, this encouragement was lacking in 1989.

General rejection of the political situation is pervasive and often bitter in all sections of Arab society in Jerusalem. But it remains largely passive and politically fragmented even now. The poor from the village quarters as well as certain elements of the new immigrant population from Hebron who are still economic underdogs (including some of those who came between 1950 and 1967) form a large group of urban poor who have been slow to identify with the "national" Arab opposition. They, along with the Israeli Arabs who were moving in slowly but in increasing numbers, can be co-opted—even since the intifada. On the other hand, many of these as well as the young are now joining the ranks of the Islamic fundamentalist movement (a social phenomenon similar in a sense to what we observe among economically marginal Muslims in Israel). In addition, as we have seen, about 40 percent of the Arab work force are employed in the Israeli economy, and most East Jerusalem Arabs also belong to the Israeli health insurance system. Workers and the less well-off have unspoken reasons for accepting the system. In addition, it is just these elements of society (and especially the females in this sector), not the upwardly mobile bourgeoisie or oligarchs, who benefit from the municipal Arab school system, which is administered by the city administration.

Histadrut (the Israeli trade union) election returns before the intifada were quite significant. In the elections in 1985 in the southern Arab village areas—Silwan, Jabal Mukaber, Sur Bahir, Beit Safafa, and so on—the Israeli Labour party received a hefty 3,055 votes, or 94 percent of the votes cast in these areas. Issawiya, A-Tur, and the Wadi Joz area (a lower middle class area in central East Jerusalem) returned 857 votes (94 percent of those cast) for Labour. These are high voter percentages: They reflect over 20 percent of all registered voters, including, of course, those not in the Histadrut in these exclusively Arab areas; and for the southern area, 40 percent of all breadwinners. This repeats the overall Israeli pattern. Arab workers care who represents them in the Histadrut.[10] They join the Histadrut and a significant minority votes for the Labour Alignment list (*Jerusalem Statistical Yearbook 1986*). There were 4,400 Arab voters, or about one-third of those eligible, in 1985. In 1989, however, only 1,300 made their way to Strauss Street in West Jerusalem to cast their ballots, after being pointedly advised by leaflets of the intifada not to vote. There are Palestinian trade unions in Jerusalem, but they are in no way as significant economically as the Histadrut, and the organizations are not nearly as large. The intifada has officially curtailed their operations. The strongest has been the union of the East Jerusalem electric company, which still exists despite the demise of the company itself, long valued as a national symbol more than as a carrier of electricity.

THE RACE FOR SPACE AND OPPORTUNITIES

The Arab community in Jerusalem remained quiet in the face of expanding Jewish building and land expropriation within the city. However, most Jewish housing expansion takes place in areas where there was previously no Arab housing; limited Arab expansion is also tolerated. A map of housing expansion within the city (figure 5–2) indicates how this mutual expansion progresses (along lines logically determined by the municipal authority, which has a pro-Jewish bias, but with some opportunities and space for the Arab community). There is an obvious Jewish housing and infrastructure ring encompassing four-fifths of Jerusalem and extending from Mount Scopus to East Talpiot. Among the newest Jewish neighborhoods are Ramot and Gilo, each with 26,500 residents, and the newer Pisgat Zeev, home to 3,700 and planned for 50,000. Arab exit routes and infrastructure develop toward Jericho and Hebron. Joint development takes place along the northern route to Ramallah, with major Jewish infrastructural grids leading west toward Tel Aviv and developing on the West Bank as well.

The combined Jewish population of the expanding areas in northern Jerusalem, northeastern Jerusalem (French Hill, Ramat Eshkol, Ramot Alon, Neve Yaakov, and Pisgat Zeev), and southern and southeastern Jerusalem (East Talpiot and Gilo) had passed the 120,000 mark by the

Figure 5–2
Jerusalem: Development of Built-up Area, 1981

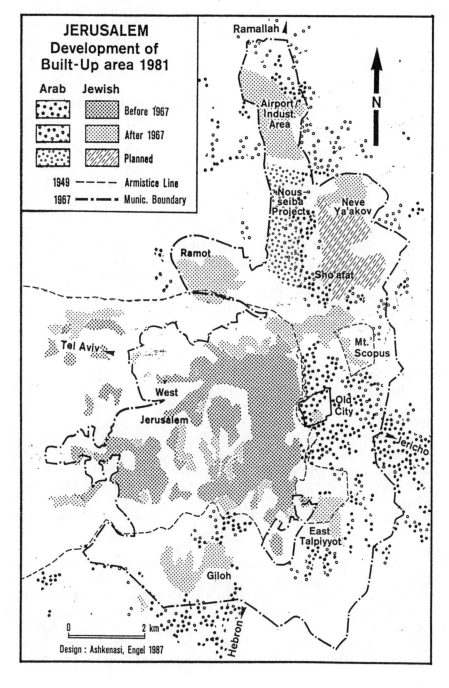

late 1980s. In addition, Jewish suburban growth to the east, west, and south of Jerusalem's city limits is considerable (some 50,000 more). The Jewish center of town is booming; all in all, there is no other word to describe the infrastructural revolution that has occurred since 1967. The intifada has not impeded this. It has, however, crippled Arab development. While building has occurred in the new northern suburbs of Beit Hanina and Shuafat (the camp has seen "illegal" unlicensed building) and in the villages that are now part of the Jerusalem municipality, the Arab business center has deteriorated. Municipal licensing has not been forthcoming. The Old City, on the other hand, is being spruced up and renovated (sewage systems, cut stone streets, and more)—a big help for the Waqf, which is a major landlord. Individual Arabs with property have been able to build new dwellings or to renovate and expand their old homes. And there has been some central Israeli and municipal development on the outskirts of Jerusalem (al-Azariya), especially for Arab civil servants. By and large, however, municipal planning for Arab housing has been impeded by the national Ministry of Housing and major bureaucratic foot-dragging. In addition, Jewish settlement in the Old City outside the Jewish Quarter, although statistically minimal, is a major source of provocation to Arabs.

But for the most part public expenditure has gone into the Jewish sector at an estimated rate of 9:1 (Romann and Weingrod 1990). To alleviate the pressure of a growing Arab population, the Jerusalem municipality has released previously reserved "farmland" in the Arab north (Beit Hanina) for development; up to 10,000 units and 40,000 to 60,000 dwellers. However, the Israeli national ministries have stubbornly refused to license Arab development here. The release of Arab land was paralleled by the progressing Jewish development of Pisgat Zeev, the difference being that Pisgat Zeev is being built with major infrastructure (highways, bus lines) connecting it to the city and to the Hebrew University campus on Mount Scopus. The city estimates that there will an Arab population of 30 percent in Jerusalem by the year 2000. It is planning new electrical grids, water lines, and sewage pipes that will make Jerusalem the hub of a modern utility network. Whatever happens politically, it seems that the municipality's plan is for the services to emanate to the entire area from a united Jerusalem with a clear Jewish majority[11]—but, again, with opportunities and benefits for Arabs who wish to cooperate, with or without Palestinian ethos.

Indeed, much parallelism is allowed within the city. Separate bus and taxi lines operate within Jerusalem (see figure 5–3; Romann 1984). Ethnic business is also successfully practiced within the city. There are virtually no long-term joint ventures, but there is also little attempt to destroy the ongoing economic activity of individual Arabs, and short-term subcontracting is prevalent. Again, political cooperation is a prerequisite for licensing (taxis, buses, restaurants). Cooperation does not necessarily mean

Figure 5–3
Jerusalem: Public Transport, 1981

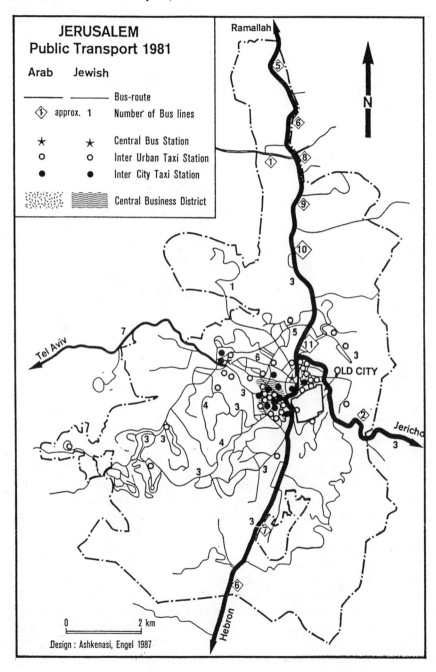

JERUSALEM
Public Transport 1981

Arab   Jewish

—————— —————— Bus-route
⟨1⟩ approx. 1 Number of Bus lines

★   ★   Central Bus Station
○   ○   Inter Urban Taxi Station
●   ●   Inter City Taxi Station

Central Business District

Ramallah

N

Tel Aviv

OLD CITY

Jericho

Hebron

0   2 km

Design : Ashkenasi, Engel 1987

more than a quiescent acceptance of the status quo, at least in deed (paying taxes, not supporting violence), if not in word. That is the limit to cooperation; despite many blandishments, Arabs have been loath to enter into joint long-term operations with Jewish capital, whether public or private. Indeed, this is one of the reasons for industrial stagnation and infrastructural weakness in Arab Jerusalem. The Jerusalem administration keeps pressuring for joint operations before licensing larger projects; here, the tug-of-war is still on. The intifada has simply highlighted the basic issues of economic inequality.

THE POLITICAL STANDOFF

The policies underlying the bundle of subtle measures used by the Kollek administration were characterized by the late Joseph Gadish, one of the administration's key advisors, in this way: (1) Ask Amman before doing anything. (2) Don't hide anything. Keep your politics open. (3) Get younger people involved in your municipal policies and keep direct contacts to all elements in the society. (4) Have no integrated housing. (5) Have no short-term expectations for any kind of national solutions.

Interestingly enough, as open, passionate, and intellectually acute a Palestinian nationalist as Ibrahim Dakkak formulated the following points a few years ago for a Palestinian position in Jerusalem: (1) Jerusalem is not a melting pot; (2) Palestinians must expect a long stay by the Israelis; (3) Arab (Palestinian) society has to be able to accept new ideas and to resolve its own internal conflicts; (4) Arab (Palestinian) society must develop under occupation. It must develop a separate infrastructure, and so be able to maintain itself until such time as it can reestablish its own control over its own destiny.[12]

These policies complemented each other, and Dakkak understood something that has evaded some other Palestinians but that the Labour Zionist movement knew quite well: Without a healthy, cohesive society, land is just dirt. But the policies pursued by both sides have implied a continued Israeli, Zionist administration of the city of Jerusalem and a continued Arab social and economic development—parallel, and indeed in opposition but not violent opposition to the Israeli administration of the city—until such time as Arab society will be up to the national tasks. There are signs that this policy has failed because the cards have been stacked against the Palestinians. Recall that Smooha argued convincingly that in Israel from 25 percent to 35 percent of the Arab community really accepts the state. Arabs are a nonassimilating, indeed dissident, minority. But this minority maintains various degrees of cooperative and accommodative political activity; never have more than 10 percent been radical and rejectionist. Growing militancy in political and social demands is a reflection of a sociopolitical learning process; Arabs are gaining the ability to use the Israeli political system and to coalesce with Jewish political groups.

This is a pattern that seems to be slowly taking hold in Jerusalem but in a different way. There Israeli presence and even expansion may be tolerated, but not Israeli sovereignty. Municipal cooperation may be another question, as the next chapter will demonstrate. The radical community seems twice as large and the rejectionists are "off the fence" politically, if not economically. Jerusalem's Arab community is loath to "formally" use the Israeli system through its own political parties and through overt political leverage in various Israeli and municipal institutions. Meron Benvenisti (1983) maintained that this situation cannot continue and that eventual violent conflict is inevitable. He argued that Israeli society would not tolerate a Palestinian Arab political party in Jerusalem and that Jerusalem's Arabs would not accept substitutes (such as the Israeli Communist party, Rakah). Benvenisti's model has always been Belfast. His theoretical approach, based on polarization, is completely different from the sort of pluralist sociology employed by Smooha. Benvenisti's position has been that the national or macronational struggle will eventually swallow the micro-ethnic disputes. No matter what strategies Israeli authorities may determine, their final course will have to be violent suppression. The intifada seems to have manuevered Arab protest between these two poles. There is periodic violent conflict in Jerusalem, often ideologically motivated, between the Israel police force and Palestinians, and between religiously motivated groups on both sides. The Jerusalem city administration and conservative elements in Palestinian society have long been able to ameliorate the situation; this constitutes damage control par excellence. Recently, marginal groups in both societies have begun to attack innocent bystanders in a complete reversal of what had been the pattern of confrontation in Jerusalem.

Certain social trends give credence to communal pessimism (or revolutionary optimism, as the case may be). It is true that the Arab community in Jerusalem is not growing appreciably faster than the Jewish community— the Arab birth rate in the city is 32.1 per 1,000 and the Jewish birth rate 28.2 per 1,000, compared to 32.9 and 24.4, respectively, for the country as a whole (in fact, in 1988 the Arab rate dipped below the Jewish rate as Orthodox religious Jews continued to follow the biblical injunction to be fruitful and multiply). Nevertheless, Jerusalem will soon be populated by a new generation of Arabs different in outlook and twice as numerous as their predecessors. The same is true for Jews. The new generation is already proving more ready to risk violent confrontation.

There is also no doubt that the West Bank is much more volatile than Jerusalem. The question is this: Does the city act to pacify the rest, or vice versa? West Bank safety valves (emigration and relative prosperity) are closing off. (Indeed there was a significant return of displaced Palestinians

Table 5–6
Distribution of Votes at Palestinian Universities, Spring 1985

University	Student Youth (Fatah)	Progress and Unity (Popular Front)	Islamic Bloc	Percentage who voted
Birzeit	38%	36.4%	24.5%	91%
Al-Najah (Nablus)	50%	13%	36%	88%
Hebron	50%	7%	44%	90%
Bethlehem	43.5%	45%	11%	93%

Source: Survey of Arab Affairs (Jerusalem), November 1985.

from the Gulf as a result of the war.) Young academics are without prospects; the number of unemployed or graduates is rising (Safadi 1987). University-wide elections held in 1985 indicate a strong emotional attachment to the PLO and, especially in the case of Bethlehem, to the rejectionist Popular Front for the Liberation of Palestine (PFLP) and Democratic Front for the Liberation of Palestine (DFLP).

In terms of nonuniversity institutes of higher education, two colleges in Jerusalem have been nonpolitical and under Jordanian influence: Abu Dis College of Science and Technology (just outside Jerusalem) and the women's college Dar al-Tifl. (Farther outside the city, the same characterization holds true for Hebron Polytechnic.) Abu Dis, however, has recently initiated an elected student council. There was also some indication that a new Jordan-oriented university may be established near Tulkarm. It is for the time being a victim of the intifada. (The Islamic Jerusalem University is really a seminary.) And the academic youth are also fragmented, as was seen in the last really free elections for any institutions in the West Bank and Gaza, in 1985 and 1986, at the universities (tables 5–6, 5–7). If Gaza is included, we find large majorities for fundamentalist Muslim organizations among students in all of the occupied territories. Outside the universities, in Israel proper and on the West Bank, fundamentalist Islam in general, the Sunni Muslim Brotherhood, and new nationally oriented Islamic organizations are forces to be reckoned with, but they have not fully cooperated with Palestinian nationalist groups.[13] Although more recently Islam has been gaining converts in Jerusalem, it is at a slower and lower rate than elsewhere.

This divisive element has been largely missing in Jerusalem; but Islamic fervor is a powerful latent force, and the religious element fused with the national can easily destroy the best-organized communal calm. The most volatile confrontations in Jerusalem have been religious; after the al-Aqsa fire in the late 1960s and as a reaction to Jewish Orthodox provocations in the 1980s, the depths of Muslim resentment and the level of potential political activism were obvious (Caplan and Caplan 1980, Elon 1989). The

Table 5–7

Distribution of Votes at Palestinian Universities, 1985

Student faction	No. of votes	Percentage
Islamic University — (Gaza), 17 Nov., 1985 Men's College		
1. Al-Kutla Al-Islamiyya (Muslim Brotherhood)	1,369	65.1
2. Harakat'l-Shabiba (Fatah)	569	27.1
3. Jab'at'l-'Aml (Popular Front)	164	7.8
Total votes	2,102	100
Women's College		
1. Al-Kutla Al-Islamiyya	884	75.4
2. Harakat'l-Shabiba	231	19.7
3. Jab'at'l-'Aml	58	5.0
Total votes	1,173	100

The Al-Kutla Al-Islamiyya wins all nine seats in each of the councils.

Student faction	No. of votes	Percentage
Hebron University — 16 December 1985		
1. Harakat'l-Shabiba	788	50.0
2. Al-Ķutla Al-Islamiyya	688	43.6
3. Al-Itihad w'al Taqadum (Popular Front and Communists)	101	6.4
Total votes	1,577	100

The Shabiba movement wins all nine seats of the student council.

Student faction	No. of votes	Percentage
Al-Najah National University — 8 January 1985 (Nablus)		
1. Harakat'l-Shabiba	1,511	49.3
2. Al-Kutla Al-Islamiyya	1,154	37.7
3. Jab'at'l-'Aml	308	10.1
4. Al-Wahda (Democratic Front for the Liberation of Palestine)	92	3.0
Total votes	3,065	100

The Shabiba movement wins all eleven seats on the student council.

Student faction	No. of votes	Percentage
Birzeit University — 16 December 1985		
1. Harakat'l-Shabiba	735	36.8
2. Al-Itihad w'al-Taqadum	693	34.7
3. Al-Kutla Al-Islamiyya	568	28.5
Total votes	1,996	100

Source: *Al-Fajr*, February 7, 1986.
Note: The official shut-down of universities beginning early in the intifada precludes the possibility of updating these figures.

established religious leadership seems to accept the religious status quo. The Supreme Muslim Council, the Waqf authorities, and so on, all reflecting Jordanian policy, could apparently keep firebrand sheikhs in line. A significant portion of the Arab population is susceptible to religious fervor, but even during the intifada the fires are dormant as long as religious sensibilities are not offended and prejudices not aroused. However, the differences between Gaza and the West Bank are already significant. Jerusalem, like Israel proper, still sees relatively little fundamentalist-nationalist violence.

The familiar pattern of fragmentation and lack of leadership make manipulation of this problem easy; the unseen boundaries between Jerusalem and the West Bank still seem to an extent to preserve the city from the upheaval around it. Social and economic differences between the dominant Jewish community and the Arab sector are mirrored within the Arab community. Spatial separation and patterns of inequality are also similar. The political structure is buttressed by this situation. City administrators know their limits and have been struggling to maintain the political status quo. There is, however, a constant nibbling at the "turf" of the minority. Jewish "micro-expansion" seems especially irritating when it occurs in the Old City and around religious shrines. In the following chapter we will try to assess what is happening psychologically and to gauge the levels of political risk-taking in Arab society. The popular national uprising (which has presented Israel with three years of discontent, beginning during the period when this chapter was researched) has not as yet changed the basic structures of the past. Property damage is the most likely threat during the intifada for Jewish Jerusalemites. They fear finding their parked cars torched in the morning, whereas those driving in the West Bank must worry about being stoned. The city administration is still thinking along Ottoman lines in terms of functional sovereignty. Of course, the key question is this: Just who is going to function under whose sovereignty, and where? Palestinians will have to have a much bigger say in the running of their own affairs, at the least, if the city is to continue to function as one entity as it did in the 25 years following 1967.

For the time being, a nationally polarized country and city have led to remarkably little organized direct confrontation. Certainly, all elements of the Arab political leadership in Israel have kept a lid on violence, despite obvious sympathies for Palestinians on the West Bank and Gaza. The situation in East Jerusalem is more complicated. But as we have seen, violence tends to be more reactive. Remarkably few people have been fatally injured. Arab municipal employees continue to work throughout the crisis. Hospitals still function on a binational basis, with Jewish and Palestinian patients and staff. Civil rights for Palestinians in Jerusalem have rarely been suspended. As in more peaceful times, the city plays an intermediate sociopolitical role between Israel and the Palestinians, different from Israel proper but different again from the West Bank and the misery of Gaza. The Arab and Jewish populations of Jerusalem, and Israel as well, seem to have recoiled from one another and are eyeing each other cautiously and not without mutual trepidation. But the events since 1987 have also shown this: It is not simply coercion that has kept ethnic conflict from erupting in Israel and Jerusalem. In fact, more coercion seems to breed more conflict.

The seething potential for violence—especially in Gaza, in the refugee camps, in fundamentalist religious circles, and among the young—can spill over into Israel and East Jerusalem, but even the intemperate, indeed provocative, Israeli national reaction to the Arab protest has not yet destroyed the pattern of the past. (The periodic proclamation of a state of emergency in East Jerusalem by the police minister, or similar national interference in the sensitively balanced East Jerusalem legal, social, or economic system, in the form of localized curfews or declaring areas closed military zones, represent significant departures.) As long as the policy of predictable, managed doses of coercion, co-optation, cultural and spatial autonomy, and limited but obvious opportunity is maintained, the power on the ground will lead to grudging accommodation and sullen resignation. Dramatic changes in the international and regional balance, in the structure of Palestinian society, or in the character of Israeli society and administration may all be in the offing but are not highly visible yet. Just how much real influence the youth—the driving and organizing force of the intifada—has over Palestinian society remains to be seen. More conservative Palestinians in and out of the PLO, Jordan's infrastructure, and the oligarchic family structures have not disappeared. In fact, what communal leadership there is, which is concentrated within bodies such as the chamber of commerce and the Supreme Muslim Council, remains dominated by the personalities of the 1960s. (The chamber of commerce has had but one major change in personnel since 1967.)[14]

No one really knows whether there will be a drastic change in U.S. policy or, if there is, how it will affect intercommunal relations. Israeli society is also changing rapidly. More conservative national or more religiously motivated national government may weaken the hold of the Jerusalem municipality on events (an administration that has also held power since before 1967, under Teddy Kollek). There is already an increasingly palpable tension between the municipality and the nationalist elements in state ministries who often deliberately run roughshod over status quo considerations in decision-making that affects the city. Already a certain disquiet seems to be growing among the reserved but cooperating notables and commercial leaders in the Arab sector. They may be questioning Teddy Kollek's ability to maintain even the unfavorable (for them) status quo. There is no guarantee that a new Jewish generation will not compete with the *shabab* (Palestinian youth) in volatility and hostility. The needs of the community—Jewish, Israeli Arab, and Palestinian—are manifest. They are at their

most obvious, and most evidently mutual, in the geographic mosaic of
Jerusalem. The struggle between integrative and exclusionary nationalist
ideology on the one hand, and the communal and psychological needs of
multi-ethnic geographic areas on the other, has never been laid out so
clearly. In chapter 6 we will attempt to come to grips with the goals and
hopes of the Palestinian community in Jerusalem in the face of their multifaceted contacts with the Jerusalem administration and Israeli national
policies and in the face of the uneven distribution of goods, services, and
security provisions that is a result of this situation.

NOTES

1. *Jerusalem Statistical Yearbook 1984.*
2. Lea Tsemel, interview (1986). This calculation is based on a ratio of about
100 cases (rather than individuals) from Jerusalem to over 900 cases from Ramallah,
and a similar number from Hebron in 1985. The figures for Nablus and Gaza are
considerably higher. Tsemel, a prominent Israeli defense attorney, states: "Being
a prisoner begins with being a Palestinian under occupation. Every youngster of
the age of 16 or more has at one time or another come under some kind of
interrogation." There was an increase of about 40 percent in security cases in
Jerusalem in 1986 (about 140 files). However, this number includes cases from
Israel proper committed by Arabs from the West Bank and Gaza. A large proportion of Jerusalem crimes are committed by Shuafat camp dwellers.
3. Compare this (perhaps unfairly) to 96,000 cases of armed robbery in New
York alone in 1989.
4. See discussion of interviews with Muslim leaders in 1990 in the next chapter.
5. The entire survey is based on an approximately 10 percent return from the
Arab community in question.
6. It should be noted, however, that through extremely low rentals on its vast
holdings in the Old City, the Waqf indirectly subsidizes Muslims. It is also a major
employer—and insures its workers through Israel's national social security system.
7. The advisor to the mayor on Arab East Jerusalem, Amir Cheshin, claims
that this is not so (interview, September 8, 1987).
8. Interview with Lotte Salzberger, May 1986. Cf. "Autonomy Mooted for
Neighborhoods," *Jerusalem Post*, January 17, 1986 ("In Jerusalem" supplement).
Two Jewish minhalot, Har Nof and Rehavia, have or will soon get this autonomy.
Neve Yaakov and Pisgat Zeev are newly formed Jewish minhalot.
9. Interview with I. Kara'een, January 1986.
10. About 20,000 East Jerusalem Arabs were members of the Histradrut in 1987.
Of these, some 12,000 were workers and the rest dependents, mostly wives, who
join for the socioeconomic benefits. Jerusalem Arab Histadrut members can and
do also vote for the central Israeli trade union leadership in Israel-wide elections
(interview, Faez Jaber, October 19, 1987). Histadrut membership is down slightly
(perhaps 10 percent) because of the intifada.
11. The political and financial benefits for the city administration are obvious.
Water rates, for example, are higher outside Jerusalem and are collected by Jerusalem (interview, Amnon Raz, February 1986). In addition, there are proposals

to incorporate some Jewish suburbs to the west into Jerusalem. The latest plan for Beit Hanina envisages 7,600 units, considerably less than the municipality's 1987 plan. The Housing Ministry seeks to maintain a national Jewish-Arab balance of 74 percent (Jewish) to 26 percent (Arab) in Jerusalem (*Jerusalem Post*, November 21, 1989).

12. Interviews with Joseph Gadish and Ibrahim Dakkak, October 1984; Dakkak, 1981. Feisal Husseini, who may be the most prominent Palestinian nationalist in East Jerusalem, also maintained that it is necessary to build a social and political infrastructure before engaging in political activity such as elections (interview, September 9, 1987). Dakkak in 1990 is still in Jerusalem, cut off from the western half, as is Husseini.

13. Cf. Said el Ghazali, "Islamic Movements vs. National Cooperation: Friendly Cooperation in a State of War," *Al-Fajr*, September 6, 1987. This was true until the winter of 1988. Just how deep the ties are between the major contenders for Palestinian loyalty is still open to question.

14. Interview with P. Wengert, November 1989.

6

PALESTINIAN VIEWS ABOUT JERUSALEM

We have seen how fragmentation within the Palestinian community in Jerusalem hindered citywide development of Palestinian political expression. We have also seen that this fragmentation enabled the Jewish administration of Jerusalem to administer the city with a minimum of friction and a maximum of benefit to Jewish Israeli citizens. Through a system of multifaceted contacts maintained with the Palestinian community, an uneven distribution of goods, services, and even security was available to its members, on the basis of their cooperation with various elements of the Jewish administration of Jerusalem and/or the government of Jordan. Various major family units whose ties were to both institutions profited most from this arrangement. We have seen as well a deep longing for a Palestinian entity that is especially profound among younger Palestinians, and that is evinced in particular among those who graduated from the various Palestinian universities in the West Bank. For years these younger Palestinians had very little influence over the oligarchic structure of Palestinian society in the city and less over the workings of city affairs, which were dominated by the almost exclusive Jewish city administration and to some extent the Ministry of Occupied Territories in the Kingdom of Jordan.

To further understand Palestinian perceptions of the situation in Jerusalem, I embarked upon in-depth polling of the city's Arab community in the summer of 1987. As in my earlier studies on the problems of ethnic conflict in divided cities generally and in Jerusalem specifically,[1] the intent of the polling was to shed light upon the political, social, and economic problems inherent in the close communal confines of an ethnically divided city. The underlying questions in all these studies were:

1. How long do communal confrontations of this type remain locally manageable?

2. How powerful are national blandishments in the urban setting?

3. How do various subgroups within the ethnic communities react to various political, economic, and social developments?

4. What, in essence, is the tolerance level of populations in divided cities?

The intifada broke out as the study was being completed. It was and is an uprising as much against the state of affairs within Palestinian society that led to fragmentation and relative docility as it is a revolt against Israeli occupation. It reflects population pressures and concomitant social changes within Arab society; it is an attempt by a new and demographically ever more powerful generation to not only gain influence but to lead. Furthermore, it has united social groups in many ways around national goals but still has left political divisions. While the intifada seems to have unified the youthful leadership, not much is known about its large and growing group of followers. Hence, the need to probe this issue.

Two questionnaires were prepared. The respondents were all Palestinians who either reside in Jerusalem, hold Jerusalem identity cards (Israeli-issued), or both. In other words, the overwhelming majority of the respondents, some 90 percent, live within an Israeli polity and are subject to Israeli law, but are not Israeli citizens. Most of them hold Jordanian citizenship, yet a significant majority report that they have contacts with Israeli institutions, such as health services and licensing offices, and for a significant minority these contacts were regular. Indeed, about half were directly dependent on the Israeli economy.

The first questionnaire was open and solicited commentary as well as simple answers. Twenty-two questions dealing with social, religious, and political preferences were circulated among the social, educational, and economic leadership of the Palestinian community in Jerusalem. Thirty-five of forty-two persons approached answered. Most of these respondents—trade union leaders, qadis, teachers—commented fully and openly. Only the businessmen did not respond, for reasons we will speculate on shortly. The second questionnaire consisted of 13 questions covering some of the same issues. It was simplified and a random sample of 419 persons representing the "public at large" responded.

In earlier research I complained that no one had really tried to assess the attitudes of the various social groups within the Palestinian community. Israelis, Jordanians, and Palestinians on all sides of the political spectrum have substituted the placatory issuing of statements for in-depth analysis of the political aspirations and qualified goals of various social groups in Palestinian society. The lack of knowledge about real Palestinian aspirations in Jerusalem was heightened by the fact that no Palestinian political organizations were developed that could openly disseminate them, and no

elections were held in which independent Palestinian institutions were represented. Thus, no true indicators of the obvious variances in Palestinian
desires could be established. In addition, no real opinion polling had ever
taken place within the Palestinian community in Jerusalem alone. There
were no published reports on community goals or social, political, and
economic desires. This was in stark contrast to the extensive polling within
the Israeli Arab community and, of course, within the Jewish community.
The lack of concrete information on indigenous Palestinian desires in Jerusalem was a function of the constant difficulty of polling within the city.
This difficulty, long evident, obviously did not abate with the uprising. A
people under occupation, be it ever so benign in the eyes of the occupier,
are loath to open themselves to detailed questioning. No one is really sure
that anonymity can be guaranteed.

Another difficulty in polling arises in that whatever element of Arab
society an investigator is from, he is likely to receive a very warm welcome
from some and a very cool reception from others. My own chief examiner
was a sociologist from Bir Zeit University. He was unable to introduce the
questionnaire into such conservative Arab circles as the Shari'a religious
court, the Arab employees of various municipal offices, and the conservative families in Jerusalem. He also had difficulties with some of the more
Islamic-oriented schools and teachers in the city. He was easily able to
enter questionnaires into the community of unemployed college graduates
in Jerusalem, members of Arab national trade unions in Jerusalem, self-
defined progressive teachers, and youth in general. In these circles another
examiner might not have been able to achieve the same level of trust and
acceptance. It became obvious that the forms that were being returned to
him in the open questionnaire were not the same as the questionnaires
that were being returned to me. It was also obvious that this had nothing
to do with our choice of subjects to interview, since we chose them together;
it was simply a reflection of where we each received the more open and
trusting reception (although mine, being a "neutral," was also invariably
open and cordial). Thus, this element of the research was asymmetrical.

The questioning extended into the period of the intifada. The last returns
of the open questionnaire were received on July 18, 1988. The closed
questionnaire was concluded in February 1989. The intifada does not seem
to have influenced the opinions of the respondents. Instead, it seems to
have crystallized long-held opinions and has not further radicalized Palestinian opinion, though sections of society have been motivated and gal-
vanized. The basic change has been in Palestinian activism, and even here,
in the case of Jerusalem, the situation has not taken on the volatility that
we find in the West Bank and even more so in Gaza. In the previous
chapter I pointed out various distinctions between Jerusalem and the occupied territories. These could not be verified in the questionnaire, since
it was exclusively Jerusalem-based. However, the situation this long after

the intifada is beginning to reaffirm the differences between Jerusalem and the West Bank that were also reflected in differences among social groups in Jerusalem, and indeed between Jerusalem and Israel. For example, as we will see, responses in Shuafat differ from those in affluent Beit Hanina.

As I pointed out in the last chapter, there is enormous difference in the level of violence and volatile confrontation between Jerusalem and the occupied territories; the city, different from Israel proper but different again from the West Bank and the misery of Gaza, plays an intermediate sociopolitical role between Israel and the Palestinians. Events have made it clear that it is not simply coercion that has kept ethnic conflict from erupting in Israel in general and in Jerusalem. The questionnaires attempted to uncover reasons for this phenomenon.

Palestinian opinion had hardened well before the intifada. The intifada also seems to reflect social differences within Arab society in Jerusalem, which themselves are a reflection of the differences in the overall Palestinian social structure. In the villages and rural areas added to greater Jerusalem after 1967, the level of political volatility and physical activity is highest. Jabal Mukaber, Sur Bahir, A-Tur, Issawiya, the Shuafat camp, Anata, and the ancient village of Silwan, all areas harboring socially intact communities with low mobility and earning power, are flash points. Family feuds are functionalized politically and nationally, and this leads to protracted internecine conflict and political radicalization.

THE OPEN QUESTIONNAIRE

The open questionnaire was sent to teachers, Arab trade union leaders, prominent university student leaders, qadis (judges) of the Shari'a courts, employees of the Waqf, employees of the Israel municipality, school administrators, Arab leaders of the Histadrut, members of the successful commercial class representing oligarchic families (there are few successful merchants not of oligarchic families), and members of the professional middle class. We attempted to choose people in leading social positions rather than exposed political leaders. We did not try to interview the PLO leadership in the city or the leaders of Arab information and scientific institutions. Their ideas are reflected in the work underlying the questionnaires, written up in the policy study that forms the basis of the previous chapter. The open questionnaire was designed to illustrate the positions of various social groups within the city. In addition, some attempt was made to single out leadership in certain more depressed areas, such as Shuafat and Silwan.

The overall random questioning of the Palestinian community in Jerusalem was deferred pending initial evaluation of the open questionnaire of leadership in the community. The random sampling was based on over 400 respondents from the Arab boroughs of Beit Hanina, the refugee camp

Shuafat, Beit Safafa, Silwan, and the old city of Jerusalem, as well as the village areas Issawiya and Sur Bahir and the boroughs of A-Tur and Abu Tor. The sampling was completed in the winter of 1989. The boroughs were also chosen on the basis of previous analysis. In some cases paradoxes are in need of explanation. Both Issawiya and Sur Bahir indicated a high percentage of electoral support for the Jerusalem municipality but have also been highly volatile in the early stages of the intifada. A-Tur had a functioning local council with funding from Jordan as well as the Jerusalem administration. Abu Tor is split down the middle—half Jewish and half Arab. Beit Safafa is half "Israeli Arab" and half "East Jerusalemite."

In the open questionnaire no attempt was made to establish hard statistical patterns within Palestinian society. I was more interested in establishing patterns of opinion and associating clusters of patterns of opinion to social divisions. The responses indicate that this strategy was useful in many ways. Furthermore, the results of the questionnaires show that many of the plans in the peace process have ignored the wishes of the Palestinian leadership of the city. This was reflected in the negative attitude toward various peace plans (before the Arafat initiatives of 1989); only a minority, under 30 percent, of the respondents reacted positively to the proposals. This means that until recently not much influence has been exerted by the indigenous Palestinian community in Jerusalem on the peace process. The Palestine National Council (PNC) meeting of November 1988 may have been an early indication that this pattern could be changing. Events are moving quickly, but the indigenous leadership and the public are also divided, as the responses indicate.

Before discussing the responses to the open questionnaire in some depth, it is interesting to know who did not respond. One of the most important results of the questionnaire is that almost everyone responded fully except for the representatives of the commercial class in Jerusalem. No representatives of the Arab chamber of commerce answered the questionnaire, nor any member of such leading families as the Barakats, Dajanis, or Nasser al-Dins. This universal rejection of any kind of polling technique by the commercial leadership of Jerusalem's Palestinian society could simply mean pecuniary mistrust. It could also reflect a certain political sophistication on the part of the commercial groups, who probably assumed that their own opinions for a possible solution in Jerusalem are at variance with the wider Palestinian population and the Jewish administration of the city. The members of the commercial class quite likely did not realize that the wider population, or at least its social leadership, holds positions that also reflect some variance from those of the Palestine Liberation Organization. They may not have expected the candor with which the various and highly divergent opinions in Palestinian society were expressed. The commercial leadership apparently felt that the PLO's position is one that must be openly accepted. They may have distrusted assurances of anonymity and felt that adhering to such positions in this kind of questionnaire could prejudice their ties to the Jerusalem municipality and the Jordanian government. Indeed, reluctance to associate oneself with Jordan, even when on the Hashemite payroll, was one of the salient findings of this questionnaire and may have been a factor in Jordan's 1988 (ostensible) decision to cut its losses in the West Bank by declaring that it was no longer responsible there.

The open questionnaire gave the respondents an opportunity to deal at some length with certain political and social complexes. The respondents made use of this opportunity and the written replies were often emotional and eloquent. There was an obvious need for expression on these issues. Most of those who answered were not the least bit reticent about expressing an opinion. At times, respondents signed their three-page question form. The respondents commented on: (1) their own occupational and geographical position in the city; (2) the status they desire eventually for the city of Jerusalem; (3) their relationship or lack of relationship to Jews and how they would like this to develop or not develop; (4) their assessment of the services received from the Jerusalem administration; (5) their assessment of the peace process; (6) their definition of and attachment to Palestinianism (which elicited the most eloquent answers); and (7) their own personal, political, and social options: what they desired and what they were willing to sacrifice for these goals.

First and foremost, our interest was in the Palestinians' relationship to their own city. How did they view Jerusalem and what were their social and political demands and goals for it? There was a universal feeling, even among Palestinians working for the municipality of Jerusalem, that services offered to the Palestinians by the city administration were insufficient. There was some qualified support for these services, but by and large negativism prevailed. A word of caution is needed here: Numerous respondents, those representing Palestinian youth, university graduates, and Palestinian trade union movements, reacted completely unfavorably toward the municipality, but their reactions were in general negative—to Jordan, the peace process, religion, and relationships with official representatives of the state of Israel, as well. In addition, almost all of these respondents were eloquent in their Palestinianism, often emotionally so, and their demands for the eventual restructuring of Jerusalem seem to indicate that they desire an exclusively Palestinian city. This was insisted upon by some directly, and by others in avoiding a direct answer to the question on the city's future. The response "other" was invariably a national Palestinian "other," judging by the responses to different questions and more in-depth, personal follow-up questioning.

Almost half of the respondents were such youth, graduates, and trade unionists. The raw numbers are probably less significant than the unanimity encountered in the answers from this social group. It is obviously the group that has the closest contacts to the intifada. It is also clear that many of the members of this group are in an unsatisfactory economic position within Jerusalem, as we saw in the previous chapter. While an educated 45-year-old Jerusalem Arab is pretty much as well off as his Jewish counterpart, a younger Arab definitely is not. The situation has probably been deteriorating. The results were predictable. Another large group of respondents, whose responses differ greatly for certain aspects of the questionnaire but in the direction of "moderation," represent the older age bracket and higher economic and social status plus a modicum of security.

Most interesting are the responses indicating various preferences for the status of Jerusalem. Almost exactly the same number of respondents opted for an open city as for a national Palestinian solution. In other words, a city without distinct national or political boundaries is attractive to the established. These responses generally came from workers in the Jerusalem municipality, representatives of the Histadrut, and members of the professional classes, whether they were self-employed, employed by the Waqf, or by the Israeli municipality. This means that an element of Palestinian society that was associated in some way with the status quo is not happy with it but is afraid of a new, highly charged national status quo led by the previously powerless and economically dependent young.

A juncture between religious organizations and Jordan emerged from the survey. All respondents who indicated a preference for religion in their lives over anything else, including a Palestinian state, indicated a much higher tolerance of Jordan and a stronger desire to include Jordan in some future restructuring of Jerusalem. The relationship to Jordan, however, is more a result of Jordan's Islamic social and legal system than of loyalty to the Hashemite kingdom. Generally, the responses indicate a certain positive appreciation of Islam and Islamic social and political influence on the part of respondents who are not on the rejectionist, socially reformist, revolutionary, or radically nationalist side of the Palestinian community. Palestinian radicals in the "national" camp reject religion in the same fashion as they do any association with Israel or Zionism. Interestingly enough, many of these Palestinians indicate desire for contact with non-Zionist, leftist, or progressive Israelis. On the whole, they have none. A certain correlation seems to be possible between generation, position, and even religiosity, and relations and contact with Jews. It appears that the more contact one has had and has with Jews in Jewish institutions, the more likely one is to opt for a less volatile political option. This confirms our assumptions stated in chapter 3.

This is true as well of the qadis who were interviewed. It may be interesting to dwell on the responses from the Shari'a court, although these respondents are not necessarily a representative group. The qadis generally do not appreciate social science researchers and research surveys. All three Shari'a court members indicate, not surprisingly, a pro-Islamic, and to a degree pro-Jordanian, bias. Their social ideology is basically conservative, and all three maintain relationships, including social ones, with Jews (although one qadi was ambivalent). All considered religion more important than a Palestinian state, and at the same time all of them expressed sympathy for and empathy with Palestinianism. This sympathy and empathy, incidentally, characterized all respondents to the questionnaire. Palestinianism has become a form of highly emotional identification for almost the entire Arab community. Only a few respondents related to the question of Palestinianism with a dry "I was born here" or "It is my nationality." For the so-called hard core or rejectionist Palestinians, the nationality takes on a chiliastic glow and becomes associated in some mythical fashion with social justice. This is, of course, typical of all burgeoning nationalisms of the nineteenth and twentieth centuries.

The qadis all supported the rapidly developing fundamentalist tendencies in Islam. This is an interesting development, because the questionnaire was formulated before the intercession of the Islamic fundamentalist group Hamas into the intifada, or the entrance of the Islamic movement into Israeli politics. The qadis' position, however, seemed to have foreshadowed much of what has developed as political Islam in Israel: a political and personal acceptance of Jews and Israel, a strong sense of social justice, a strict morality, and a desire for Islamic and conservative Palestinianism. Among our other respondents only a limited group supported fundamentalist Islam. The "nationalist" or "radical" group rejected it out of hand. It is obvious that this questionnaire did not reach potential religious nationalists. However, these were not evident as "leaders" as late as summer 1988. Yet the qadis who responded then seemed to consider the growth of Islamic fundamentalism as a positive development. The random samples later revealed strong support among 30 percent of Muslims for an Islamic state and Islamic city. In the open questionnaire, the Christian leadership in the city was not polled. My basic thesis, based on demographic developments, is that Islamic groupings in the city and Muslims in general will be the deciding factor in determining policy and opinion in Jerusalem. In the random sample, Christians were overwhelmingly secular in their responses.

Of more than parenthetical interest were interviews with a different (more political) set of Muslim leaders in the fall of 1990.[2] These were "official leaders" who indicated that much of official Islamic opinion reflects institutional and organizational considerations within the various Islamic organizations, rather than overall policy. All seemed to favor the redivision of the city.[3] The three interviewees are all employees of Jordan and all acknowledge the completeness of official Islam's tie to the Jordanian government. They uniformly reject contact or cooperation under "present" conditions with Jewish religious authorities, but again the intensity of rejection varies. (All acknowledge "dealings" with the Israeli municipality, but no "ties or relations" with it. In other words, whenever they have no choice but to contact the municipality or, less often but despite their rejectionism, the Ministry of Religion, they do it. Their justification is that the good of the community demands the concession.) Their answers also indicate Jordan's continuing formal and informal interest in Jerusalem; the influence of personal preference, religious interpretation, and Jordanian proclivities all come into play.[4]

A representative of Hamas leadership (as he described himself), also interviewed in 1990, displayed more finality. He holds official Islam in the city in contempt, as one body with Jordan. He rejects any contact with Israelis: "Binational coexistence is dead, killed by the Jews." He advocates an Islamic Palestinian administration of the entire city. He sees no need for any contacts of any kind with the Western part of the city at present.[5]

Another interesting outcome of the questionnaire is the apparent difference in attitude among school teachers. They did not provide a unified picture. Obviously, on a basis of four or five respondents one can say very little about the teaching community at large, but it does seem obvious that certain schools are far more radically national than others. Instruction personnel are more nationalist and so are the students. From one girls' elementary school (Tori) in the Abu Tor neighborhood we received the type of answers associated with more moderate Arab opinion (open city, religiosity, contacts with Jews, high element of Palestinianism), but at the same time more traditionally and religiously oriented responses as well. On the other hand, almost all the young teachers who responded to the questionnaire and were graduates of national Palestinian universities (all of whom were employees of Jerusalem municipality schools drawing an Israeli salary) were totally committed to a Palestinian state and a Palestinian Jerusalem. They maintained no contact with Jews. They also rejected Islamic religion out of hand as reactionary and antifemale. This was a uniform reaction in the group, whether men or women were answering.

The open questionnaire reflected the decline in the influence of mukhtars. Three were interviewed, two from Shuafat and one from Silwan. The mukhtars reflected the attitudes of their areas rather than their status as mukhtars. The Silwan mukhtar is one of the few elderly members of the hard-core national group in the sample. He seemed to represent the feelings in his borough, which, as the random samples show, is less religious and highly nationalist. (Silwan is also perhaps the poorest borough in Jerusalem.) Municipal services have been lacking. It is a base for criminal activity, such as drug dealing, and the home of the *hamula* of Abu Musa, a radical paramilitary leader outside the territories. It is also a borough with a high level of internal feuding. The Shuafat mukhtars, both of whom entertain closer relationships with the Jewish community, also represent to a degree social groups within the Arab area. They do not come from large and significant families and their position vis-à-vis religion and the Jewish community is more flexible (or perhaps opportunist). Many of these individuals, especially in the refugee camp, have established themselves through financial and social contact with Jews. The Shuafat camp mukhtar is one of the few respondents who opted for an eastern Arab and a western Jewish partition of the city, although he qualified his answer by expressing a desire for a particular kind of Palestinian state, not specifying if he wanted this state to dominate both portions of the city or just one. Interestingly enough, in the random samples the east-west option seems more popular.

The survey highlighted the contrast in attitudes between the members of the Histadrut's Arab leadership and members of the Arab worker's associations in East Jerusalem, most of whom were from the electrical workers' union. The Arab worker's association leadership is to a man hardcore. They reject Israel out of hand. They profess Marxism and by and large are for a socialist Palestinian state. The few Histadrut respondents gave very differentiated answers to the questions, and almost all of them favor an open city. They support a Palestinian state; material possessions are not a decisive factor in their lives. One tended toward the religious camp, citing religion as the key to a future. All indicated a strong attachment to Palestinianism, and their argumentation in opposition to the Israeli administration of Jerusalem is based on their assessment of it as oppressive and not cognizant of the rights of Palestinian workers.

This is significant in many ways. The Histadrut is by far the largest organization of Palestinians in East Jerusalem. These Arabs care who administers their organization and must trust those whom they elect. Consequently, the Histadrut leadership is probably the only Palestinian leadership even indirectly elected or supported by Arab society in Jerusalem. Whether their political opinions have any influence is something else again.[6]

Generally, it is difficult to say whether respondents are speaking purely for themselves or for their institutions, and how much effect their opinions have on others. The fact that distinct clusters of opinions do develop is, however, highly significant. Nevertheless, in one respect there is little difference. As we have already seen, opinions are determined by generation, position, income, religiosity, and contact with the Jewish community or its institutions. Political positions harden around these social paradigma. There is very little crossover. If this had been a quantitative questionnaire we would have seen an enormous percentage supporting the Palestinian state as a basic desire. Approximately 75 percent of the respondents indicated such a preference. This preference was trailed by religion, standard of living, and family and society (the answer of the only doctor interviewed). Most respondents were reticent to admit what preference they would sacrifice in order to achieve a major goal. Of those who answered, however, a majority of the small sample were ready to sacrifice a high standard of living; a second significant group, religion; and a few, a Palestinian state, and family and society. It seems strange that a highly family-oriented society should care so little for perhaps the single most important social phenomenon of its community. This was true of the random samples as well. This may mean a real change in social values or a self-deceptive way out of a tricky question. Again, the rejection of a high living standard and especially of religion was a major feature of the "hard-core" group of nationalist respondents.

As we pointed out previously, there was only limited support for fundamentalist Islam but a strong attachment on the part of many respondents to Islam and Islamic values. The peace process was judged negatively by a small majority of all respondents, who cited lack of Palestinian input (this was before the Palestinian initiative of 1989). Services by the Jerusalem administration were judged negatively by almost all respondents, with small numbers indicating qualified acceptance and limited support. Many responses stressed the self-serving nature of administration services. Roads or schools built shortly before elections or minor social or economic concessions were criticized as social bribery. An "only when they need us" consensus prevailed among those who did not reject it all out of hand. The future hopes and demands for the city did not reflect any great inclination to redivide the city; only 10 percent of the respondents answered in this way. A large majority of the respondents either wished for a completely Palestinian Jerusalem or an open city. The interpretation of just what is an open city is also open to question. In other words, perhaps these individuals had reason to beg the question.

A very small minority of the respondents favored a Palestinian-Israeli joint administration of Jerusalem (recall that seven of thirty-five respondents are upper-level officials of the city or the Histadrut), two respondents opted for a Jordanian-Israeli Jerusalem, and two for a religiously oriented Jerusalem. Boundaries were never specified. Only four preferred redivision of Jerusalem into an eastern and western city. As we pointed out before, the "elite" or "leadership" responses differ markedly here from those of the random samples. Perhaps an elitist group is more aware of the dislocations involved in redivision. Or perhaps they may be better able to insulate themselves against the hardships of the intifada and the occupation, which, despite everything we have said about Jerusalem, still makes life insecure and unstable, especially for the young and disadvantaged.

Since some respondents opted for more than one solution on many questions and some did not answer certain questions, the statistical value of this questionnaire is not its greatest contribution. It does, however, verify what was indicated earlier: that there are broad differences in opinion within Palestinian society in Jerusalem, but that almost all Jerusalem Arabs have a strong relationship to Palestinianism. Palestinianism may mean different things to the different people attached to it, but almost all Palestinians desire the establishment of a Palestinian state. Whether or not they eventually wish to be a part of this state is not clear. What the questionnaire's responses implied, however, was that the social structure of this Palestinian state has not been a matter of deep thought or open discussion. The social structure of a Palestinian state seems less important now than the emotional necessity of its establishment. This means that the fragmentations in the society will definitely swell if and when such a state is established. There are indications that many respondents are apprehensive about this. The large number of respondents who opt for a tempered national solution for the city is significant. These are the individuals with the most to lose. Conservative fear of new, as yet undefined institutions and a new generation first becoming involved politically are responsible for this hesitation to espouse radical change in Jerusalem. Arab-Israeli society also evinces this attachment to Palestinianism, but not to the necessity of holding a Palestinian passport. The differences in attitudes among the generations according to social position, propensities toward contact with the Jewish community, and religion that we saw in the last chapter were verified to a degree in the open questionnaire. The random samples further strengthened the analysis and point in some of the same directions. Even before in-depth examination of these samples was undertaken, they served to round out a multifaceted picture of Jerusalem's Palestinian community.

THE RANDOM CLOSED QUESTIONNAIRE

The random samples were first distributed in the boroughs of Beit Hanina, Beit Safafa, Silwan, Shuafat (including the refugee camps), and the Old City. The boroughs of A-Tur, Issawiya, Sur Bahir, and Abu Tor were polled later. Wide differences in mobility levels and income were found between the new, upwardly mobile Beit Hanina area and the others, but especially between Beit Hanina, the Shuafat camp, and Silwan. Beit Safafa and the Old City seem to exemplify a middle social position within Palestinian Arab society in Jerusalem. A bit more caution is required about national labeling here, in Beit Safafa, and to a more limited extent in Beit Hanina. Israeli Arabs were also included in the 1983 census, which provided the data for the tables analyzed in chapter 5. The extent to which Israeli Arabs consider themselves Arabs or Palestinians may be unclear to them. But for Jerusalem's non-Israeli-citizen Arabs there is no ambivalence. They are Palestinians. Nonetheless, concretization of this national identity is as complicated for the randomly sampled respondents as it was for the elite group questioned before them. The attachment to Palestine and Palestinianism is fiercely held, but nationalism is always a diffuse ideology. In other words, almost all of the respondents may have had trouble imagining what a Palestinian state would be like—but unequivocally they wanted it.

The open questionnaire was started and completed in the fall of 1988. The closed random samples were taken during the summer and fall of 1988 and continued into 1989. There were no significant variances in response during this time. Because certain boroughs had evinced more volatility than others by then, we included Sur Bahir, Issawiya, and A-Tur.[7] Analysis of responses indicates that middle and lower middle class Palestinians were the most accessible to our research team. General difficulties in reaching and obtaining cooperation from religiously oriented members of society were compounded by the intifada. (The whole investigation was carried out under aggravated and, indeed, sometimes dangerous conditions.)

Fifty-six respondents were Christian, or 13 percent, and 352 were Muslim. The representation of Christians here, as compared to the selective open survey, reflects this sample's random character and the relative accessibility of Christians. In the open questionnaire a special effort was made to question Muslims as the determinant element in Palestinian society. The percentage of Christians reached is another indicator of "middle class" bias. The Christian population of Jerusalem was 14,300, or about 8 percent of the Palestinian population (based on the 1986 census). (There were then 118,500 Muslims and 336,000 Jews counted in Jerusalem.) The raw percentage of Christians among the Palestinian or non-Jewish population may also be misleading. Palestinian Christians are not necessarily "100 percent" Arabs. While they may very well be Palestinian nationalists, they may also be ethnic Greek, or Armenians with divided loyalties. However, the median Christian age is 30.0, while the figure for Muslims is 17.4 (25.2 for Jews), so that the percentages are not quite as lopsided as they may at first seem.

Statistical evidence indicates that Jerusalem's Arab population is altogether "middle class," relative to the rest of the population of the West Bank and Gaza. This is especially true in terms of employment by profession, with only 1,580 of 19,650 Muslims and 75 of 3,880 Christians listed as unskilled workers by the 1986 *Jerusalem Statistical Yearbook*. If we primarily consider those employed or in the registered work force (not including many younger unemployed or marginally employed Palestinians), we are dealing with a society that is accurately represented in the samples. The researchers maintain that this is definitely the case. In Jerusalem we have an economically "privileged" Palestinian society that is nonetheless on the bottom rungs of Jerusalem's economic ladder. This is true despite the fact that areas of selection such as Issawiya, Sur Bahir, Silwan, Shuafat camp, and to a lesser extent the Old City and A-Tur rank at the bottom of a socioeconomic index developed by statistical area[8] and make up 70 percent of the random sample. The index's analysis complements the data used in chapter 4. Even our weighted polling procedures in terms of reaching these more depressed areas produced a majority of Palestinian middle class respondents. In fact, they would classify themselves as such.

The questions in the closed questionnaire were simple versions of the open questions in the elite sample (table 6–1). One of the most significant results of the broad sample is that more than half the subjects preferred

Table 6–1
Palestinian Views: The Random Closed Samples

Question			
1	Religion	Christian	56
		Muslim	352
2	Status of Jerusalem	Jerusalem should be:	
		East and West (Divided)	223
		An Open City	106
		Jordanian and Palestinian	29
		Other (Independent Palestinian)	60
3	Contacts with Israeli Institutions	Do you have contact with Israeli institutions?	
		Yes	156
		No	262
4	Regular Contacts with Israeli Institutions	Do you have regular contacts with Israeli institutions?	
		Yes	68
		To some extent	90
		No	257
5	Satisfaction with Municipal Services	Are you satisfied with the services rendered by the Jerusalem municipality?	
		Yes	15
		To some extent	53
		No	178
		Not at all	171
6	Peace and Palestinian Rights	Does the current peace process take into consideration Palestinian legitimate rights?[1]	
		Yes	13
		Partly	44
		No	212
		Not at all	149
7	Support for Jordan	The Jordanian regime is attempting to gain Palestinian support. What is your position?	
		Support	19
		Support under conditions	89

a redivided city. As we have pointed out, this differs significantly from the open questionnaire. This may reflect the simple desire of many at this point to free themselves from constant physical harassment by the national Israeli police force and territorial guards (the latter, many of them Druze and a few Christian Arabs from Israel, have been particularly brutal, frightening, and insulting). In addition, the high percentage of young people polled and the relatively high desire for an Islamic polity (30 percent of all Mus-

Table 6–1 (Continued)

Question			
		Against	175
		Totally against	134
8	Nature of a Palestinian State	A future Palestinian state must be:	
		Secular	185
		Islamic	93
		Socialist	46
		Not important	88
9	Priorities: to Choose	If confronted with a choice, which would you select?	
		Palestinian state	366
		Economic well-being	7
		Family and community	—
		Religion	41
10	Priorities: to Sacrifice	Which of the four would you be willing to sacrifice?	
		Palestinian state	12
		Economic well-being	151
		Family and community	31
		Religion	190

Note: Where results do not tally to 419, questions were not answered by all respondents.

1 Asked before Arafat's initiatives of the late 1980s.

lims; see discussion of question 8) may have combined to produce the high percentage favoring redivision.

As might have been expected, more of the elite, especially those over age 30, had contacts with Israeli institutions. In fact, with the exception of the "hard core," 100 percent maintain a connection. About 15 percent of the respondents in the closed questionnaire had contacts on a regular basis and another 25 percent had some contact.

The answers to question 5, concerning satisfaction with services offered by the Jerusalem municipality, showed an even lower level of content than the elite sample; obviously even less is trickling down to the less highly placed.

There seems to be no doubt that most Palestinians in Jerusalem feel discrimination and deprivation from the municipality. However, they have not taken organizational steps to change this situation. There have been no demands on the city administration directly tied to the intifada. No formal quid pro quos have been established. The informal network of contacts and elite compromise that led to this dissatisfaction is still in place and treading water. An open Palestinian political organization with concrete demands for a reorientation of services has yet to surface.

General dissatisfaction with the peace process also characterizes Palestinian society in Jerusalem. The random sample differs from the elite in its highly negative reaction to the process. Nine elite members answered positively, without reservation, and eight gave qualified support for the process (this was before Arafat's Algiers conference); these figures represent almost 50 percent of those answering. The results of the random sample were 86 percent negative. Although the open questionnaire lacks statistical validity, the difference between 50 percent and 14 percent approval is stark. Again, this seems to reflect the helplessness and frustration felt by much of the Palestinian population at large. Their larger sense of being without influence and hope in the present system is expressed as well in their responses to questions 2 and 4.

Support for the Jordanian regime was surprisingly high in the random samples, considering King Hussein's supposed unpopularity in Jerusalem and his overt withdrawal from the internal Palestinian political process in Jerusalem. Over 25 percent qualified support shows how tenacious is Jordanian and conservative influence in the city—and probably Islamic sentiment as well. (Close analyses of the responses showed a consistently significant relationship of over 50 percent between "pro-Jordanian" and "Islamic.") Recall that a large segment of the "pro-Jordanian elite" chose to remain silent in the open questionnaire.

Two distinct preferences for a secular Palestinian state or for any kind at all (44 percent and 21 percent, respectively) reflect Palestinian secularism. These are apparent from responses to question 8. The political preference for Islam is relatively weak in Jerusalem, although 30 percent of all Muslims preferred an Islamic Palestinian state. Analysis of the samples indicated that the less educated and lower income groups, as well as some of the young, are more susceptible to Islam as a political force. These results tended to vary from quarter to quarter. Islamic strength, then, may very well be subject to particularities and concentrated in regional pockets, as well as being an economic phenomenon. Closer analysis of the responses bears this out, as we shall see.

The question of determination of value choices reaffirms the open questionnaire's illustration of a deep commitment to a Palestinian state in all segments of Palestinian society in Jerusalem. The results speak for themselves.

Readiness to sacrifice also seemed more pronounced in the public at large than among the elite. But again, the seemingly inconsistent relationship to the complex "family and community" makes one wonder (it was picked by no one as most desirable, yet by the lowest number as able to be sacrificed). Perhaps it is accepted as an immutable given. Or we may again be dealing with self-deception. Thirty-five respondents, by far the highest number for a single question, did not answer this.

The raw data in the random closed questionnaire are given more detailed scrutiny in the following discussion. Quantitative relationships will be established between factors such as region (borough or quarter), origin, age, sex, social position, religion, contact with Jews, political preferences, attitudes toward Jerusalem's future, the Jordanian connection, the Islamic state, and so on. The relatively simple, impressionistic exercise with the data of the open questionnaire is more complicated given the social structure and pure numbers of the closed questionnaire; analysis becomes richer and more rigorous. However, preliminary conclusions can be drawn on the basis of correlation of the two samples:

1. Jerusalem's Palestinian community overwhelmingly desires sovereignty for the Palestinian people and a Palestinian polity.

2. Within the community there are wide differences of opinion as to the desirable political form and social structure of the political "state" of Palestine.

3. A significant percentage of the population (50 percent of the elite and 25 percent of the "public at large") wants some kind of "open" solution for Jerusalem.

4. There is strong support, especially among the young and the religious, for total separation from any Jewish polity.

5. Some of the same attitudes, probably held by the same separatists, emerge in relation to current contacts and the desire to maintain them with Jews and Jerusalem's institutions of municipal authority. Tentative readiness by other Palestinians for significant relations is countered by this total negation.

6. The desire to maintain contacts holds despite the overwhelming dissatisfaction with services rendered by the city administration (an opinion held as well, apparently, by those in its employ).

AN IN-DEPTH ANALYSIS

Overall analysis of the random samples in correlation with the selected open questionnaire has given us an impressionistic yet detailed picture of Palestinian political goals in East Jerusalem. Examining the impact that Palestinian fragmentation has had on political goals in the past demands in-depth analysis, subjecting the raw data of the random closed questionnaire to more rigorous scrutiny. Fragmentation in Palestinian society, as we have seen, was considered a major source of Israeli strength in the policy conflicts between the state of Israel and Palestinians. The municipal administration of Jerusalem was also able to manipulate Palestinian fragmentation to buttress its control of the city. Examination of the Palestinian community in Jerusalem in social and economic terms showed broad differences that were verified to a degree in the initial analysis of the questionnaires. Just how deep these fissures might be, and how significant they were, was the central question for in-depth analysis of the random samples.

Differentiation by Borough

The first element to be analyzed was response by boroughs. The borough results are given in tables 6–2 through 6–10. These give the number of people questioned in each borough (column total), the number of those answering each particular segment of the question (row total), the percentage of those polled, the row percentage of those answering questions in a certain fashion, and the the percentage of those of the entire number of respondents answering in a given fashion (column percentage).

Question A2. Significant for question A2 on the future status of Jerusalem are the boroughs with high percentages opting for an open city: Issawiya and Beit Safafa, with 39.1 percent and 39.7 percent, respectively. This represents significantly more than the 25.4 percent of all those polled. A large percentage of those polled in Beit Safafa were Israeli citizens, since the village was divided between Israel and Jordan between 1948 and 1967. Thus, the high percentage of those opting for an open city is not surprising. Issawiya, as we pointed out previously, has had a large percentage of its population working in the Jewish sector in Jerusalem. In Issawiya and Beit Safafa, the lowest percentages (34.8 percent and 37.9 percent, respectively) opt for an East-West division of Jerusalem. Given indications that an answer of "other" means a desire for more radical Palestinian solutions to the problem of Jerusalem, it is noteworthy that the refugee camp Shuafat leads all other boroughs polled in this preference. But it also has the highest percentage (11.8 percent) of those supporting a Jordanian-Palestinian Jerusalem. These results may very well reflect the Islamic orientation of the refugee camp, which will be analyzed later.

Results in Silwan are significant in that a high percentage opt for an open city although it is a highly volatile borough that could be expected to be more radical than the rest. Indeed, Silwan has the second highest "other" response as well, and it appears to be one of the most divided boroughs internally. A certain trend that will recur is already evinced in the responses of A-Tur and Beit Hanina and, to a lesser extent, Abu-Tor and the Old City. These areas opt for positions supported by the Palestine Liberation Organization. This is especially true for A-Tur throughout the survey.

Questions A3, A4. Half-Israeli Beit Safafa, not surprisingly, shows the

Table 6–2
Status of Jerusalem (Question A2)

Count Row Pct Col Pct	Area	East- West	Open city	Jordan & Palestine	Other	Row total
	Issawiya	8 34.8 3.6	9 39.1 8.5	2 8.7 6.9	4 17.4 6.7	23 5.5
	A-Tur	27 65.9 12.1	11 26.8 10.4	3 7.3 10.3		41 9.8
	Abu Tor	8 57.1 3.6	4 28.6 3.8	1 7.1 3.4	1 7.1 1.7	14 3.3
	Old City	50 57.5 22.4	17 19.5 16.0	6 6.9 20.7	14 16.1 23.3	87 20.8
	Sur Bahir	15 50.0 6.7	8 26.7 7.5	2 6.7 6.9	5 16.7 8.3	30 7.2
	Shuafat	16 47.1 7.2	6 17.6 5.7	4 11.8 13.8	8 23.5 13.3	34 8.1
	Beit Hanina Dahri	50 65.8 22.4	13 17.1 12.3	5 6.6 17.2	8 10.5 13.3	76 18.2
	Silwan	27 49.1 12.1	15 27.3 14.2	3 5.5 10.3	10 18.2 16.7	55 13.2
	Beit Safafa	22 37.9 9.9	23 39.7 21.7	3 5.2 10.3	10 17.2 16.7	58 13.9
	COLUMN TOTAL	223 53.3	106 25.4	29 6.9	60 14.4	418 100

Number of missing observations = 1

Table 6–3
Contact with Israeli Institutions (Question A3)

Count Row Pct Col Pct Area	Yes	No	Row total
Issawiya	8 34.8 5.1	15 65.2 5.7	23 5.5
A-Tur	13 31.7 8.3	28 68.3 10.7	41 9.8
Abu Tor	3 21.4 1.9	11 78.6 4.2	14 3.3
Old City	26 29.9 16.7	61 70.1 23.3	87 20.8
Sur Bahir	17 56.7 10.9	13 43.3 5.0	30 7.2
Shuafat	6 17.6 3.8	28 82.4 10.7	34 8.1
Beit Hanina Dahri	23 30.3 14.7	53 69.7 20.2	76 18.2
Silwan	18 32.7 11.5	37 67.3 14.1	55 13.2
Beit Safafa	42 72.4 26.9	16 27.6 6.1	58 13.9
COLUMN TOTAL	156 37.3	262 62.7	418 100

Number of missing observations = 1

Table 6–4
Regular Contact with Israeli Institutions (Question A4)

Count Row Pct Col Pct	Area	Yes	To some extent	No	Row total
	Issawiya	5 21.7 7.4	3 13.0 3.3	15 65.2 5.8	23 5.5
	A-Tur	2 5.0 2.9	13 32.5 14.4	25 62.5 9.7	40 9.6
	Abu Tor	1 7.1 1.5	2 14.3 2.2	11 78.6 4.3	14 3.4
	Old City	5 5.9 7.4	19 22.4 21.1	61 71.8 23.7	85 20.5
	Sur Bahir	7 23.3 10.3	5 16.7 5.6	18 60.0 7.0	30 7.2
	Shuafat	2 5.9 2.9	6 17.6 6.7	26 76.5 10.1	34 8.2
	Beit Hanina Dahri	7 9.2 10.3	20 26.3 22.2	49 64.5 19.1	76 18.3
	Silwan	13 23.6 19.1	7 12.7 7.8	35 63.6 13.6	55 13.3
	Beit Safafa	26 44.8 38.2	15 25.9 16.7	17 29.3 6.6	58 14.0
	COLUMN TOTAL	68 16.4	90 21.7	257 61.9	415 100

Number of missing observations = 4

133

Table 6–5
Satisfaction with Municipal Services (Question A5)

Count Row Pct Col Pct	Area	Yes	To some extent	No	Not at all	Row total
	Issawiya		2 8.7 3.8	17 73.9 9.6	4 17.4 2.3	23 5.5
	A-Tur			28 68.3 15.7	13 31.7 7.6	41 9.8
	Abu Tor			11 78.6 6.2	3 21.4 1.8	14 3.4
	Old City	3 3.5 20.0	16 18.6 30.2	25 29.1 14.0	42 48.8 24.6	86 20.6
	Sur Bahir		2 6.7 3.8	13 43.3 7.3	15 50.0 8.8	30 7.2
	Shuafat		4 11.8 7.5	8 23.5 4.5	22 64.7 12.9	34 8.2
	Beit Hanina Dahri	1 1.3 6.7	1 1.3 1.9	44 57.9 24.7	30 39.5 17.5	76 18.2
	Silwan	1 1.8 6.7	15 27.3 28.3	16 29.1 9.0	23 41.8 13.5	55 13.2
	Beit Safafa	10 17.2 66.7	13 22.4 24.5	16 27.6 9.0	19 32.8 11.1	58 13.9
	COLUMN TOTAL	15 3.6	53 12.7	178 42.7	171 41.0	417 100

Number of missing observations = 2

Table 6–6
Do Peace Initiatives Take into Account Palestinian Rights? (Question A6)

Count Row Pct Col Pct Area	Yes	Partly	No	Not at all	Row total
Issawiya			15 65.2 7.1	8 34.8 5.4	23 5.3
A-Tur			32 78.0 15.1	9 22.0 6.0	41 9.8
Abu Tor		1 7.1 2.3	12 85.7 5.7	1 7.1 .7	14 3.3
Old City	3 3.4 23.1	9 10.3 20.5	43 49.4 20.3	32 36.8 21.5	87 20.8
Sur Bahir		4 13.3 9.1	16 53.3 7.5	10 33.3 6.7	30 7.2
Shuafat	2 5.9 15.4	5 14.7 11.4	10 29.4 4.7	17 50.0 11.4	34 8.1
Beit Hanina Dahri	3 3.9 23.1	4 5.3 9.1	37 48.7 17.5	32 42.1 21.5	76 18.2
Silwan	1 1.8 7.7	5 9.1 11.4	28 50.9 13.2	21 38.2 14.1	55 13.2
Beit Safafa	4 6.9 30.8	16 27.6 36.4	19 32.8 9.0	19 32.8 12.8	58 13.9
COLUMN TOTAL	13 3.1	44 10.5	212 50.7	149 35.6	418 100

Number of missing observations = 1

135

Table 6–7
Support for Jordan (Question A7)

Count Row Pct Col Pct	Area	Support	Support conditionally	Against	Totally against	Row total
	Issawiya	1 4.3 5.3	5 21.7 5.6	13 56.5 7.4	4 17.4 3.0	23 5.5
	A-Tur	1 2.4 5.3	4 9.8 4.5	28 68.3 16.0	8 19.5 6.0	41 9.8
	Abu Tor		3 21.4 3.4	10 71.4 5.7	1 7.1 .7	14 3.4
	Old City	6 6.9 31.6	20 23.0 22.5	29 33.3 16.6	32 36.8 23.9	87 20.9
	Sur Bahir	2 6.7 10.5	9 30.0 10.1	7 23.3 4.0	12 40.0 9.0	30 7.2
	Shuafat	3 8.8 15.8	5 14.7 5.6	9 26.5 5.1	17 50.0 12.7	34 8.2
	Beit Hanina Dahri	3 3.9 15.8	13 17.1 14.6	34 44.7 19.4	26 34.2 19.4	76 18.2
	Silwan	2 3.7 10.5	18 33.3 20.2	19 35.2 10.9	15 27.8 11.2	54 12.9
	Beit Safafa	1 1.7 5.3	12 20.7 13.5	26 44.8 14.9	19 32.8 14.2	58 13.9
	COLUMN TOTAL	19 4.6	89 21.3	175 42.0	134 32.1	417 100

Number of missing observations = 2

136

Table 6–8
Preference for a Palestinian State (Question A8)

Count Row Pct Col Pct	Area	Secular	Islamic	Socialist	Not important	Other	Row total
	Issawiya	16 69.6 8.6	3 13.0 3.2	4 17.4 8.7			23 5.5
	A-Tur	3 0 73.2 16.2	3 7.3 3.2	7 17.1 15.2	1 2.4 1.1		4 1 9.8
	Abu Tor	9 64.3 4.9	3 21.4 3.2	2 14.3 4.3			1 4 3.3
	Old City	3 2 36.8 17.3	2 0 23.0 21.5	8 9.2 17.4	2 6 29.9 29.5	1 1.1 16.7	87 20.8
	Sur Bahir	8 26.7 4.3	6 20.0 6.5	5 16.7 10.9	1 1 36.7 12.5		3 0 7.2
	Shuafat	1 1 32.4 5.9	1 4 41.2 15.1	1 2.9 2.2	7 20.6 8.0	1 2.9 16.7	3 4 8.1
	Beit Hanina Dahri	3 7 48.7 20.0	2 6 34.2 28.0	5 6.6 10.9	6 7.9 6.8	2 2.6 33.3	76 18.2
	Silwan	2 6 47.3 14.1	7 12.7 7.5	7 12.7 15.2	1 5 27.3 17.0		5 5 13.2
	Beit Safafa	1 6 27.6 8.6	1 1 19.0 11.8	7 12.1 15.2	2 2 37.9 25.0	2 3.4 33.3	5 8 13.9
	COLUMN TOTAL	185 44.3	9 3 22.2	4 6 11.0	8 8 21.1	6 1.4	418 100.0

Number of missing observations = 1

Table 6-9
Priorities (Question A9)

Count Row Pct Col Pct	Area	Palestinian state	Economic well- being	Religion	Row total
	Issawiya	23 100.0 6.3			23 5.6
	A-Tur	41 100.0 11.2			41 9.9
	Abu Tor	13 92.9 3.6		1 7.1 2.4	14 3.4
	Old City	75 90.4 20.5	1 1.2 14.3	7 8.4 17.1	83 20.0
	Sur Bahir	27 90.0 7.4		3 10.0 7.3	30 7.2
	Shuafat	24 70.6 6.6	2 5.9 28.6	8 23.5 19.5	34 8.2
	Beit Hanina Dahri	66 86.8 18.0		10 13.2 24.4	76 18.4
	Silwan	53 96.4 14.5		2 3.6 4.9	55 13.3
	Beit Safafa	44 75.9 12.0	4 6.9 57.1	10 17.2 24.4	58 14.0
	COLUMN TOTAL	366 88.4	7 1.7	41 9.9	414 100

Number of missing observations = 5

138

Table 6–10
Which Could You Sacrifice? (Question A10)

Count Row Pct Col Pct	Area	Palestinian state	Economic well- being	Family & community	Religion	Row total
	Issawiya		9 40.9 6.0		13 59.1 6.8	22 5.7
	A-Tur		6 14.6 4.0	1 2.4 3.2	34 82.9 17.9	41 10.7
	Abu Tor		5 41.7 3.3		7 58.3 3.7	12 3.1
	Old City	8 9.9 66.7	30 37.0 19.9	7 8.6 22.6	36 44.4 18.9	81 21.1
	Sur Bahir	1 4.3 8.3	9 39.1 6.0	1 4.3 3.2	12 52.2 6.3	23 6.0
	Shuafat		19 65.5 12.6	1 3.4 3.2	9 31.0 4.7	29 7.6
	Beit Hanina Dahri		28 40.6 18.5	3 4.3 9.7	38 55.1 20.0	69 18.0
	Silwan		21 38.2 13.9	7 12.7 22.6	27 49.1 14.2	55 14.3
	Beit Safafa	3 5.8 25.0	24 46.2 15.9	11 21.2 35.5	14 26.9 7.4	52 13.5
	COLUMN TOTAL	12 3.1	151 39.3	31 8.1	190 49.5	384 100

Number of missing observations = 35

highest level of contact with Israeli institutions, whereas the refugee camp Shuafat manifests the least. Interestingly enough, Silwan with 23.6 percent maintains the second highest total of regular contact with Israeli institutions. This may account for the high percentage of open city responses there. The interesting aspect of question A3 is the high percentage of Palestinians in the village of Sur Bahir who have some relation with Israeli institutions. If we look at the intensity of contact, or regular relationships with institutions (question A4), we then see Issawiya creeping up on Sur Bahir. Again, A-Tur and Beit Hanina, Abu Tor and the Old City give very low responses for intense contact with Israeli institutions. This is surprising with regard to A-Tur, since it has a minhelet, a neighborhood council that is funded in part by the city administration. Having a neighborhood council does not seem to have led to an intense regular relationship with Israeli institutions, or if it has, people are not admitting to it.

Question A5. The general dissatisfaction with services rendered by the Jerusalem administration is indicated in the responses to question A5. The highest levels of satisfaction are to be found, again and not surprisingly, in Beit Safafa (39.6 percent; more than twice the average for Jerusalem). In A-Tur and Abu-Tor there is virtually no satisfaction, even though A-Tur not only enjoyed a neighborhood council with a city budget but was actually the Jerusalem administration's model for cooperative development in both sewage system and road building. Abu Tor's dissatisfaction may result from invidious comparisons that Palestinians there make with their nearby Jewish neighbors (the borough has contiguous Jewish and Arab sections). Beit Hanina's negativism toward the administration of Jerusalem continues; the richest borough is one of the least satisfied.

Question A6. The negative attitude toward the peace process is shared by almost all boroughs, but here again Beit Safafa seems the most optimistic.

Question A7. Interestingly enough, under certain conditions support for Jordan is highest in Silwan. This indicates once again that Silwan is a highly polarized borough. Apparently, family contacts account for the differences in responses to these questions. Particularistic interests in Silwan seem to be stronger than in some of the other boroughs. The agrarian village borough of Sur Bahir, with its conservative social structure, is the second highest supporter of a Jordanian role in the future of Jerusalem. The impression given so far by Beit Hanina and A-Tur of high PLO identification and support continues with this item. This is all the more interesting because, as we previously mentioned, A-Tur was receiving funds from Jordan for its neighborhood council until the intifada. (This funding was continuing as of fall 1989, according to the council's Israeli Arab secretary, despite Jordan's supposed abdication of responsibility for the West Bank.)

Question A8. Preferences for the political and social future of a Palestinian state were surprising. Shuafat, the poorest borough, and Beit Hanina, the richest, indicated the most support for an Islamic state. A-Tur, Issawiya, and Sur-Bahir, despite their conservative social structure, returned the highest preferences (though not very high) for socialism. The large number of "not important" responses in Beit Safafa may reflect the many Israelis there who might not be citizens of a future Palestinian state. Yet the number of Islamic-oriented Palestinians is highest among Israeli Arabs, so that some of these may have opted for the Islamic future.

Question A9. Responses to question A9, which deals with priorities.and major goals, confirms the impression received so far from A-Tur. Its unanimous choice of a Palestinian state above any other goal in life is astonishingly emphatic. In only three boroughs did preference for a Palestinian state sink below 90 percent: Shuafat, Beit Hanina, and Beit Safafa. Here there were minority preferences for a religious state, in all instances Islamic. Only in its limited Islamic preferences does Beit Hanina leave the PLO consensus—perhaps. (The PLO is striving to absorb Islamically oriented Palestinians. Conversely, Hamas tries to absorb the secular nationalists.) The lower percentage in Beit Safafa can probably be attributed to its Israeli citizens. Beit Safafa is also clearly a borough that evinces a degree of religious polarization within its Muslim community. It returned the lowest percentage of those willing to sacrifice religion to achieve other goals. A lower percentage in Shuafat reflects the high incidence of Islamic preference that was also indicated in question 2A.

Question A10. Generally, the answer to this question about readiness to sacrifice confirmed a high level of secularism in A-Tur, Abu-Tor, Sur Bahir, Beit Hanina, and Issawiya. The low figures for those willing to sacrifice religion indicate that these boroughs have the highest level of Islamic preference. In Silwan, once again, answers are polarized. The fact that almost no one in either Israeli or Palestinian Arab society in East Jerusalem (28 of our respondents were Israeli Arabs) wished to sacrifice a Palestinian state simply verifies our overall impressions.

However, there are differences within the boroughs in Jerusalem as to political preferences. The refugee camp Shuafat, with its high level of Islamic preference, and Beit Safafa, with its high percentage of Israeli respondents, differ significantly from other boroughs. A-Tur and Beit Hanina seem the most pro-PLO in orientation, although there is significant support for Islam in Beit Hanina. The Old City of Jerusalem seems to most accurately reflect the Palestinian community at large. Other differentials between the boroughs reflect particularist developments. This seems particularly clear in Silwan.

Differentiation by Generation

It is clear to any observer that the intifada is being sustained by the younger generation. Many observers see the uprising as planned and car-

ried out by youth below the age of 30. In order to assess the opinions of
this portion of Arab society, our random sample was divided into those
below 30 and those above 30. A word of caution is needed here: Date of
birth was not stipulated, so that the cutoff age—in any event a heuristic,
statistical cutoff—is less an expression of actual date of birth than of occupational and social standing within the community. This information was
readily derived from the questionnaire. The possibility of actual age error
is very low. Our expectation was for a far more radical society in the
younger age bracket. The young are thought of as being far more oppositional, not only toward the Israeli authorities but toward their elders as
well; far more attuned to a confrontational course; and inclined to activism.
However, analysis proved our expectation to be incorrect, at least according to the questionnaire, as tables 6–11 through 6–19 show.

Question B2. Preferences for the future of Jerusalem indicated widespread differentials among the generation below age 30. This implied a
more differentiated opinion in the younger generation, or a higher level
of fragmentation, than in the respondents above age 30. The latter adhered
to the strategy of having an East-West city. Over two-thirds of those polled
preferred a redivision of Jerusalem. In other words, the over–30 group
seems to be more firmly in the camp of mainline Fatah opinion. The below–
30 generation, which probably includes most of the intifada's leaders,
showed a 38 percent response in support of an East-West division. The
two interesting statistics are 28.9 percent for an open city and 24.7 percent
answering "other," which is the code response for a more radical Palestinian position. The radicalism might have been expected, since the below–
30 group includes many university and high school graduates without suitable employment or without employment at all. But the more moderate
preference for an open city, almost 30 percent higher than that of the
respondents above 30, could not have been predicted.

Many of the other responses were also surprising. More members of the
below–30 generation have contact with Israeli institutions and their relations tend to be far more intensive (questions B3 and B4). Astonishingly,
the younger generation is more satisfied with the services rendered by the
Jerusalem administration (question B5); over 20 percent indicate some
degree of satisfaction. But again, at the opposite spectrum of complete
negation, 46.4 percent reject services completely, as compared to 36.4
percent of their elders.

The same differentiation emerges clearly in responses to question B6.
The below–30 generation is more optimistic with regard to the peace process, but they also are more heavily represented at the extreme of complete
negation. In all instances negation outweighs acceptance—yet in all instances acceptance is higher than in the above–30 generation.

While the same tendency is discernible in the question dealing with
Jordan (B7), the spread is not quite as significant. The answers to question

Table 6–11
Status of Jerusalem (Question B2)

Count Row Pct Col Pct	Age	East- West	Open city	Jordan & Palestine	Other	Row total
	Under 30	63 38.0 28.9	48 28.9 48.0	14 8.4 50.0	41 24.7 78.8	166 41.7
	Over 30	155 66.8 71.1	52 22.4 52.0	14 6.0 50.0	11 4.7 21.2	232 58.3
	COLUMN TOTAL	218 54.8	100 25.1	28 7.0	52 13.1	398 100

Number of missing observations = 21

Table 6–12
Contact with Israeli Institutions (Question B3)

Count Row Pct Col Pct	Age	Yes	No	Row total
	Under 30	73 44.0 48.0	93 56.0 37.8	166 41.7
	Over 30	79 34.1 52.0	153 65.9 62.2	232 58.3
	COLUMN TOTAL	152 38.2	246 61.8	398 100

Number of missing observations = 21

Table 6–13
Regular Contact with Israeli Institutions (Question B4)

Count Row Pct Col Pct	Age	Yes	To some extent	No	Row total
	Under 30	36 22.0 54.5	33 20.1 37.5	95 57.9 39.4	164 41.5
	Over 30	30 13.0 45.5	55 23.8 62.5	146 63.2 60.6	231 58.5
	COLUMN TOTAL	66 16.7	88 22.3	241 61.0	395 100

Number of missing observations = 24

Table 6–14
Satisfaction with Municipal Services (Question B5)

Count Row Pct Col Pct	Yes	To some extent	No	Not at all	Row total
Under 30	10 6.0 71.4	24 14.5 47.1	55 33.1 32.2	77 46.4 47.8	166 41.8
Over 30	4 1.7 28.6	27 11.7 52.9	116 50.2 67.8	84 36.4 52.2	231 58.2
COLUMN TOTAL	14 3.5	51 12.8	171 43.1	161 40.6	397 100

Number of missing observations = 22

Table 6–15
Do Peace Initiatives Take into Account Palestinian Rights? (Question B6)

Count Row Pct Col Pct	Yes	Partly	No	Not at all	Row total
Under 30	6 3.6 54.5	26 15.7 63.4	62 37.3 30.1	72 43.4 51.4	166 41.7
Over 30	5 2.2 45.5	15 6.5 36.6	144 62.1 69.9	68 29.3 48.6	232 58.3
COLUMN TOTAL	11 2.8	41 10.3	206 51.8	140 35.2	398 100

Number of missing observations = 21

Table 6–16
Support for Jordan (Question B7)

Count Row Pct Col Pct	Age	Support	Support conditionally	Against	Totally against	Row total
	Under 30	7 4.2 46.7	38 23.0 44.2	57 34.5 33.3	63 38.2 50.4	165 41.6
	Over 30	8 3.4 53.3	48 20.7 55.8	114 49.1 66.7	62 26.7 49.6	232 58.4
	COLUMN TOTAL	15 3.8	86 21.7	171 43.1	125 31.5	397 100.0

Number of missing observations = 22

Table 6–17
Preference for a Palestinian State (Question B8)

Count Row Pct Col Pct — Age	Secular	Islamic	Socialist	Not important	Other	Row total
Under 30	46 27.7 26.0	41 24.7 47.1	23 13.9 52.3	53 31.9 62.4	3 1.8 60.0	166 41.7
Over 30	131 56.5 74.0	46 19.8 52.9	21 9.1 47.7	32 13.8 37.6	2 .9 40.0	232 58.3
COLUMN TOTAL	177 44.5	87 21.9	44 11.1	85 21.4	5 1.3	398 100

Number of missing observations = 21

Table 6–18
Priorities (Question B9)

Count Row Pct Col Pct — Age	Palestinian state	Economic well-being	Religion	Row total
Under 30	131 80.4 37.6	6 3.7 85.7	26 16.0 66.7	163 41.4
Over 30	217 93.9 62.4	1 .4 14.3	13 5.6 33.3	231 58.6
COLUMN TOTAL	348 88.3	7 1.8	39 9.9	394 100

Number of missing observations = 25

Table 6–19
Which Could You Sacrifice? (Question B10)

Count Row Pct Col Pct — Age	Palestinian state	Economic well-being	Family & community	Religion	Row total
Under 30	10 6.8 83.3	74 50.7 52.9	16 11.0 53.3	46 31.5 25.1	146 40.0
Over 30	2 .9 16.7	66 30.1 47.1	14 6.4 46.7	137 62.6 74.9	219 60.0
COLUMN TOTAL	12 3.3	140 38.4	30 8.2	183 50.1	365 100

Number of missing observations = 54

145

B8 also reinforce this trend. The most interesting response is probably the higher attachment to an Islamic polity that the younger generation evinces, as well as their relative indifference to the political construction of a future Palestinian state: Almost three times as many answer "not important" as in the generation above 30. Again, the above–30 generation espouses the middle-of-the-road Fatah position, desiring a secular Palestinian state alongside Israel.

Responses to question B9 show a high (16.0 percent) preference for religion over a Palestinian state. The significance of this should not be exaggerated; more than 80 percent of the younger generation would still choose a Palestinian state over anything else—but the preference for religion is three times that of the older Palestinians. And some of the young were willing to choose "economic well-being" as first on their list. While the proportion is tiny, this "unpatriotic" answer called for a great deal of candor.

Responses to question B10 confirm the rest of the sampling. Only a third of the youth would be willing to sacrifice religion, as compared to two-thirds of the older respondents. A small percentage would be willing to sacrifice a Palestinian state, something the older respondents would not do. On the other hand, over half of the younger Palestinians would be willing to sacrifice economic well-being, compared to a third of their elders. These responses seem to indicate that (1) the younger generation is less bound to the political positions of Fatah and (2) has more secular radicals and more religious fundamentalists than does the above–30 generation. As we have pointed out previously, Jerusalem's Palestinian society has always been generally secular and relatively moderate in its political goals. Despite the strong element of moderation and secularism in the below–30 group, the cohesiveness of the secular moderate society seems to be weakening at the extremes.

Opinion Trends among the High School–Aged

Because we felt that age 30 might have been too advanced for generational differentiation, we decided to poll high school students in the 12th grade—those working toward the *taujihe* matriculation examination in the East Jerusalem school system with its Jordanian curriculum and those Israeli Arabs working toward the *bagrut* matriculation examination in the Israeli-curriculum Beit Safafa school. (Beit Safafa is the only Jerusalem school with two curriculum systems, one Jordanian and one Israeli. The *bagrut* qualifies students for admission to Israeli universities; most of the Palestinians work toward the *taujihe*, required by the universities of the Arab world.)

The sample included 278 Arab students from Jerusalem, 134 males and 144 females. We concentrated somewhat on females because they had been notably absent in the random samples. When we were polling randomly in the city, men usually came forward to answer questions; women stayed in the background. This characteristic of Arab society could be avoided in the school polling since the Arab schools with Jordanian curriculum are divided by gender. We polled (1) 60 male students at Abdullah High School, administered by the city of Jerusalem; (2) 60 female students at Ma'mouniya High School, likewise administered by the city of Jerusalem; (3) 40 females at Dar al-Tifl, a private Muslim school; (4) 20 males at the private Christian school Mitre (also attended by Muslims); (5) 36 males at the Amal vocational school administered by the city; and (6) 33 students at Beit Safafa High School on the Jordanian curriculum, as well as 29 students on the Israeli curriculum. Almost all of the students professed a middle class socioeconomic position in society. We did not differentiate between males and females at Beit Safafa High School.

The high schools in Jerusalem that have remained open throughout much of the intifada are relatively moderate ones. Some publicly administered high schools such as Rashadiya (males) were closed because of repeated demonstrations. Ibrahamiya, for males, probably the most prestigious private school in the city, was also closed. In addition, some of the Christian schools refused to allow polling. Nonetheless, the data that emerged were interesting both in verifying the random sample results and in and of themselves (tables 6–20 through 6–22).

Question B11. The high percentage of Christian youth opting for an open city is certainly significant. As later analysis of random samples will show, Christians in almost all their responses demonstrate more moderation than Muslims, and more openness to compromise with Jewish authorities. What is also interesting in this particular poll is female rejection of an open city, as well as strong female attachment to the East-West division solution— shown by fully 83 percent of the secularly educated girls in Ma'mouniya and half of those in Dar al-Tifl. (These students are all approximately 18 years old.) The most interesting result, however, is the strong male orientation toward an Islamic polity: Half of the boys at Abdullah supported a Muslim orientation in East Jerusalem, compared to only 17 percent of the girls from a similar social background and in a similar school, Ma'mouniya. The percentage supporting a Muslim polity at Muslim Dar al-Tifl was high at 38 percent, but small compared with Beit Safafa's Israeli-curriculum students (52 percent), and similar to the percentage among the Jordanian-curriculum students there (39 percent). This last figure is a further indication that Israeli Arabs in Jerusalem are more prone to support an Islamic political orientation than are their Jerusalem Palestinian compatriots.

Two additional points of interest arise here. The Israeli Arabs in Beit Safafa are not interested in a joint open city with Israeli-Arab cooperation either. The students studying the Jordanian curriculum are more inclined

Table 6–20
The Preferred Solution for East Jerusalem at the Current Stage (in Percentages) (Question B11)

School	Open city with Israeli-Arab competition	East Jerusalem belongs to Palestinians	East Jerusalem with Islamic orientation
Abdullah	2	37	50
Ma'mouniya	0	83	17
Dar al-Tifl	13	50	38
Mitre	45	36	0
Amal Vocational	11	61	31
Beit Safafa			
General	19	30	46
Israeli curriculum	15	27	52
Jordanian curriculum	24	33	39

Table 6–21
Readiness to Live in Jerusalem Sharing Rights and Responsibilities with a Jewish Majority (in Percentages) (Question B12)

School	Yes, if possible	Maybe, if possible	No, even if possible
Abdullah	5	5	90
Ma'mouniya	6	11	80
Dar al-Tifl	15	15	70
Mitre	28	39	33
Amal Vocational	17	17	66
Beit Safafa			
General	5	33.5	52
Israeli curriculum	10	52	34
Jordanian curriculum	15	15	70

Table 6–22
Relations with Jews (in Percentages) (Question B13)

School	Yes	Seldom	Hardly ever	None
Abdullah	15	13	10	62
Ma'mouniya	15	12	9	61
Dar al-Tifl	13	12	10	60
Mitre	15	10	5	70
Amal Vocational	17	19	6	58
Beit Safafa				
Israeli curriculum	83	17	0	0
Jordanian curriculum	40	22	10	28

to favor this solution and, indeed, are the second highest group polled with this orientation. Among the potential graduates of the Jerusalem high school system, the vocational students—young men studying to be electricians, mechanics, and so on—showed the strongest PLO orientation.

Question B12 dealt with readiness to live in Jerusalem with a Jewish majority, sharing equal rights and duties. The results verified the answers to question B11 and also showed a significant readiness for some sort of cooperation with Jews among young Arabs (about 30 percent on average). This is true not only, as expected, of Israeli Arabs studying in Beit Safafa, but also for the Christians who were polled and, interestingly enough, for over a third of the vocational students. And it holds even though large majorities from Abdullah, Ma'mouniya, and Amal (63, 73, and 64 percent, respectively), and a smaller majority from the Jordanian-curriculum Beit Safafa students, indicated (when they were asked to list effects of the intifada on them) the beginning of hatred for Jews.

We also wished to know about current relationships with Jews. In the random sample the younger generation had indicated a higher rate of contact with Israeli institutions than the older generation. We asked the 12th graders about relations with Jews and non-Israeli institutions (question B13). Four of the six schools polled are municipal schools. Teachers' salaries are paid by the administration of Jerusalem, but most students seem unconcerned by this. Approximately 15 percent of all the students indicated that they had steady contacts with Jews, and another 10 to 19 percent indicated that they had such contacts off and on. Naturally, the *bagrut*-track students at Beit Safafa, who are Israeli citizens, have more extensive relations with Jews, and this of course influences the high number of their Jordanian-curriculum peers who are more open to Jewish society (62 percent have some or continuing contacts with Jews.) What is interesting is that the Christian students, who were astonishingly moderate in their answers and surprisingly open to an Israeli polity, have the least contact with Jews. (This may actually be one reason for their relative moderation: Contact can also mean encounter with the police or other unpleasant authorities.) They have less off-and-on contact than the female Muslim students at Ma'mouniya and Dar al-Tifl, although the same percentage of Christian and female Muslim students have ongoing contact with Jews.

The readiness for some sort of cooperation among some 30 percent of the students is similar to the results of the random sample of those below the age of 30. The preferences for Islamic social and political solutions are even more pronounced among the male Muslim students, and especially, apparently, among Israeli Arabs in Jerusalem—a fact that was confirmed in the random sample, as we shall see in tables 6–23 through 6–31. Large numbers of the Muslim students reported that they have been physically assaulted by the police or that they or members of their families have been arrested. The figures for being assaulted or arrested are much lower among the girls, and lower again among the Christians, whose percentages are similar to those of Beit Safafa. For example, no member of a Christian respondent's family had been arrested, as compared to 36 percent of the families of the girls in Ma'mouniya. Arab youth in Jerusalem, although they seem to be suffering more proportionally than any other group within the Palestinian community, have not been disproportionately radicalized. Nor does there seem to be one unifying polity that could unite this youth. Here, as elsewhere, the dominant political opinion is shaped by Fatah. More and more male students, however, seem to be gravitating toward Islamic movements. And the attitudes of women in the school system who are not working for a high school diploma—in other words, women who leave school earlier in their lives, with lower career expectations and opportunities and, perhaps, a more traditional attitude—are unknown at present.

Differentiation by Religion within the Random Samples

Although Christian spokesmen and Palestinian leaders generally deny any difference of opinion between Muslims and Christians, my own research into this question indicates that significant differences do exist. These also emerge from the random samples—not with the surprising clarity of the questionnaires in the Jerusalem school system, but with definite statistical significance.

The results in tables 6–23 through 6–31 verified these differences. In responses to question C2, we see that Christians are far more positive toward an open-city solution than Muslims—although, interestingly enough, Fatah positions are supported by almost the same percentage of Christians as Muslims. Where Muslims differ from Christians is in the answer "other"; in other words, in the preference for a more radical solution. Very few Christians opted for this fourth alternative. There is a higher level of Christian relationship with Israeli institutions (questions C3 and C4), and twice as many Christians are satisfied with the services rendered by the administration in Jerusalem, compared to Muslims (question C5). The question on peace prospects (C6) shows no significant difference between Christians and Muslims, but a higher percentage of Christians support Jordanian attempts to find a solution for the Palestinian problem (question C7). Obviously, the Christians do not support an Islamic polity, although in our random sample one Christian consistently responded in a pro-Islamic fashion (which may reflect misunderstanding on his part, a mistaken marking of his own religion, or our clerical error). Nevertheless, the overall results are clear, and the growing strength of political support for Islam probably accounts for subliminal Christian moderation in dealing with the Jewish polity as well.

Yet Christians, by an overwhelming majority, support the creation of a

Table 6–23
Status of Jerusalem (Question C2)

Count Row Pct Col Pct		East-West	Open city	Jordan & Palestine	Other	Row total
	Christian	31 55.4 14.1	21 37.5 20.4	2 3.6 7.1	2 3.6 3.6	56 13.8
	Muslim	189 53.8 85.9	82 23.4 79.6	26 7.4 92.9	54 15.4 96.4	351 86.2
	COLUMN TOTAL	220 54.1	103 25.3	28 6.9	56 13.8	407 100

Number of missing observations = 12

Table 6–24
Contact with Israeli Institutions (Question C3)

Count Row Pct Col Pct		Yes	No	Row total
	Christian	28 50.0 18.4	28 50.0 11.0	56 13.8
	Muslim	124 35.3 81.6	227 64.7 89.0	351 86.2
	COLUMN TOTAL	152 37.3	255 62.7	407 100

Number of missing observations = 12

Table 6–25
Regular Contact with Israeli Institutions (Question C4)

Count Row Pct Col Pct		Yes	To some extent	No	Row total
	Christian	11 19.6 16.9	18 32.1 20.2	27 48.2 10.8	56 13.9
	Muslim	54 15.5 83.1	71 20.4 79.8	223 64.1 89.2	348 86.1
	COLUMN TOTAL	65 16.1	89 22.0	250 61.9	404 100

Number of missing observations = 15

Table 6–26
Satisfaction with Municipal Services (Question C5)

Count Row Pct Col Pct		Yes	To some extent	No	Not at all	Row total
	Christian	1 1.8 7.1	13 23.2 25.0	28 50.0 15.8	14 25.0 8.6	56 13.8
	Muslim	13 3.7 92.9	39 11.1 75.0	149 42.6 84.2	149 42.6 91.4	350 86.2
	COLUMN TOTAL	14 3.4	52 12.8	177 43.6	163 40.1	406 100

Number of missing observations = 13

Table 6–27
Do Peace Initiatives Take into Account Palestinian Rights? (Question C6)

Count Row Pct Col Pct		Yes	Partly	No	Not at all	Row total
	Christian	2 3.6 18.2	7 12.5 15.9	32 57.1 15.3	15 26.8 10.5	56 13.8
	Muslim	9 2.6 81.8	37 10.5 84.1	177 50.4 84.7	128 36.5 89.5	351 86.2
	COLUMN TOTAL	11 2.7	44 10.8	209 51.4	143 35.1	407 100

Number of missing observations = 12

Table 6–28
Support for Jordan (Question C7)

Count Row Pct Col Pct		Support	Support conditionally	Against	Totally against	Row total
	Christian	2 3.6 10.5	1 5 26.8 17.2	2 4 42.9 14.0	1 5 26.8 11.6	5 6 13.8
	Muslim	1 7 4.9 89.5	7 2 20.6 82.8	147 42.0 86.0	114 32.6 88.4	350 86.2
	COLUMN TOTAL	1 9 4.7	8 7 21.4	171 42.1	129 31.8	406 100

Number of missing observations = 13

Table 6-29
Preference for a Palestinian State (Question C8)

Count Row Pct Col Pct	Secular	Islamic	Socialist	Not important	Other	Row total
Christian	40 71.4 21.9	1 1.8 1.1	10 17.9 22.7	5 8.9 6.1		56 13.8
Muslim	143 40.7 78.1	92 26.2 98.9	34 9.7 77.3	77 21.9 93.9	5 1.4 100.0	351 86.2
COLUMN TOTAL	183 45.0	93 22.9	44 10.8	82 20.1	5 1.2	407 100

Number of missing observations = 12

Table 6-30
Priorities (Question C9)

Count Row Pct Col Pct	Palestinian state	Economic well- being	Religion	Row total
Christian	53 96.4 14.9	1 1.8 16.7	1 1.8 2.4	55 13.6
Muslim	303 87.1 85.1	5 1.4 83.3	40 11.5 97.6	348 86.4
COLUMN TOTAL	356 88.3	6 1.5	41 10.2	403 100

Number of missing observations = 16

Table 6-31
Which Could You Sacrifice? (Question C10)

Count Row Pct Col Pct	Palestinian state	Economic well- being	Family & community	Religion	Row total
Christian		7 13.0 4.8	3 5.6 10.0	44 81.5 23.7	54 14.4
Muslim	12 3.8 100.0	139 43.4 95.2	27 8.4 90.0	142 44.4 76.3	320 85.6
COLUMN TOTAL	12 3.2	146 39.0	30 8.0	186 49.7	374 100.

Number of missing observations = 45

Palestinian state as the most important thing in their lives (question C8). Only 1.8 percent of the Christians indicated that economic well-being was the most important option for them (question C9). Again, the religious option was almost exclusively chosen by Muslims. And Christians profess a high degree of secularism (question C10). Some 81.5 percent of them would sacrifice religion, whereas only 44.4 percent of the Muslims would be willing to do so. There are major sociological differences between Christians and Muslims, as well as differences in their goals for the future. Since Christian society in Jerusalem has diminished in size, perhaps their positions are not as important as they were in the past. Many of the spokesmen for the traditional Fatah factions, however, are Christian: *Al-Fajr* editor Hanna Siniora, attorney Jonathan Kuttab, his journalist brother Daoud, the writer Saman Khouri, and so on. But the Christian community as a whole seems (based on our sample) to be seeking some way out of what threatens to be hard and fast polarization in Jerusalem. In the Muslim community some of the same fears of a radicalized society exist, but there is growing support for Islamic political orientation. In the meantime, many of the older or secular Jerusalem Muslims are uniting behind the political organizational framework offered to them by a newly moderate Fatah. As long as this secular bridge can be maintained, most Christians and a high percentage of Muslims will support Fatah positions in Jerusalem.

For the Christians, a minimalistic Palestinian solution in cooperation with the Jerusalem administration, if not Israel, appears to be an acceptable outcome of the intifada. That means a compromise in the future that would not leave them totally at sea within an Islamic polity.

Analysis of Differentiation by Employment

The random samples were divided into two economic categories: occupational status (unemployed or student, salaried or self-employed) and place of employment or "national dependency" in employment (Israeli business, Palestinian business, foreign company or agency, or self-employed). Occupational status is indicated in tables 6–32 through 6–40; place of employment in tables 6–41 through 6–49.

The analysis of Palestinian society by occupational status was not as significant as the generational, religious, and borough analyses. Nevertheless, certain interesting patterns emerged. The question on the future status of Jerusalem (D2) showed, not surprisingly, that the unemployed and the students shared opinions held by the young in our generational analysis. Over twice the percentage of the unemployed and students opted for the radical "other" solution than did the salaried or self-employed workers. The 35.1 percent positive answer for an open city seems surprising in this group. The self-employed generally were the most constant in support of the Fatah positions in Jerusalem. Many of the salaried employees work

Table 6–32
Status of Jerusalem (Question D2)

Count Row Pct Col Pct		East- West	Open city	Jordan & Palestine	Other	Row total
	Unemployed	14 24.6 6.3	20 35.1 18.9	3 5.3 10.3	20 35.1 33.3	57 13.6
	Salaried	102 55.1 45.7	43 23.2 40.6	14 7.6 48.3	26 14.1 43.3	185 44.3
	Self- employed	107 60.8 48.0	43 24.4 40.6	12 6.8 41.4	14 8.0 23.3	176 42.1
	COLUMN TOTAL	223 53.3	106 25.4	29 6.9	60 14.4	418 100

Number of missing observations = 1

Table 6–33
Contact with Israeli Institutions (Question D3)

Count Row Pct Col Pct		Yes	No	Row total
	Unemployed	6 10.5 3.8	51 89.5 19.5	57 13.6
	Salaried	94 50.8 60.3	91 49.2 34.7	185 44.3
	Self- employed	56 31.8 35.9	120 68.2 45.8	176 42.1
	COLUMN TOTAL	156 37.3	262 62.7	418 100

Number of missing observations = 1

Table 6–34
Regular Contact with Israeli Institutions (Question D4)

Count Row Pct Col Pct		Yes	To some extent	No	Row total
	Unemployed	1 1.8 1.5	5 8.9 5.6	50 89.3 19.5	56 13.5
	Salaried	57 31.1 83.8	38 20.8 42.2	88 48.1 34.2	183 44.1
	Self- employed	10 5.7 14.7	47 26.7 52.2	119 67.6 46.3	176 42.4
	COLUMN TOTAL	68 16.4	90 21.7	257 61.9	415 100

Number of missing observations = 4

Table 6–35
Satisfaction with Municipal Services (Question D5)

Count Row Pct Col Pct		Yes	To some extent	No	Not at all	Row total
	Unemployed	3 5.3 20.0	7 12.3 13.2	9 15.8 5.1	38 66.7 22.2	57 13.7
	Salaried	10 5.4 66.7	33 17.8 62.3	71 38.4 39.9	71 38.4 41.5	185 44.4
	Self- employed	2 1.1 13.3	13 7.4 24.5	98 56.0 55.1	62 35.4 36.3	175 42.0
	COLUMN TOTAL	15 3.6	53 12.7	178 42.7	171 41.0	417 100

Number of missing observations = 2

Table 6-36
Do Peace Initiatives Take into Account Palestinian Rights?
(Question D6)

Count Row Pct Col Pct	Yes	Partly	No	Not at all	Row total
Unemployed	3 5.3 23.1	8 14.0 18.2	16 28.1 7.5	30 52.6 20.1	57 13.6
Salaried	6 3.2 46.2	22 11.9 50.0	92 49.7 43.4	65 35.1 43.6	185 44.3
Self- employed	4 2.3 30.8	14 8.0 31.8	104 59.1 49.1	54 30.7 36.2	176 42.1
COLUMN TOTAL	13 3.1	44 10.5	212 50.7	149 35.6	418 100

Number of missing observations = 1

Table 6-37
Support for Jordan (Question D7)

Count Row Pct Col Pct	Support	Support conditionally	Against	Totally against	Row total
Unemployed	1 1.8 5.3	15 26.3 16.9	12 21.1 6.9	29 50.9 21.6	57 13.7
Salaried	8 4.3 42.1	49 26.6 55.1	70 38.0 40.0	57 31.0 42.5	184 44.1
Self- employed	10 5.7 52.6	25 14.2 28.1	93 52.8 53.1	48 27.3 35.8	176 42.2
COLUMN TOTAL	19 4.6	89 21.3	175 42.0	134 32.1	417 100

Number of missing observations = 2

Table 6–38
Preference for a Palestinian State (Question D8)

Count Row Pct Col Pct		Secular	Islamic	Socialist	Not important	Other	Row total
	Unemployed	1 3 22.8 7.0	1 7 29.8 18.3	8 14.0 17.4	1 7 29.8 19.3	2 3.5 33.3	5 7 13.6
	Salaried	7 5 40.5 40.5	4 3 23.2 46.2	2 5 13.5 54.3	4 1 22.2 46.6	1 .5 16.7	185 44.3
	Self- employed	9 7 55.1 52.4	3 3 18.8 35.5	1 3 7.4 28.3	3 0 17.0 34.1	3 1.7 50.0	176 42.1
	COLUMN TOTAL	185 44.3	9 3 22.2	4 6 11.0	8 8 21.1	6 1.4	418 100

Number of missing observations = 1

Table 6–39
Priorities (Question D9)

Count Row Pct Col Pct		Palestinian state	Economic well- being	Religion	Row total
	Unemployed	4 5 80.4 12.3		1 1 19.6 26.8	5 6 13.5
	Salaried	160 87.9 43.7	4 2.2 57.1	1 8 9.9 43.9	182 44.0
	Self- employed	161 91.5 44.0	3 1.7 42.9	1 2 6.8 29.3	176 42.5
	COLUMN TOTAL	366 88.4	7 1.7	4 1 9.9	414 100

Number of missing observations = 5

Table 6–40
Which Could You Sacrifice? (Question D10)

Count Row Pct Col Pct		Palestinian state	Economic well- being	Family & community	Religion	Row total
	Unemployed	1 2.0 8.3	30 60.0 19.9	5 10.0 16.1	14 28.0 7.4	50 13.0
	Salaried	8 4.8 66.7	70 41.7 46.4	14 8.3 45.2	76 45.2 40.0	168 43.8
	Self- employed	3 1.8 25.0	51 30.7 33.8	12 7.2 38.7	100 60.2 52.6	166 43.2
	COLUMN TOTAL	12 3.1	151 39.3	31 8.1	190 49.5	384 100

Number of missing observations = 35

Table 6–41
Status of Jerusalem (Question E2)

Count Row Pct Col Pct	Employer	East- West	Open city	Jordan & Palestine	Other	Row total
	Israeli	50 46.3 23.6	32 29.6 32.7	8 7.4 28.6	18 16.7 34.6	108 27.7
	Palestinian	56 50.0 28.4	26 23.2 26.5	9 8.0 32.1	21 18.8 40.0	112 28.7
	Foreign	5 31.3 2.4	6 37.5 6.1		5 31.3 9.6	16 4.1
	Self- employed	101 65.6 47.6	34 22.1 34.7	11 7.1 39.3	8 5.2 15.4	154 39.5
	COLUMN TOTAL	212 54.4	98 25.1	28 7.2	52 13.3	390 100

Number of missing observations = 29

Table 6–42
Contact with Israeli Institutions (Question E3)

Count Row Pct Col Pct	Employer	Yes	No	Row total
	Israeli	71 65.7 47.3	37 34.3 15.4	108 27.7
	Palestinian	24 21.4 16.0	88 78.6 36.7	112 28.7
	Foreign	1 12.5 1.3	14 87.5 5.8	15 4.1
	Self- employed	53 34.4 35.3	101 65.6 42.1	154 39.5
	COLUMN TOTAL	149 38.5	240 61.5	389 100

Number of missing observations = 29

Table 6–43
Regular Contact with Israeli Institutions (Question E4)

Count Row Pct Col Pct	Employer	Yes	To some extent	No	Row total
	Israeli	49 45.8 74.2	20 18.7 23.5	38 35.5 16.0	107 27.6
	Palestinian	6 5.4 9.1	16 14.4 18.8	89 80.2 37.6	111 28.6
	Foreign		3 18.8 3.5	12 81.3 5.5	15 4.1
	Self- employed	11 7.1 16.7	46 29.9 54.1	97 63.0 40.9	154 39.7
	COLUMN TOTAL	66 17.0	85 21.9	236 61.1	388 100

Number of missing observations = 31

Table 6–44
Satisfaction with Municipal Services (Question E5)

Count Row Pct Col Pct Employer	Yes	To some extent	No	Not at all	Row total
Israeli	8 7.4 61.5	25 23.1 50.0	32 29.6 19.0	43 39.8 27.7	108 27.8
Palestinian	2 1.8 15.4	10 8.9 20.0	41 36.6 24.4	59 52.7 37.3	112 28.8
Foreign	1 6.3 7.7	1 6.3 2.0	5 31.3 3.0	9 56.3 5.7	16 4.1
Self- employed	1 1.3 15.4	14 9.2 28.0	90 58.8 53.6	47 30.7 29.7	152 39.3
COLUMN TOTAL	12 3.3	50 12.9	168 43.2	158 40.6	389 100

Number of missing observations = 30

Table 6–45
Do Peace Initiatives Take into Account Palestinian Rights? (Question E6)

Count Row Pct Col Pct Employer	Yes	Partly	No	Not at all	Row total
Israeli	5 4.6 50.0	19 17.6 44.2	48 44.4 23.9	36 33.3 26.5	108 27.7
Palestinian		9 8.0 20.9	55 49.1 27.4	48 42.9 35.3	112 28.7
Foreign	1 6.3 10.0	2 12.5 4.7	6 37.5 3.0	7 43.8 5.1	16 4.1
Self- employed	4 2.6 40.0	13 8.4 30.2	92 59.7 45.8	45 29.2 33.1	154 39.5
COLUMN TOTAL	10 2.6	43 11.0	201 51.5	136 34.9	390 100

Number of missing observations = 29

Table 6–46
Support for Jordan (Question E7)

Count Row Pct Col Pct Employer	Support	Support conditionally	Against	Totally against	Row total
Israeli	4 3.7 22.2	3 1 29.0 36.9	3 5 32.7 21.1	3 7 34.6 30.6	107 27.5
Palestinian	5 4.5 27.8	3 0 26.8 35.7	3 8 33.9 22.9	3 9 34.8 32.2	112 28.8
Foreign		3 18.8 3.6	6 37.5 3.6	7 43.8 5.8	1 6 4.1
Self-employed	9 5.8 50.0	2 0 13.0 23.8	8 7 56.5 52.4	3 8 24.7 31.4	154 39.6
COLUMN TOTAL	1 8 4.6	8 4 21.6	166 42.7	121 31.1	389 100

Number of missing observations = 30

Table 6–47
Preference for a Palestinian State (Question E8)

Count Row Pct Col Pct Employer	Secular	Islamic	Socialist	Not important	Other	Row total
Israeli	3 3 30.6 18.9	3 1 28.7 35.2	1 6 14.8 37.2	2 6 24.1 33.3	2 1.9 33.3	108 27.7
Palestinian	5 3 47.3 30.3	2 3 20.5 26.1	1 3 11.6 30.2	2 1 18.8 26.9	2 1.8 33.3	112 28.7
Foreign	4 25.0 2.3	3 18.8 3.4	3 18.8 7.0	5 31.3 6.4	1 6.3 16.7	1 6 4.1
Self-employed	8 5 55.2 48.6	3 1 20.1 35.2	1 1 7.1 25.6	2 6 16.9 33.3	1 .6 16.7	154 39.5
COLUMN TOTAL	175 44.9	8 8 22.6	4 3 11.0	7 8 20.0	6 1.5	390 100

Number of missing observations = 29

Table 6–48
Priorities (Question E9)

Count Row Pct Col Pct	Employer	Palestinian state	Economic well- being	Religion	Row total
	Israeli	89 82.4 26.1	3 2.8 50.0	16 14.8 41.0	108 28.0
	Palestinian	97 89.0 28.4		12 11.0 30.8	109 28.2
	Foreign	14 93.3 4.1		1 6.7 2.6	15 3.9
	Self- employed	141 91.6 41.3	3 1.9 50.0	10 6.5 25.6	154 39.9
	COLUMN TOTAL	341 88.3	6 1.6	39 10.1	386 100

Number of missing observations = 33

Table 6–49
Which Could You Sacrifice? (Question E10)

Count Row Pct Col Pct	Employment	Palestinian state	Economic well- being	Family & community	Religion	Row total
	Israeli	5 5.2 41.7	47 49.0 33.3	11 11.5 44.0	33 34.4 18.4	96 26.9
	Palestinian	3 3.0 25.0	37 37.4 26.2	7 7.1 28.0	52 52.5 29.1	99 27.7
	Foreign	1 6.3 8.3	8 50.0 5.7	1 6.3 4.0	6 37.5 3.4	16 4.5
	Self- employed	3 2.1 25.0	49 33.6 34.8	6 4.1 24.0	88 60.3 49.2	146 40.9
	COLUMN TOTAL	12 3.4	141 39.5	25 7.0	179 50.1	357 100

Number of missing observations = 62

for Israeli businesses, so there is a certain tendency in this group toward more moderation in dealing with Israel. There is much more contact with Israelis and Israeli institutions on the part of the salaried members of the Palestinian community, as assessed in questions D3 and D4. And in terms of satisfaction with services rendered by the Jerusalem administration (question D5), over 20 percent of the salaried Palestinians responded positively, twice the percentage for the entire community and three times as high as the self-employed.

The relation to the peace initiatives (question D6) does not vary significantly within the three groups, but in terms of attitude toward Jordanian political efforts in Jerusalem (question D7), the salaried group evinced more positive reactions than either of the other two groups. A relatively large percentage of the unemployed and the students, over 25 percent, would under certain conditions support a Jordanian regime's attempts to influence the future of Jerusalem. Again, the self-employed are least likely to support Jordan or are the least susceptible to Jordanian blandishments. However, as within the younger generation, those who are "totally against" (the category of strongest rejection) prevail among the students and unemployed. The tendency toward Islamic orientation (question D8) is much higher among the unemployed; the self-employed evinced the strongest support for the Fatah position. As was expected, the self-employed are less oriented toward socialism than either salaried employees or the unemployed. While socialist feeling in Jerusalem is definitely a minority point of view, it is more significant among the unemployed, students, and salaried employees.

Answers about priorities and willingness to sacrifice verify the trends already developed in the questionnaire returns (questions D9 and D10). Religion plays a greater role in the political desires of the unemployed and students. The difference between the salaried and self-employed here is not overly significant. The single interesting exception is in the readiness to sacrifice. Only 30 percent of the self-employed would be willing to sacrifice economic well-being, whereas 41.7 percent of the salaried would be so inclined. Both the unemployed and students show a high number— 60 percent—ready to sacrifice an economic well-being that they do not have.

Tables 6–41 through 6–49 indicate responses to the questionnaire by those who work for Israeli businesses, those who work for Palestinian businesses, those who are employed by foreign agencies, and those who are self-employed. There is a slight differential between those who called themselves self-employed and those who were so classified on the basis of their answers to the sociological questions introducing the questionnaire. Not unexpectedly, those employed by Israeli businesses indicated a higher preference than average for having an open city (question E2), but interestingly enough, the highest percentage of supporters for an open city are employed by foreign concerns in Jerusalem. These include a variety of agencies and businesses that are neither Israeli nor Palestinian, such as the United Nations. Only 16 of the respondents to the questionnaire are so employed, but through their foreign connections these Palestinians have an influence on outside opinion disproportionate to their numbers. A high percentage of foreign employees opt for "other," the more radical of the Palestinian positions. Those employed by Israeli businesses have, as we saw, a higher level of contact with Israeli institutions (questions E3, E4). The self-employed must also maintain a rather high degree of contact with Israeli institutions, whereas Palestinians who work for foreign concerns have the least contact with Israeli institutions, even less than those who work for Palestinian businesses. The returns of the random sample verified an impressionistic analysis made in Jerusalem that Palestinians employed by foreign agencies try to ignore Israeli authorities and the Jerusalem administration.

In terms of satisfaction with services (question E5), those employed by Israeli businesses evince a far higher level of satisfaction than anyone else. Although once again the peace process question (E6) does not show a very wide differentiation, those who work for Israeli businesses are the most positively inclined, both toward the peace process and, interestingly enough, toward the Jordanian regime as well (question E7). Here, however, the differentiation between the groups is much less than was found along generational or other sociological lines. The high preference for an Islamic polity (question E8) by those working for Israeli businesses again confirms the trend seen throughout the questionnaire: The relationship with Israel leads to a strengthened pro-Islamic position. For the larger percentage of those employed by foreign agencies, the unimportance of a specific political form for a future Palestine is also interesting, albeit puzzling.

The analysis of desires and readiness to sacrifice (questions E9, E10) shows that economic differentiation does not lead to great differences in attitude. Only the category "religion," again strongest with Arabs employed by Israeli businesses, reaffirms previously salient trends. Generally, it is interesting that place of employment does not seem to have as much of an effect on the political desires of the Palestinian community as might have been expected. Economic influences seem to play less of a role than particularist social influences—family, community, religion, or generation—in forming an opinion as a Palestinian.

CONCLUSION

The in-depth analysis of Palestinian opinion in Jerusalem shows two major trends.

First, a majority take a moderate Fatah position. This support is especially strong among "established Jerusalemites" (including the self-employed, Christians, and Muslims over age 30) and in large boroughs such as Beit Hanina, A-Tur, and the Old City. However, these Jerusalemites have not crystallized politically. They still encompass many disparate groups (Christian intellectuals, conservative Hebronite families—some of whom, like the Sonqrat family, support Hamas leaders), and as long as no formal structure exists to organize and hold these groups together, Palestinians in Jerusalem will continue to be disadvantaged politically. Articulation, action, and compromise are determined in various centers and current majorities in opinion have not been molded into clear statements of political goals.

Second, at the edges of Jerusalem's Palestinian society—among youth, especially high school students and young academics, and in some of the boroughs—majority opinions are fraying. The chances are that if there is no satisfactory solution for Palestine and Jerusalem in the near future, the current consensus around the intifada will start to crack. The Jerusalem administration knows how to deal with fissures in Palestinian society in Jerusalem. The Israeli government, however, in recent years has shown a remarkable, if inadvertent, ability to foster unity in the Palestinian community through its heavy-handed policies. The fragmentation in Palestinian society in Jerusalem will not become politically critical if Israeli pressure and the attempt to resist it continue to fuse the society into a whole. But even here time is not necessarily the friend of Jerusalem's Palestinians, since a radicalization of their society—which is a distinct possibility among the young, among Muslim men, and in certain boroughs—will likely work against them.

Despite the difficulties in aspects of our polling and in some areas of response, the results of these polls still make one thing clear: Changes must be made in the method of administration, probably in the political processes, and in the political structure if the city is to avoid stagnation or, worse, the violent ethnic conflict that has scarred Beirut, Belfast, and Nicosia.

Time is running out for a city that has continued to be relatively peaceful and unified. The dissatisfaction of the young and the dynamism of the demographic development operative in Jerusalem bode ill for any polity. The growth of religious fundamentalism and political intolerance, especially in the young, will be fueled by failed political and economic programs. Beyond the evidence provided by the open and closed samples, results of the school surveys carried out in the spring of 1989 further support this conclusion.

The polls indicate that there are elements in the Palestinian community that can be approached and worked with. In any peace process, Jerusalem must be the key. It is at the emotional heart of the national problems. More than that, it is already a north-south hub for Palestinians of the area, and it would continue to be that as well as an east-west hub for the entire region if a solution could be reached. Both sides will have to decide for themselves how much they can offer the other. The least the Palestinians can be asked to accept is a significant and binding say over their own development and the social, economic, and political tools with which to develop. Otherwise, the city will degenerate into a functional breakwater against the ever-rising tides of national aspiration.

NOTES

1. See Ashkenasi (1988) (upon which the previous chapter is based), as well as Ashkenasi ("Nationalism," 1990) and Ashkenasi, "Communal Policy, Conflict Management and International Relations," *Jerusalem Journal of International Relations* 10, no. 2 (1988): 109.

2. Interviews were conducted with Sheikh Ismael al-Jamal, the head qadi in Jerusalem, Sheikh Akramah Sabri, the head of religious training at al-Aqsa, and Adnan al-Husseini, chief of the Waqf's building program.

3. Jamal's position was most forceful: "Wherever Arabs [Muslims] once lived in Jerusalem must be returned to Islamic suzereignty." (This includes, presumably, such neighborhoods as Bakaa and Talbieh, primarily Arab until 1948 and now high-priced and trendy areas in Jewish Jerusalem.) Husseini, being an engineer and therefore the most cognizant of the infrastructural problems a Palestinian city would face, was the most moderate.

4. There is broad unanimity but within it a certain flexibility. This is evident in their assessment of their relations with the Israeli Islamic movement. Again, it is an interpretation of the meaning of contacts (*alakat*); they have, variously, "as much contact as possible" or just "advisory" and "spiritual," rather than monetary or structural, contact. All this implies active informal commitment and indicates the attempt to gain influence, especially in spiritual and educational matters.

5. Hamas's leader claims that the official Islamic leadership in Jerusalem maintains extensive contacts with the Islamic movement in Israel, providing direction to youth groups and religious education. He contends that the ties of Hamas itself to the Israeli Islamic movement are excellent and extend to administrative "assistance" and help in local elections. Apparently the battle is on for the souls of Israel's Muslims, and this may be more important and simpler for the time being than contacts with any Jewish institutions. (Here as elsewhere opinions differ. See Lilly Weissbrod, "Hamas: A Force To Be Reckoned With," *Jerusalem Post*, September 16, 1990.)

6. In addition to the nearly 20,000 members in East Jerusalem (including spouses), the Histadrut in East Jerusalem represents 7,000 residents of the West Bank who work in Jerusalem. While they are not members, some have taken positions of responsibility nonetheless. They are represented in the organization's various professional committees, and in four East Jerusalem factories there are individuals from the West Bank who have been voted onto workers' councils.

7. For levels of violence in the various boroughs, see Zilberman (1988).

8. *Jerusalem Statistical Yearbook, 1986.*

7

CONCLUSION

HOPES AND GOALS—CONCRETE ALTERNATIVES

As we have seen, Israel's Arabs and the Palestinian Jerusalem community are quite similar in sociological structure. Both groups conceive of themselves in middle class terms, although they are by and large working-class and low-salaried communities. Their middle class ethos is highly subjective and they see their ability to achieve upward mobility very much in terms of educational opportunity. Israel's Arabs may be more modern, in the sense that sociologists conceive of modernity, than the Palestinians in Jerusalem. Their society has certainly been more deeply penetrated by Western ideas. But again, most Palestinians in Jerusalem are part of a Western urban economic structure, while many of Israel's Arabs live in villages; some of their boroughs show the "modern" social and economic mobility, educational achievement, and nuclear family structure that are the hallmarks of Western society. Both communities show a low tendency toward violence, all the more so when compared to the West Bank and especially Gaza. And members of both communities have been, by and large, quiescent and law-abiding citizens in the Jewish polity—although each group subjectively rejects this polity. Jerusalem's Palestinian Arabs probably share many of the ideological preferences and propensities, in terms of options, that characterize Israel's Arabs according to the model that Smooha has developed. The differences between the two groups—and especially the differences between them and the rest of their compatriots—lie in the alternatives available to them. Their perception of reality is tempered by their relation to the Jewish community surrounding them and the obvious power of the Israeli state that represents this community.

But readiness to cooperate with the state or even the Jerusalem municipal administration is dependent on the Jewish polity's ability to open its society to fair competition. This is especially true for economic opportunity and cultural development. "How much national aspiration are you willing to sacrifice for economic development and cultural autonomy?" is not a question that has been satisfactorily posed within the Palestinian community. It has not really had a chance for consideration, because attractive alternative solutions have not been offered in a concrete fashion by Israel. To the degree that Palestinians have room to cooperate and even develop economically, Israel has achieved a certain measure of accommodation and co-optation. Because this degree of cooperation demands far more national self-abnegation and accommodation in the geographical and social context of Jerusalem that it did for Israeli Arabs, the successes in Jerusalem with much the same kind of limited policy have been negligible. However, Israel has bought grudging quiescence in Jerusalem, and it has bought time that was used to counter the Arab population of Jerusalem, including its 100 percent demographic growth, with Jewish expansion into previously all-Arab, Israel-annexed East Jerusalem. It has kept the lid on the volatile situation inherent in transplanting populations.

The intifada has heightened the questions of political choice open to both Arabs and Jews. But this has proven to be far more uncomfortable for Arabs. Much of the support for Islamic fundamentalist groups in Israel seems to represent a flight from the unpleasant choice posed by the intifada. If one cannot decide whether one's future lies as a minority in Israel or as a citizen of a Palestinian community, no matter where this Palestinian state is established, then one can easily fall between the two political poles into a psychological no-man's land. The conflict in Jerusalem is more starkly etched, but here the young and the poor are faced with the future possibility of political compromise with the goal of the Palestinian national movement. Many are slowly opting for other solutions that (1) conform to emotional, uncompromising national principles and (2) are essentially far broader in scope and perhaps less realistic than those professed by the mainstream PLO. As time passes, so too do the opportunities for a solution. Israeli society manifests a certain fatalistic complacency. It confronts the intifada with relative ease within the geographical limits of its own civil authority and psychological perception. The intifada challenges the army, and Israelis are used to this type of confrontation. Fewer than three percent of all Israeli Jews live in the occupied territories outside of Jerusalem. Most of these live clustered around the 1948 borders of the state of Israel and the municipal boundaries of Jerusalem. The intifada forces less pressure for a solution upon them than upon Arab society. Palestinians outside the civil boundaries of Israel have made their choice. They really have no other to make, because they are in essence offered no other alternative than to struggle for a Palestinian state. Within the green line, for as long as there are other options, a significant segment of Arab society will continue to cooperate and accommodate rather than endure the hardships of direct confrontation. This enhances the difficulty of those Israeli Arabs who wish to support the intifada with more than just lip service.

In Jerusalem the situation is mixed. There are distinct benefits to be had by continued accommodation with the Jerusalem municipal authority, if not the state of Israel, even when and if a Palestinian state is established. On the other hand, the negative pressures grow every day, especially among the young, for a complete break with any kind of Jewish polity. This break, however, is difficult to make without a concrete alternative. The only alternative that is overtly considered, a Palestinian state with East Jerusalem as its capital, is not yet a viable solution given the complexity of geographical development and power structure in the area. Jerusalem's Palestinian elite is aware of this complexity and of the power relationships unfavorable for them on the ground, which will inhibit for the foreseeable future this kind of a solution. These include Jewish economic and military domination, demographic and infrastructural imbalances, and lack of international support for an Arab Jerusalem. The flap that occurred when President Bush called Jerusalem "occupied territory" in the spring of 1990 indicated the depth of Israeli attachment to the city. Moreover, whereas a retreat from most of the West Bank and Gaza seems feasible at least politically, a truncated East Jerusalem on the wrong side of all the physical infrastructure (electricity, water, sewage, and telephone systems), even if it were acceptable to Israel, is not a judicious alternative. Whether or not there is a Palestinian state, the Palestinian population in the area will be tied in many ways to the economic structure of Israel, Israeli infrastructure, and perhaps its social system as well—which, arguably, would be advantageous in terms of jobs, insurance, and so forth. Redivision of the city of Jerusalem in absolute terms is probably economically unfeasible and politically unrealistic. The question of alternatives, then, looms large for the Palestinian community in Jerusalem. They have not developed the institutions to face the question concretely. The pressures of the intifada make action imperative but do not help policy implementation for an essentially politically inexperienced Arab communal leadership. There are sympathetic Israeli citizens who would help if they could, but their ability and means to do so are limited. The city administration of Jerusalem seems fatally tied to old policies it actually deems liberal. The Jewish electorate in Jerusalem is notoriously nationalist and conservative, while the new generations grow apart along a void of mistrust and nascent hatred that bode ill for a united city.

EPILOGUE

The events at the Temple Mount, in which some 17 Arabs were killed and many more wounded, seem to belie many of the trends discussed in this book. Jerusalem was a relatively "violence-free" city even during the intifada. Major confrontations occurred elsewhere—in the West Bank and Gaza; on the Israeli side of the green line they were even rarer than in Jerusalem. Israeli Arabs paid lip service to Palestine, but little more than that. But many trends we have seen remain valid, even as violence in Jerusalem escalates in the wake of the tragedy. Note, for example, that the revenge attacks that have followed in the city, whether directed against civilians or policemen, have been perpetrated by Palestinians from the outside. Demonstrations in Israel, although intense, have been local and limited.

The "moderates" all around will try to exercise damage control. But it is highly unlikely that the memory of violence and the growing hatreds can be exorcised. What are some of the political and social structures analyzed and developed in this book that contributed to the confrontation at the Temple Mount?

1. The increasingly disenchanted, polarized, and volatile Arab and Jewish youth.

2. A political and economic reality, on both the domestic and international fronts, that seems to condemn the Arab youth to a life of second-class citizenship.

3. A national Israeli police force and territorial guard with a disturbing propensity for "independent" and inflammatory behavior. The failure to protect Arabs against Jews who rioted earlier in the summer when the bodies of two boys who had been hitchhiking were found murdered, and the Temple Mount carnage are but recent examples of a deep-seated anti-Palestinianism in some segments of the police.

4. The growing destabilization of the area by powerful international actors. The Temple Mount demonstration, although obviously a function of domestic frustration, was encouraged and capitalized upon by outside actors. An obviously neuralgic area in Jerusalem, the scene of emotional but less tragic confrontations in the past, was exploited to further ends that are only tangentially associated with Jerusalem.

5. A burgeoning religious intolerance, which was not significant in the city in the past but by now is a volatile catalyst. The previous political supremacy of secular and pragmatic consideration is under assault. Should the relatively moderate religious leaders on both sides continue to avoid direct cooperation with one another, the embattled Jerusalem minority may not be able to douse the flames lurking in the embers.

6. There is a growing sense of empathy between Israeli Arabs and

Palestinians. It may be easier for the Israeli authorities to deal with this than to deal with Jerusalem, but it will not be simple.

Without reform of the structure of control and relationships, both social and economic, Israel and the city of Jerusalem are headed for an increase in ethnic conflict.

BIBLIOGRAPHY

Abdul-Hadi, M. *Thoughts on Israel's Policies and Practices in Jerusalem*. Cambridge, Mass., 1985.

Amiran, D. H. K., A. Sahar, and I. Kimhi, eds. *Urban Geography of Jerusalem*. New York, 1973.

Ansprenger, Franz. *Juden und Araber in einem Land. Die politischen Beziehungen der belden Völker im Mandatsgebiet Palästina und im Staat Israel*. Munich, 1978.

Arab Studies Quarterly. "Israel and the Question of Palestine" (special issue). Spring-Summer 1965.

Aruri, N. H., *Occupation: Israel over Palestine*. Belmont, Mass., 1983.

Ashkenasi, Abraham. "The Structure of Ethnic Conflict and Palestinian Political Fragmentation." Occasional paper, Forschungsgebeitsschwerpunkt Aussenpolitik (FGS AP), Free University of Berlin, February 1981.

————. "Social Ethnic Conflict and Paramilitary Organization in the Near East." In *Political Violence and Terror*, edited by P. H. Merkl. Berkeley, 1986.

————. Jerusalem Data Project. The Hebrew University of Jerusalem, 1987, unpublished. Collection of statistical compilations based on the 1983 Israel census.

————. "Communal Policy, Conflict Management and International Relations." *Jerusalem Journal of International Relations* 10, no. 2 (1988).

————. "Israeli Policies and Palestinian Fragmentation: Political and Social Impacts in Israel and Jerusalem." Policy Studies #24. Jerusalem, Leonard Davis Institute for International Relations, June 1988.

————. "Palestinian Views about Jerusalem." Policy Studies #30. Jerusalem, Leonard Davis Institute for International Relations, May 1989.

————. "Opinion Trends among Jerusalem Palestinians." Policy Studies #36. Jerusalem, Leonard Davis Institute for International Relations, n.d. [1990].

————. "The International Institutionalization of a Refugee Problem: The Palestinians and UNRWA." *Jerusalem Journal of International Affairs*, March 1990.

————. "Nationalism and National Identity." Ethnizitat und Gesellschaft Occasional Papers, no. 23. Berlin, 1990.

Azar, E., P. Jureidini, and R. McLaurin. "Protracted Social Conflict: Theory and Practice in the Middle East." *Journal of Palestine Studies* 8, no. 1 (Autumn 1978).

Baker, Douglas. *Race, Ethnicity and Power*. London, 1983.

Barth, Ernest, and Donald L. Noel. "Conceptual Frameworks for the Analysis of Race Relations: An Evaluation." *Social Forces* 50 (March 1972).

Barth, Fredrik, ed. *Ethnic Groups and Boundaries: The Social Organization of Cultural Difference*. Bergen-Oslo, 1969.

Baumgarten, Helga. *Die Enstehung des palästinensischen Nationalismus*. Berlin, Arbeitsheft des Berliner Instituts für Vergleichende Sozialforschung, 1985.

————. *Befreiung in dem straat: Die Palestinensischer national Bewegung seit 1948*. Frankfurt am Main, 1991.

Ben-Artzi, Yossef. "Residential Patterns and Intra-Urban Migration of Arabs in Haifa." Occasional Papers on the Middle East (New Series), no. 1. Jewish-Arab Center, University of Haifa, 1980.

Ben-Dor, Gabriel. *The Druzes in Israel: A Political Study*. Jerusalem, 1979.

Benvenisti, M. *Jerusalem, the Torn City*. Minneapolis, 1976.

————. *Jerusalem, Study of a Polarized Community*. Jerusalem, 1983.

————. *The Jerusalem Question: Problems, Procedures and Options*. Rev. ed. Jerusalem, 1985.

————. *1986 Report: Demographic, Economic, Legal, Social and Political Developments in the West Bank*. Jerusalem, 1986.

————. *The Shepherds' War: Collected Essays (1981–1989)*. Jerusalem, 1989.

Birnbaum, Pierre. "Le petit chaperon rouge et le pouvoir local." *Revue Française du Sociologie* 15 (April-June 1974).

Brass, P. R. *Ethnic Groups and the State*. London, 1985.

Bruno, E., A. Korte, and K. Mathey. *Umgang mit städtischen Wohnquartieren unterer Einkommensgruppen in Entwicklungsladern*. Darmstadt, 1984.

Caplan, Gerald, and Ruth Caplan. *Arab and Jew in Jerusalem: Explorations in Community Mental Health*. London, 1980.

Castells, M. "Urban Sociology and Urban Politics: From a Critique to New Trends of Research." *Comparative Urban Research* 3 (1975).

————. *The Urban Question*. London, 1977.

Clarke, C., D. Ley, and C. Peach, eds. *Geography and Ethnic Pluralism*. London, 1984.

Clarke, S. E. "Urban Ethnic Conflict: Selected Theoretical Approaches." In *Urban Ethnic Conflict: A Comparative Perspective*, edited by S. E. Clarke and J. L. Obler. Chapel Hill, 1976.

Cohen, A., ed. *Urban Ethnicity*. London, 1974.

Cohen, Erik. *Integration vs. Separation in the Planning of a Mixed Jewish-Arab City in Israel*. Jerusalem, 1973.

Cohen, R. "Processes of Political Organization and Voting Patterns of Israeli Arabs." M. A. thesis, Tel Aviv University, 1985.

Committee to Confront the Iron Fist. "Fact Sheet on Deportation." Mimeographed. Jerusalem, February 1986.

Dakkak, Ibrahim. "Jerusalem during the Ten Years 1967–1977." Jerusalem, 1981 (Arabic).

———. "The Transformation of Jerusalem: Juridical Statute and Physical Change. In *Occupation: Israel over Palestine*, edited by N. H. Aruri. Belmont, Mass., 1983.

Dekmejian, R. H. "Consociational Democracy in Crisis: The Case of Lebanon." *Comparative Politics* 10 (1978).

Despres, L. A. "Toward a Theory of Ethnic Phenomena." In *Ethnicity and Resource Competition in Plural Societies*, edited by L. A. Despres. Paris, 1975.

Deutsch, Karl W., and W. Foltz, eds. *Nation-Building*. New York, 1963.

Dunleavy, P. C. "The Urban Basis of Political Alignment." *British Journal of Political Science* 9, pt. 4 (1979).

Efrat, Elisha. "Spatial Patterns of Jewish and Arab Settlements in Judea and Samaria." In *Judea, Samaria and Gaza: Views on the Present and Future*, edited by D. J. Elazar. Washington, D. C., 1982.

Ehlers, E., "Sfax/Tunesien, Dualistische Strukturen in der Orientalisch-Islamischen Stadt." *Erdkunde* 37 (1983).

Eisenstadt, S. N. "Introduction: Some Reflections on the Study of Ethnicity. In *The Study of Israeli Society*, vol. 1, edited by Ernest Krausz. New Brunswick, N.J./London, 1980.

Elime, Farouk. "Die arabische Minorität in Israel: Zur Analyse der soziopolitischen Orientierung der konfessionellen und familiären Gruppierungen in Nazareth." Ph.D. diss., Free University of Berlin, 1985.

Elkin, Stephen L. *Politics and Land Use Planning*. London, 1973.

———. "Comparative Urban Politics and Interorganizational Behaviour." *Comparative Urban Research* 2 (1974).

Elliot, B., and D. McCrone. "Power and Protest in the City." In *New Perspectives in Urban Change and Conflict*. London, 1981.

Elon, Amos. *Jerusalem: The Torn City*. Boston, 1989.

Enloe, C. *Ethnic Change and Urban Development*. Boston, 1973.

Erlanger, Howard S. "The Empirical Status of the Subculture of Violence." In *Urban Ethnic Conflict: A Comparative Perspective*, edited by S. E. Clarke and J. L. Obler. Chapel Hill, 1976.

Fahri, David. "Der muslimische Rat in Ost-Jerusalem, Judäa und Samaria seit dem Sechstagekreig." *Neur Orient* 1–2 (1979).

Falk, A. "The Meaning of Jerusalem: A Psychohistorical Viewpoint. In *Maps of the Mind: Readings in Psychogeography*, edited by Howard F. Stein and William G. Nederland. Norman, Okla., 1989.

Flores, Alexander, and Alexander Schölch. *Palestinenser in Israel*. Frankfurt am Main, 1983.

Frisch, Hillel. "From Armed Struggle over State Borders to Political Mobilization and Intifada within It: The Transformation of PLO Strategy in the Territories." *Plural Societies* 19, no. 2/3 (1990).

Gabai, M. *The Arabs of Israel: A Question of Identity*. Givat Haviva: Institute for Arab Studies, 1984 (Hebrew).

Gaube, H., and E. Wirth. *Aleppo*. Weisbaden, 1984.

Gensicke, Klaus. *Der Mufti von Jerusalem: Amin el-Husseini und die National-*

sozialisten. Ethnien Regionen und Konflikte, no. 1. Frankfurt am Main, 1988.

Ginat, Joseph. "Analysis of the Arab Vote in the 1984 Elections." Occasional Papers, no. 100. Dayan Center for Middle Eastern and African Studies, Shiloah Institute, Tel Aviv University, 1987.

———. "The Elections in the Arab Sector: Voting Patterns and Political Behavior." *Jerusalem Quarterly* no. 53 (Winter 1990).

Haas, M. *Husseins Konigreich: Jordaniens Stellung im Nahen Osten*. Munich, 1975.

Habash, Awni H. "Society in Transition: A Social and Political Study of the Arab Community in Israel." Ph.D. diss., Cornell University, 1973.

Haidar, Aziz. "The Different Levels of Palestinian Ethnicity." In *Ethnicity, Pluralism and the State in the Middle East*, edited by M. J. Esman and L. Rabinovich. Ithaca, 1988.

Al-Haj, Majid. "The Status of the Arab *Hamula* in Israel." Master's thesis, University of Haifa, 1979 (Hebrew).

———. "Adjustment Patterns of the Arab Internal Refugees in Israel." *International Migration* 24, no. 3 (September 1986).

———. "The Changing Arab Kinship Structure: The Effect of Modernization in an Urban Community." *Economic Development and Cultural Change* 36, no. 2 (1988).

———. "Elections in the Arab Street in the Wake of the Intifada: Propaganda and Results." In *The Arab Vote in Israel's Parliamentary Elections*, edited by J. M. Landau. Jerusalem, 1989.

Al-Haj, M., and A. Yaniv. *Uniformity and Diversity: A Reappraisal of Voting Behavior of the Arab Minority in Israel*. Jewish-Arab Center, University of Haifa, 1983. Also in *The Elections in Israel—1981*, edited by A. Arian. Tel Aviv, 1983.

Harari, Yechiel. *The Arabs in Israel—1976: Facts and Figures*. Givat Haviva, 1976.

———. "The Elections in the Arab Sector in 1977, Knesset and 1978, Histadrut." Mimeographed. Givat Haviva, Center for Arab and Afro-Asian Studies, 1978a (Hebrew).

———. "The Elections in the Municipal Councils in the Arab Sector, 1978." Givat Haviva, Center for Arab and Afro-Asian Studies, 1978b (Hebrew).

———. "Additional Data on the Arabs in Israel 1978." Mimeographed. Givat Haviva, Center for Arab and Afro-Asian Studies, 1980 (Hebrew).

Harris, L. "Finance and Money with Underdeveloped Banking." Paper presented at the Symposium on Economic Development under Prolonged Occupation: West Bank and Gaza. Oxford, 1986.

Harvey, D. *Social Justice and the City*. Baltimore, 1973.

———. "The Urban Forces under Capitalism." *International Journal of Urban and Regional Research* 2 (1978).

Al-Histadrut: Kel'a Hasina min Ajil al-'Omel (The Histadrut: A fortress for the worker, who must protect it). Tel Aviv, August 1989 (Arabic).

Hofman, John E. "Readiness for Social Relations between Jews and Arabs in Israel." *Journal of Conflict Resolution* 16, no. 2 (June 1972).

———. "National Images of Arab Youth in Israel and the West Bank." *Megamot* 20, no. 3 (July 1974) (Hebrew).

———. "Identity and Intergroup Perception in Israeli Jews and Arabs." Occasional

Papers on the Middle East, no. 7. Jewish-Arab Center, University of Haifa, 1976.

———. "Stereotypes and Identity of Arab Youth in Israel." Mimeographed. Institute for Research and Development of Arab Education, University of Haifa, 1977 (Hebrew).

———. "Transformations in the Evaluation of Religious-National Images of Arab Youth in Israel." *Megamot* 24, no. 2 (August 1978) (Hebrew).

———. "Social Identity and the Readiness for Social Relations between Jews and Arabs in Israel." *Human Relations* 35 (1982).

Hofman, John E., and Benjamin Beit-Hallahmi. "The Palestinian Identity and Israel's Arabs." *Peace Research* 9 (January 1977). Reprinted in *The Palestinians and the Middle East Conflict*, edited by Gabriel Ben-Dor. Ramat Gan, 1978.

Hofman, John E., and S. Debbiny. "Religious Affiliations and Ethnic Identity." *Psychological Reports* 26 (1970).

Hofman, John E., and Nadim Rouhana. "Young Arabs in Israel: Some Aspects of a Conflicted Identity." *Journal of Social Psychology* 99 (1976).

Horowitz, Donald. "Direct, Displaced and Cumulative Ethnic Aggression." *Comparative Politics* 6 (October 1973).

———. "Dual Authorities Polities." *Comparative Politics* 14, no. 3 (1982).

———. *Ethnic Groups in Conflict*. Berkeley, 1985.

Horowitz, D., and M. Lissak. *The Origins of the Israeli Polity: Palestine under the Mandate*. Chicago, 1978.

Hudson, Michael C. "Social Mobilization Theory of Arab Politics." In *From National Development to Global Community*, edited by R. L. Merrit and Bruce M. Russet. Boston, 1981.

Huntington, S. P. *Political Order in Changing Societies*. New Haven, 1968.

Institute for Israeli Arabs Studies. "Survey: 60% of Arab Children Live Below the Poverty Line." *Arabs in Israel* 1, no. 24 (1992): 5–8.

Jerusalem Institute for Israel Studies. *The Dynamics of Urban Population: Coping with Changing Needs*. Jerusalem, May 1983.

Jerusalem Statistical Yearbook 1986. Jerusalem, 1986.

Journal of Palestine Studies. "The Palestinians in Israel and the Occupied Territories" (special issue). Vol. 14, no. 2 (Winter 1985).

Kamon, Charles. *After the Tragedy: The Arabs in the State of Israel from 1948 to 1950*. Haifa, 1984 (Hebrew).

Kanaana, Sharif. "Survival Strategies of Arabs in Israel." *MERIP Reports*, no. 41 (October 1975).

———. *Socio-Cultural and Psychological Adjustment of the Arab Minority in Israel*. San Francisco, 1976.

Kapeliouk, Amnon. "Les Arabes Chrétiens en Israël 1948–1967." Ph.D. diss., University of Paris, 1968.

———. "L'état social, économique, cultural et juridiques des Arabes Chrétiens en Israël." *Asian and African Studies* 5 (1969).

Korpi, Walter. "Conflict, Power, and Relative Deprivation." *American Political Science Review* 68 (December 1974).

Kraemer, J. L. *Jerusalem: Problems and Prospects*. New York, 1980.

Landau, J. M. *The Arabs in Israel: A Political Study*. London, 1969.

——. "The Arab Vote." In *The Elections in Israel—1969*, edited by A. Arian. Jerusalem, 1972.

——. "The Israeli Arabs and the Elections to the Fourth Knesset." In *Middle Eastern Themes: Papers in History and Politics*, edited by J. M. Landau. London, 1973.

——. "The Arab Vote." In *The Roots of Begin's Success: The 1981 Israel Election*, edited by D. Caspi, A. Diskin, and E. Gutman. London and Canberra, 1984.

——. "The Arabs and the Histadrut." In *Labor and Society in Israel*, edited by I. Avrech and D. Giladi. Tel Aviv, n.d.

——, ed. *The Arab Vote in Israel's Parliamentary Elections, 1988*. Research Studies Series, no. 35. Jerusalem Institute for Israel Studies, 1989 (Hebrew).

Lee, Alfred M. "Insurgent and Peace Keeping Violence in Northern Ireland." In *Urban Ethnic Conflict: A Comparative Perspective*, edited by S. E. Clarke and J. L. Obler. Chapel Hill, 1976.

Leeds, A. "Locality Powers in Relation to Supralocal Institutions." In *Urban Anthropology: Cross-Cultural Studies of Urbanization*, edited by Aidan William Southall. New York, 1973.

Lembruch, G. "Noncompetitive Patterns of Conflict Management in Liberal Democracies: The Case of Switzerland, Austria and Lebanon." In *Constitutional Democracy*, edited by K. McRae. Toronto, 1974.

Liebman, C. S; and E. Don-Yehiya. *Civil Religion in Israel: Traditional Judaism and Political Culture in the Jewish State*. Berkeley, 1983.

Licbman, C. S., and E. Don-Yehiya. *Religion and Politics in Israel*. Bloomington, Ind., 1984.

Lijphart, Arend. *The Politics of Accommodation*. Berkeley, 1968.

Lustick, J. "Stability in Deeply Divided Societies: Consociationism versus Control." *World Politics* 31 (1979).

——. *Arabs in the Jewish State: Israel's Control of a National Minority*. Austin and London, 1980.

Mar'i, Sami Khalil. *Arab Education in Israel*. Syracuse, 1978.

Masotti, L., and J. Walton. "Comparative Urban Research: The Logic of Comparisons and the Nature of Urbanism." In *The City in Comparative Perspective: Cross-National Research and New Directions in Theory*, edited by L. Masotti and J. Walton. New York, 1976.

Mattar, Ibrahim. "From Palestinian to Israeli Jerusalem, 1948–1982." *Journal of Palestine Studies* 48 (1973).

Meari, Mahmoud. "Identity of Arab Academics in Israel." Mimeographed. Research Report no. 700. Jerusalem, Israel Institute of Applied Social Research, 1978.

Meir, Avinoam, and Joseph Ben-David, eds. *The Bedouin in Israel and Sinai: A Bibliography*. Beersheba, Department of Geography, Ben-Gurion University of the Negev, 1989.

MERIP Middle East Report. Washington, D.C., 1987.

The Metropolitan Area of Jerusalem: The Urban Development of Metropolitan Jerusalem. Publication no. 1. Jerusalem Institute for Israel Studies, 1984.

Milson, Menachem. *Jordan and the West Bank*. Jerusalem, 1984.

Mishal, S. *West Bank/East Bank: The Palestinians in Jordan 1949–1967*. New Haven, 1978.

Nakhleh, Emile A. "The Arabs in Israel and Their Role in a Future Arab-Israeli Conflict: A Perception Study." Mimeographed. Alexandria, Va., 1977.

Nakleh, Khalil. "Shifting Patterns of Conflict in Selected Arab Villages in Israel." Ph.D. diss., Indiana University, 1972.

———. "The Direction of Local-Level Conflict in Two Arab Villages in Israel." *American Ethnologist* 23 (August 1975).

Nashef, J. "On Either Side of the Green Line: A Comparison of the Dreams of Refugee Children in a Camp of the West Bank and Children in an Arab Village in Israel." Manuscript. Jerusalem, 1984 (Hebrew).

———. "The Psychological Impact of the Intifada on Palestinian Children Living in Refugee Camps on the West Bank as Reflected in Dreams, Drawings and Behavior." Ph.D. diss., Free University of Berlin, 1991.

Nordlinger, Eric A. "Conflict Regulation in Divided Societies." Occasional Paper, Harvard University, 1972.

Oppenheimer, Jonathan. "The Druze in Israel as Arabs and Non-Arabs: An Essay on the Manipulation of Categories of Identity in a Non-Civil State." *Cambridge Anthropology* 4, no. 2 (1978).

Parkin, Frank. *Marxism and Class Theory: A Bourgeois Critique*. London, 1978.

Paz, R. "The Islamic Movement in Israel and the Municipal Elections of 1989." *Jerusalem Quarterly*, no. 53 (Winter 1990).

Porath, Yehoshua. *The Emergence of the Palestinian-Arab National Movement, 1918–1929*. London, 1974 (also in Hebrew, 1976).

———. *The Palestinian Arab National Movement, 1929–1939: From Riots to Rebellion*. London, 1977.

———. *In Search of Arab Unity, 1930–1945*. London, 1986.

Rekhess, Eli. "A Survey of Minority Graduates from Institutions of Higher Education in Israel 1961–71." Mimeographed. Shiloah Center, Tel Aviv University, 1974.

———. "The Israeli Arabs since 1967: The Issue of Identity." Mimeographed. Sekirot no. 1. Shiloah Center, Tel Aviv University, 1976 (Hebrew).

———. "Arabs in Israel and Land Expropriations in the Galilee: Background, Events and Implications, 1975–1977." Mimeographed. Sekirot no. 53. Shiloah Center, Tel Aviv University, 1977 (Hebrew).

———. "Arabs in a Jewish State: Images versus Realities." *Middle East Insight* 7, no. 1 (1990).

Rivlin, Helen Anne B., and Katherine Helmer, eds. *The Changing Middle East City*. Binghamton, N.Y., 1980.

Romann, M. "Inter-Relations between the Jewish and Arab Sectors in Jerusalem." Jerusalem, Jerusalem Institute for Israel Studies, 1984 (Hebrew).

———. "Bridging the Divisions in the Relations between the Jewish and Arab Sectors in Jerusalem: Methodological Aspects (special issue). *Ir V'Ezor*, (Sept. 1989) (Hebrew).

Romann, M., and Alex Weingrod. *Living Together Separately: Arabs and Jews in Jerusalem*. Princeton, 1990.

Rouhana, K. "Economic Trap in the Territories." In *Al-Fajr (English)*, November 15, 1985.

Rouhana, Nadim. "Collective Identity and Arab Voting." In *The Elections in Israel—1984*, edited by A. Arian and M. Shamir. Tel Aviv, 1986.

Rubenstein, D. *The People of Nowhere: The Palestinian Vision of Home*. New York, 1991.

Rubinstein, A. *From Herzl to Gush Emunim and Back*. Tel Aviv, 1980.

Safadi, Akram. "Employment Patterns and Problems among University Graduates in the Occupied Territories." Manuscript. Jerusalem, Truman Institute, 1987.

Sahalka, Salman. "Manpower in the Arab Sector." *Rivon Lekalkala* 23, no. 9 (1976) (Hebrew).

Samed, Amal. "Palestinian Women: Entering the Proletariat." *MERIP Reports*, no. 50 (August 1976). Reprinted in *Journal of Palestine Studies* 6, no. 1 (Autumn 1976).

Sandler, S. "The Compound Arab-Israeli Conflict." Manuscript. Jerusalem, 1986.

Sandler, S., and Hillel Frisch. *Israel, the Palestinians and the West Bank*. Lexington, Mass., 1984.

Scheffler, T. "Ethnisch-religiöse Konflikt und Gesellschaftliche Integration im Vorderen und Mittleren Orient." Literaturstudie, Ethnizitat und Gesellschaft. Berlin, 1985.

Schermerhorn, R.A. *Comparative Ethnic Relations*. New York, 1970.

Schiel, Tilman. *Fiktion und Realität einer politischen Ethnologie*. Berlin, Arbeitshefte des Berliner Instituts für Vergleichende Sozialforschung, 1985.

Schiller, David Thomas. *Palästinenser zwischen Terrorismus und Diplomatie*. Munich, 1982.

Schmalz, I. *Das vereinigte Jerusalem: Demographische Struktur der massgebenden Bevölkerungsgruppen*. Jerusalem, 1977.

Schnore, L., and E. E. Lampard. "Social Science and the City: A Survey of Research Needs." In *Urban Research and Policy Planning*, edited by L. Schnore and H. Fagin. Beverly Hills, Ca., 1967.

Schwedler, H. U. *Arbeitsmigration und urbaner Wandel: Eine Studie über Arbeitskräftewanderung und Räumliche Segregation in Orientalischen Städten am Beispiel Kuwait*. Berlin, 1985.

Seger, M. *Zum Dualismus der Struktur Orientalischer Städte: Das Beispiel Teheran*. Mitglieder der österreichischen geographischen Gesellschaft 121, Vienna, 1979.

Shalev, Aryeh. *The Intifada: Causes and Effects*. Jaffee Center for Strategic Studies, Study no. 16. Tel Aviv, 1991.

Shibutani, T., and K. M. Kwan. *Ethnic Stratification*. New York, 1965.

Shinar, D. *Palestinian Voices: Communication and Nation Building on the West Bank*. Boulder, 1987.

Al-Shuaibi, I. "The Development of Palestinian Entity Consciousness," *Journal of Palestine Studies* 9, no. 3 (Spring 1980).

Smith, M. G. "Social and Cultural Pluralism." *Annals of the New York Academy of Sciences* 83 (Jan 20, 1960).

———. "Some Developments in the Analytical Framework of Pluralism." In *Pluralism in Africa*, edited by L. Kuper and M. G. Smith. Los Angeles, 1969.

Smith, P. A. "The Exiled Bourgeoisie of Palestine." *MERIP Reports*, no. 142 (1986a).

———. "The Palestinian Diaspora, 1948–1985." *Journal of Palestine Studies* 15, no. 3 (1986b).

Smith, S. J. "Negotiating Ethnicity in an Uncertain Environment." *Ethnic and Racial Studies* 3 (1984).

Smooha, Sammy. "Arabs and Jews in Israel: Minority-Majority Relations." *Megamot* 22 (September 1976) (Hebrew).

———. *Israel: Pluralism and Conflict*. London, 1978.

———. "Control of Minorities in Israel and Northern Ireland." *CSSH* 22 (1980a).

———. "The Orientation and Politicization of the Arab Minority in Israel." Occasional Papers on the Middle East (New Series), no. 2. University of Haifa, Jewish-Arab Center, 1980b, 1984.

———. "Arab Political Orientation in Israel." Unpublished address. Jerusalem, 1985.

———. *Arabs and Jews in Israel*. Vol. 1, *Conflicting and Shared Attitudes in a Divided Society*. Boulder, 1989.

———. *Arabs and Jews in Israel*. Vol. 2, *Change and Continuity in Mutual Intolerance*. Boulder, 1991.

Smooha, Sammy, and John E. Hofman. "Some Problems of Arab-Jewish Coexistence in Israel." *Middle East Review* 9, no. 2 (Winter 1977).

Snider, Lewis W. "Minorities and Political Power in the Middle East." In *The Political Role of Minority Groups in the Middle East*, edited by R. D. McLaurin. New York, 1979.

Southall, A. "The Density of Role-Relationship as Universal Index of Urbanization." In *Urban Anthropology*, edited by A. Southall. New York, 1973.

Survey of Arab Affairs. Jerusalem, August 1985, November 1985, February 1986.

Tessler, Mark A. "Israel's Arabs and the Palestinian Problem." *Middle East Journal* 31, no. 3 (Summer 1977).

———. "The Identity of Religious Minorities in Non-Secular States: Jews in Tunisia and Morocco and Arabs in Israel." *Comparative Studies in Society and History* 20, no. 3 (July 1978).

Tsimhoni, Daphne. "Demographic Trends of the Christian Population in the West Bank 1948–78." *Middle East Journal* 37 (Winter 1983).

UNRWA Report of the High Commissioner to the General Assembly, 1987. New York, 1988.

van den Berghe, Pierre L. "Pluralism." In *Handbook of Social and Cultural Anthropology*, edited by J. J. Honigmann. Chicago, 1973.

———. *The Ethnic Phenomenon*. New York, 1981.

Walton, John. "Internal Colonialism: Problems of Definitions and Management." Comparative Urban Studies Program, Center for Urban Affairs, Northwestern University, 1974.

West Bank Data Project. "Study on Population, Employment, and Public Funding on the West Bank." Jerusalem, n.d. (1985).

Wolfsohn, Michael. *Politik in Israel*. Opladen, 1983.

Zilberman, Ifrach. "The Palestinian Uprising in Jerusalem." Jerusalem, Leonard Davis Institute, 1988 and 1990 (Hebrew).

Zureik, E. "Toward a Sociology of Palestinians." *Journal of Palestine Studies* 6, no. 4 (Spring 1977).
———. "Consequences of Zionism for Palestinian Class Structure." In *Zionism, Imperialism and Racism*, edited by A. W. Kayyali. London, 1979a.
———. *The Palestinians in Israel: A Study in Internal Colonialism*. London, 1979b.

INDEX

Abu Dis, 84, 106
Abu Dis College of Science and
   Technology, 106
Abu Musa, 121
Abu Snan, 63
Abu Tor, 117, 121, 128, 130, 140, 141
Academicians, 39-42
Accommodation, 31, 52-54, 59, 66, 73,
   104, 109, 170
Acre, 46, 60
Al-Ard movement, 62
Al-Awda, 99
Al-Azariya, 79, 84, 102
Al-Fajr, 154
Al-Haj, Majid, 48
Al-Ittihad, 59
Al-mal land, 55
Al-Najah University, 60
Al-Rashid, Haroun, 71
Anata, 116
Arab Democratic Party, 47
Arabists, 58
Arab-Jewish contact, 42-45, 119-122.
   See also Questionnaire
Arabs (groupings): ethnic Arabs, vii;
   with Israeli citizenship, vii, 8, 27-30,
   34-36; Jerusalem Arabs, vii, 8, 114.
   See also Palestinians
Arab society: structure, 17, 18; world,
   78, 79

Arafat, Yassir, 61
A-Ram, 84
Arara-Ara, 49
Armenians, 125
Arnona, 98
Arraba, 33, 55
Aspirations, 114, 118. *See also*
   Questionnaire
A-Tur, 97, 98, 116, 117, 130, 140, 141,
   166

Bagrut, 75, 146
Balata, 77
Baqa al-Gharbiya, 41, 42
Barakat family, 99, 117
Bedouins, 28-31, 45, 63; in Smooha's
   typology, 52
Beit Hanina, 89-90, 92, 94, 97-98, 102,
   116, 124, 130, 140, 166
Beit Jalla, 75
Beit Safafa, 88, 90, 92, 94, 95, 97-98,
   100, 117, 124, 130, 140, 141, 146-
   147, 149, 153
Beit Sahur, 75
Benvenisti's, Meron: Belfast model,
   105
Bethlehem, 74, 79
Biculturalism, 38, 40
Bilingualism, 29, 38, 44
Bir Zeit University, 60, 76

Bourgeois nationalism, 52
Bush, George, 170

Chauvinism, Jewish, 68
Christian Arabs, 21, 22-23, 26, 29-30
51-52; accommodation of, 31;
economic success, 29, 38, 87;
educational patterns, 30-31, 35, 90;
in Galilee, 27-28; identity, 50-56, 58;
in Jerusalem, 73, 79, 87, 125, 126,
147, 149, 153; in Jordan, 9; in
Lebanon, 4; political and social
development, 31-32, 58, 60; youth,
42-43, 147, 149, 153
Citizens' Rights party, 62-63, 98
Clans, 21, 22-23, 26, 28, 30, 45, 48,
59, 64, 99, 121
Committee for Defense of Arab
Lands, 47
Committee of Heads of Arab Local
Councils, 47, 64
Communal pessimism, 105
Communal policies, ix
Comparative analysis, ix
Competitive ideologies, 2
Cooptation, 72

Dajani family, 99, 117
Dakkak, Ibrahim, 104
Damage control, 105
Dar al-Tifl, 106
Darawshe, Abdul Wahab, 47
Darwish, Sheikh Abdallah, 60
Deir Hanna, 33, 55, 65
Democratic Front for Peace and
Equality (Hadash), 41, 47, 56, 62.
See also Rakah
Democratic Front for the Liberation
of Palestine (DFLP), 106
Dissatisfaction: "ethnic," 2; "working-
class," 2
Dissidents, 52
Druze, 27-30, 51, 52, 58, 126;
economic success, 31, 38;
educational patterns, 30-31; in
Galilee, 27-28; in Smooha's
typology, 52-54; youth, 42-43, 50-52,
63

Dynastic empires: Hapsburgs, 4;
Ottomans, Ottoman empire, 4, 6, 22

East Talpiot, 96, 97, 100
Education, 30-31, 38, 40, 75-77, 86;
and political attitudes, 54; of
women, 38. See also Israel's Arabs;
Youth
Eilabun, 33, 55
Ethnic conflict, ix, 113-114; Balkans,
6; in domestic politics, ix; historical
roots, 12-13; in international affairs,
ix; minorities, 10; and nationalism,
4-5; Near East, 6; patterns of, 13-
15; social theories of, 18-19
Ethnic minority, vii
Ethno-class, 2

Fatah, 9, 17, 18, 99, 142, 153, 154. See
also Palestine Liberation
Organization
Fellah, 23
Fence sitters, 52, 73
Fragmentation in Arab society, vii, 2,
10, 17, 19, 21, 28, 29, 43, 49-52, 66,
79, 106, 113, 129, 142, 166
French Hill, 100
Furadies, 24, 33

Gadish, Joseph, 104
Galilee, 24, 27, 31, 47-49, 54-56, 64
Gaza, viii, 8, 60, 74, 75, 77, 78, 106,
108-109, 115, 116
Geographic regions and regional
patterns, 5, 24, 27-29, 31, 45-49, 52-
56, 109. See also Galilee; South;
Triangle
Gilo, 100
Greeks, 125
Grids: "ethnic" social and political, 2;
types, 3

Habash, George, 62
Haifa, 22, 40
Hamas, 60, 65, 120, 121, 141
Hamula. See Clans
Hebrew University of Jerusalem, the,
39, 41

Hebron, 79
Hebronites, 72, 74, 166
Hebron Polytechnic, 106
Histadrut, 45, 63, 100, 119, 122, 123;
    Arab leadership, 122; Arab support
    in Jerusalem, 99; elections, 63
Hussein, Saddam, 80
Husseini family, 22, 23

Income in Jerusalem, Arab vs. Jewish,
    85-87
Integratory option, vii
International actors, 11
Intifada, viii, 15, 59, 73, 74, 75, 76,
    84, 104, 114-115, 116, 125-127, 141,
    170-171
Intra-ethnic violence, 83
Irredentism, 3
Islam: Hebronite, 74; in Jerusalem,
    106-108, 119, 123, 128, 141, 147, 164
Islamic Jerusalem University, 106
Islamic Jihad in Gaza, 60
Islamic movement, 47, 65. See also
    Muslims
Israeli Arab education, 27-30, 38;
    expanded educational opportunities
    after 1967, 35-36
Israeli authority , 32, 66, 71-74, 83,
    109
Israelization, 71, 76
Israel's Arabs: demography, 27-29, 44-
    45, 78-89; increased contacts after
    1967, 34; political activity after
    1967, 39-42; political articulation,
    38, 39, 58-62; political development
    pre–1967, 31; political and social
    development, 31-32; relations with
    Arab states, 34; segregatory
    patterns, 32, 33, 39, 44, 66, 92, 106;
    social and ideological fragmentation,
    50-52; voting trends, 62-65. See also
    Beit Safafa
Issawiya, 97, 98, 116, 117, 125, 130,
    140, 141
Issue-oriented cleavages, 49-56

Jabal Mukaber, 98, 100, 116
Jaffa, 22

Jaljulya, 48, 65
Jenin, 60
Jerusalem, areas of Jewish expansion,
    100
Jerusalem, in the peace process, 166-
    167
Jerusalem, Palestinian preferences for:
    East-West division, 120, 122, 127,
    130, 142, 147; Islamic city, 123, 126,
    141, 147; Israeli-Palestinian
    administration, 123, 142, 143;
    Jordanian-Israeli administration,
    123; Jordanian-Palestinian
    administration, 130; Open city, 119,
    121, 123, 129, 130-131, 142, 147,
    153, 154, 164; Palestinian city, 118,
    119, 130, 142, 154, 164
Jerusalem Arabs, viii, 30, 71, 72;
    connection with intifada, viii;
    contact with Jews, 76; crime and
    violence, 83-84; demography, 78,
    102, 105; educational differences,
    30, 75-77, 85-86; Hashemite
    monarchy, 72; historical distinctions,
    72-73; influence on Israeli Arabs,
    42; Islamic population, 73-75;
    occupational status, compared to
    Jews, 87-90; outside contact, 78;
    refugees, 77-78; voting patterns, 97-
    100
Jerusalem municipality, 30, 76, 99,
    100, 102, 104, 105, 115, 118, 120-
    121, 127, 129, 154, 165, 171
Jewish Quarter, 102
Jews, 19, 28, 76; economic standing in
    Jerusalem, 87-90; in Jerusalem, 19,
    79-80, 92, 105, 106, 109; Jewish
    religious authority, 120
Jezira al-Zarka, 24, 33
Jordan, 9, 30, 60, 72, 96, 113, 118,
    120, 121, 128, 140, 142, 146, 153,
    164, 165

Kalandia, 77
Kara'een, Ibrahim, 99
Kemalism, German influence, 6
Kewan, M., 61
Kfar Bara, 48, 65

Kfar Kana, 60, 64-65
Kfar Qara, 33, 41, 48
Kfar Qassem, 48, 65
Khouri, Samar, 154
Koenig, Yisrael, 67
Kollek, Teddy, 71, 84, 96;
    administration, 99
Kurds, 7, 8
Kuttab, Daoud, 154
Kuttab, Jonathan, 154
Kuwait, 80

Labour party, 63
Land Day, 44, 55, 65
Land expropriation, by Jerusalem
    municipality, 85, 100
Land question, 28, 54-55, 98, 104
Lenin, 1
Likud party, 63, 99
Lynn, Uriel, 67

Madani, 23
Maghar, 56
Mahajinah, Sheikh Raid, 65
Maki (Israel Communist party), 31
Mapam party, 63
Marx, Karl, 1
Messianic movements: nationalism, ix,
    1, 2, 4; socialism, 1
Miari, Muhammad, 59
Military occupation, viii
Minhalot, 94-97
Ministry of Occupied Territories in the
    Kingdom of Jordan, 113
Minority status, viii
Mukhtars, 94-97, 121-122
Multi-ethnic polities, 4
Muslim Brotherhood, 60, 66
Muslim Quarter, 88, 92
Muslims: economic success, 31, 38, 87,
    99; educational patterns, 30-31, 40;
    in Galilee, 27-28; identity issues, 50-
    52, 58; in Jerusalem, 35, 73, 79-87,
    120, 125, 126-127, 128, 147, 149,
    153, 154; in Smooha's typology, 52-
    56; in the Triangle, 31-32, 43;

youth, 42-43, 147, 149. See also
    Islam

Nablus, 60, 76
Nasserism, 34
National Committee of Arab Students,
    47
National Committee of Secondary
    School Students, 47
National conflict, 2
Nationalism, 118, 123; late blooming,
    3, 7; and messianism, ix, 1, 2, 4;
    organization of national goals, 16-
    18, 118; Palestinian, "Pales-
    tinianism," 10, 22-23, 59-60, 98,
    109, 124; relation to ethnicity in
    refugee camps, 77; Turkish, 6
Nationalist agitation, 4
Nationalist state, viii
National minority, vii, 21
National minority status, 4
National movements, 3, 15;
    paramilitary organization, 15
National Religious Party (Mafdal), 63
Nation-state, 3, 5, 6; "emancipatory"
    model, 5
Nazareth, 27, 33, 64
Neve Yaakov, 100
Nusseibeh family, 99
Nusseibeh quarter, 95

Occupational status in Jerusalem, Jews
    vs. Arabs, 87-90
Old City, 88, 90, 102, 108, 117, 124,
    125, 140, 141, 166
One Jerusalem list, 97
Opinion trends in Jerusalem, 165-166
Opinion trends in Jerusalem
    Palestinian community, 113-114,
    130-164; differentiation by borough,
    130-141; differentiation by
    employment, 154-165;
    differentiation by generation, 141-
    146; differentiation by religion, 153-
    154; opinions among high school-
    aged, 146-153. See also
    Questionnaires

Opinions, aspirations, goals, 113-114.
  See also Questionnaire

Palestine Liberation Organization
  (PLO), 9, 117, 141, 149. *See also*
  Fatah
Palestine National Council (PNC), 117
Palestinian activism, 115; Jerusalem
  vs. the West Bank, 106, 115-116
Palestinians, vii, 8-9; contact with
  Israeli institutions, 114, 121, 122,
  129, 130-140, 142, 149, 164; contact
  with Israelis, 119, 120, 121, 122,
  127, 149, 164; Diaspora, 9; families,
  72, 74; in Israel, (*see* Israel's
  Arabs); in Jerusalem, viii, 72-173;
  protests, viii; ties to West Bank and
  Jordan, viii
Particularism, 2, 19
Patriotic/National Action Front, 62
Peace process, 128, 142, 153, 164, 165
Pizgat Zeev, 100, 102
Pluralism and conflict in Israeli
  society, Sammy Smooha, 12
Political action in ethnic confrontation,
  determinants of, 15-16
Popular Front for the Liberation of
  Palestine, (PFLP), 106
Preferences and priorities, 128, 129,
  140; family and society, 122-123,
  128; Islamic State, 141, 146, 154;
  material well-being, 122-123, 146,
  154; by occupational status, 154,
  164-165; Palestinian state, 122, 123,
  124, 128, 129, 141, 146, 153-154;
  religion, 122-123, 141, 146, 153-154,
  164, 165; socialism, 164. *See also*
  Questionnaires.
Progressive List for Peace (PLP), 47,
  56, 59
Progressive National Student
  Movement (PNSM), 41, 61, 62, 65

Qadis, 116, 119, 120
Questionnaire, open selected, 114,
  116-124; broad differences of
  opinion, 123; importance of Islam,
  119, 120, 123; Palestinians'
  relationship to Jerusalem, 118;
  patterns of opinion, 117; population
  polled, 116; status of Jerusalem, 119
Questionnaire, random closed, 124-
  129; boroughs involved, 124;
  "middle class bias," 125; opinion of
  services by municipality, 127-128,
  140, 142, 153, 164, 165; Palestinian
  secularism, 128; "privileged"
  Palestinian society, 125; reaction to
  peace process, 128; readiness to
  sacrifice, 128, 164, 165; status of
  Jerusalem, 126; support for
  Jordanian regime, 128

Rabin, Yitzhak, 59
Rahat, 45, 48
Rakah (Israel Communist party), 40,
  41, 47, 58-59, 60, 61, 68
Ramallah, 74, 79, 100
Ramat Eshkol, 100
Ramot, 100
Refugees, refugee camps, 18, 26, 77-
  78, 119
Rejectionism, 52-55, 65, 66, 73, 104
Rekhess, Eli, 30, 34
Religion, 33, 44, 66, 73, 80, 119, 120,
  141, 154. *See also* Christian Arabs;
  Druze; Islam; Jews; Muslims

Saint-Simon, 1
Sakhnin, 24, 31, 55
Sayigh, R., 23
Self-administration in Arab Jerusalem,
  minhalot, 95; mukhtars, 94-95
Self-identification, Israeli Arabs, viii;
  Palestinians in Jerusalem, viii
Shabab, 109
Shari'a court, 115, 116, 120. *See also*
  Islam
Sharon, Ariel, 67
Sheikh Jarrah area, 78
Shfaram (Shafr-Amr) , 27, 41, 43, 51,
  60, 61
Shinui party, 63, 98

Shuafat, 77, 78, 88, 102, 116, 117, 121, 124, 125, 130, 140, 141

Silwan, 92, 96, 100, 116, 121, 124, 125, 130-131, 140, 141

Siniora, Hanna, 154

Six-Day War, 34

Smooha, Sammy, 12, 37, 71, 104

Smooha's typology, 52-55, 65-66, 73. *See also* Accommodation; Fence sitters; Rejectionism

Social conflict, 2, 3

Socialism, 1, 141, 164

Social mobility, 5

Social structures, Arab, 22; pre–1948, 21-24; 1948-1967, 24-27, 31-32; self-segregatory, 22

Sonqrat family, 166

Sons of the Village (Homeland), 40, 55, 61

South, the, 28-29, 45, 48. *See also* Bedouins

Spatial segregation in Jerusalem of Jews and Arabs, 90-94

Sruhr family, 55

Subcultures, 4

Supreme Muslim Council, 108, 109

Sur Bahir, 96, 97, 98, 100, 116, 117, 125, 140, 141

Taibeh, 28, 44, 48, 51

Talpiot, 98

Tarabaya, Jamal, 55

Taujihe, 146

Temple Mount incident, 171-172

Toubi, Tewfik, 59, 62

Triangle, the, 24, 28, 30, 31, 43, 47-48, 50, 63, 65

Tsemel, Lea, 84

Turkey, 6

Umm el-Fahm, 28, 44, 47, 48, 49, 50, 51, 53-54, 55, 60, 65, 79

Universities, 39-42, 75-76. *See also* Youth

UNRWA (United Nations Relief & Works Agency), 77

Urbanization, 29-30

Usifiya, 42

Villages, incorporated in Jerusalem municipality, 85

Vilner, Meir, 59

Voting patterns in East Jerusalem, 97-100

Waqf, 85, 87, 119

Weber, Max, 4, 11

West Bank, vii, viii, 5, 8, 10, 19, 30, 60, 72, 74, 77, 78, 79, 84, 95, 105-106, 108, 113, 115, 116, 118

Youth, 141-146, contacts between, 33; high-school aged, 42-44, 51, 85, 113, 121, 146-153; university aged, 39-42, 44, 60, 61-62, 85, 106, 109, 113, 118

Zionism, Zionists, 4, 7, 8, 22

Zureik, E., 22, 23

Zureik family, 55

About the Author

ABRAHAM ASHKENASI is a professor at the Free University of Berlin and at the Hebrew University of Jerusalem. He has published books in the United States and in Germany, and has served as editor for various journals in Germany.